A PARIS COOK BOOK

A *CassCanfield* BOOK

A
PARIS
COOK
BOOK

F.L. Stagg

HARPER & ROW, PUBLISHERS
New York • Evanston • San Francisco • London

For those who love French cuisine

FIRST EDITION

Designed by Dorothy Schmiderer

Library of Congress Cataloging in Publication Data
Stagg, Frederick L
  A Paris cook book.
  "A Cass Canfield book."
  Includes index.
  1. Cookery, French. I. Title.
TX719.S73 1975   641.5'944   74-1858
ISBN 0-06-013909-9

75 76 77 78 79 10 9 8 7 6 5 4 3 2 1

Contents

PART II

MENUS 297

PART III

FOREIGN AND EXOTIC DISHES 313

Illustrations

Drawings by the author

Publisher's Note

ALREADY THERE IS a plethora of published material on the French cuisine, including works excellent in quality and encyclopedic in scope. So why is still another book in this crowded field called for?

Because Frederick Stagg, an Englishman educated in the United States, has a special contribution to make.

In addition to his intelligence, taste, and talent for cooking, he has an advantage given to very few American cooks. In the very heart of France—he has lived in Paris since 1959—he has had many years to pursue his love affair with French cookery, eagerly seeking to enlarge his knowledge of the art and all the while testing it in his own kitchen.

Not many Frenchmen can boast a working knowledge of Parisian household cookery to match Mr. Stagg's. He knows which French dishes should be useful and pleasing for Americans; he knows what is likely to be difficult for them—whether ingredients, utensils, or procedures; he knows how to write a recipe so that it will yield an authentically Parisian dish but that is easy for Americans to grasp and follow.

The key word here is *practical*: his recipes *work*. But make no mistake: *"practical"* does not necessarily mean simple or easy. Indeed, in Part I he offers recipes of every degree of complexity, including much to interest even the most expert *chef de cuisine*. In Part II he suggests menus for meals that would truly be memorable, and in Part III he presents an array of foreign and exotic dishes that have captured his fancy over the years and that he is eager to share.

For many years, those who have been Mr. Stagg's guests in his house have been proclaiming that he is one of the best cooks in Paris as well as one of its most delightful hosts. But, alas, he cannot have us all to dine with him there. What he can do, and has done here, is to let us in on what goes on in his kitchen.

You will enjoy the charm of this book and even the experienced cook will learn much from it.

CASS CANFIELD

Author's Introduction

In these days of irascible nationalisms, one hears the supremacy of French cooking challenged in many places. That supremacy is for me a cardinal article of faith. I believe that France possesses the greatest variety of foods and the greatest literature on gastronomy in the world. Not so long ago French beef and lamb did not measure up to that of other countries. Now that has been corrected. Pastry was a weak point in Gallic cookery at the turn of the nineteenth century. Now it is unexcelled. What other country can match what flows from the French cornucopia—the large variety of cheeses, the selection of tender vegetables, the peerless fruit, the choice of mushrooms, the tasty poultry, and the immensely varied seafood? And where but in France do so many people of all classes pay so much attention and know so much about food, from the raw material to the dish placed in front of you?

Those who go to France and suffer from upset stomachs after a few days of French food generally deserve the punishment. They gorge. They concentrate on a succession of rich dishes. They drink too much and too unwisely of unaccustomed beverages. And likely as not they take too little exercise.

French cooking pays special attention to digestibility. If you follow its rules, you need have no qualms in this respect. With regard to food values or dietetics, I shall have little to say in this book. How-ever, as one who has had ample opportunities to observe the French, I may state that they are generally not given to fat, even though no nation devotes itself more than they do to food and its preparation. The author prays the indulgence of the reader in introducing a personal note: after more than twenty-five years of practicing French cooking daily and enjoying its benefits, he has not varied much in weight, although, as my friend George Higginson says, "The cargo has shifted," which is all too natural for a septuagenarian pushing eighty. The Greek one-word maxim *Metron* ("the just measure") is the best general guide for a person in normal health. Then, of course, French cuisine is very moderate in the combination of fats and starches; and it is these, we are told, which are principally re-sponsible for tipping the scales. As the reader will see in this book, French gastronomy does not major in sweets, which are a concentra-tion of those two components.

In Paris we often complain that the quality of restaurant food is not so high as it was thirty or forty years ago. We look about and find many tables filled with diners obviously on expense accounts. We oldsters remark that the clientele determines the quality and that people busy with matters other than the relative perfection of the dishes in front of them cannot be an incentive to an inspired *chef de cuisine* or a dedicated *restaurateur*. Almost the same reflections are in order when we buy foodstuffs. Democracy with its great boon for the greatest numbers and its corollary, mass production, can not stimulate quality in preference to quantity—where the money is.

Yet the French tradition of gastronomy is so strong and the pro-portion of people who discriminate with knowledge so great that the foods available in Paris are still envied the world over. Meats, poultry, game, seafood, fruits, vegetables are found in their proper season, excellent in quality. Of course, they are very expensive. And that is one reason why the cook in Paris must learn to make the most of them.

My distinguished friend William Dinsmore used to entertain and educate a roomful of music lovers in Martha's Vineyard by playing portions of famous compositions by great geniuses, pointing out how they could all be accused of plagiarism—of actual "cribbing." The same holds true for cookery books: absolute originality would be difficult to discern, as a very small addition, or subtraction, of an ingredient or a slight change in the manner of cooking can alter the nature of a dish. Besides, only a very few dishes can be traced to their originators. This is a statement in self-defense.

Weights and measures are indispensable in the kitchen, but in many preparations cannot be given with absolute precision. The reader will come across frequent mentions of "more or less," "about," etc. Vinegar, for example, varies greatly in acidity. Some wheat flours are "thirstier" than others; some sugars, sweeter. And when spoonfuls are referred to, tablespoons are always meant.

Certain preserved foods are decidedly recommended. Powdered milk for most preparations is preferable to the fresh article: it never turns sour. Tomato paste in *small* tins is much preferable to the homemade product requiring long cooking: in larger containers it is likely to be wasted. Some brands of beef consommé in tins can challenge the best cook in the world for quality—as I often repeat—and save time and labor by a great margin. Such foodstuffs could be put in the same class as smoked bacon. Under the usual circumstances, who would wish to cure and smoke his own bacon? Render his own lard? Press his own oil?

For the amateur cook—and here I use the word *amateur* in the true French sense of being a *lover* of the subject—a beautiful kitchen is an inspiration. It need not be large. But it must *not* be squalid. It should have on its walls things that please the eye: colorful pots and pans and other utensils, pictures of subjects related to cooking, food, drink, fruits, flowers. Yes, and at least one shelf with cookery books. It should be a kitchen you love to come into and hate to leave.

I have waxed parquet floors in my kitchen and some of my best rugs. A crumb or a drop that falls on the floor is immediately removed. The implements in daily use are on view, spotless; whatever is not constantly on tap is put away perfectly clean. Readers with children may scoff at all this: children, they may say, just will make messes in kitchens. Then why not in living rooms, bedrooms, bathrooms? It is all a matter of training.

I feel I must apologize to my reader for many items of advice or instruction which she or he will probably find unnecessary. In extenuation I say that I set down every step—with its possible pitfalls —as I see it in the preparation of each recipe: I feel impelled to continue with my thought, just as if I were putting it into action.

F. L. STAGG

February 1975

The beginning and the root of all good is the pleasure of the stomach; even wisdom and culture must be referred to this.

Epicurus, *Ethics*. Vatican Coll. LIV.

To grow accustomed therefore to simple and not luxurious diet gives us health to the full . . . and, when after long intervals we approach luxuries, disposes us better towards them.

Epicurus, *Letter to Menoeceus*. Ibid.

PART I

Selected Parisian Recipes

CHAPTER 1

Sauces

MORE THAN ONCE the great cuisine of France has been accused of hiding poor food under its sauces. This is no more true, of course, than the French jibe that English cooks have three taps in the kitchen: one for cold water, another for hot water, and a third for white sauce. No other cuisine has a repertory of sauces comparable with that of France, and there they are used to improve the flavor and appearance of the dishes they grace. In a way they are the highest achievement of the culinary art.

Having said this, let us begin with the sauce that for a very long time and without any certainty of its origin has been known as Sauce Espagnole.

SAUCE ESPAGNOLE or SAUCE BRUNE
[Brown Sauce and Its Derivatives]

A well-run kitchen should always have on hand a reasonable supply of this basic brown sauce, which not only brings out the flavor of meats but can actually make an impressive dish out of simple ingredients.

For 1½ cups

Into a fairly heavy enameled cast-iron saucepan, about 4 inches deep and 8 inches wide, put 1 cup smoked bacon (cut into small dice); 2 cups roughly diced carrots (first peeled, quartered lengthwise, and centers removed); 2 cups finely chopped onion; 4 spoonfuls unsalted butter; 2 bay leaves; a sprig of fresh thyme (or ¼ teaspoon dried); and ½ teaspoon white peppercorns. Set the pan on high heat, and as soon as it is hot, begin stirring with a wooden or stainless steel spoon (preferably one with a straight end, to make scraping of the bottom of the pan easier). Do not let anything stick to the bottom: it would burn, ruin the taste of the sauce, and spoil your pan. (Do not reduce the heat; removing the pan from the heat when necessary, while stirring, is far preferable.) After half an hour or so of stirring and scraping, the carrots should be cooked enough to yield to the pressure of the spoon, as if you were going to mash them.

Sprinkle the contents with 3 spoonfuls of all-purpose flour, a spoonful at a time, stirring it in well. Reduce the heat as the flour browns at the bottom of the pan, and if necessary remove the pan from the heat to prevent burning.

Add 1 tin of concentrated beef consommé and stir thoroughly to mix with the cooked flour. Add another tin, and a third one if the mixture is too thick (the quality of the flour decides this, some qualities absorbing more liquid than others; at this point the sauce should be as thick as a thick soup). Then add 3 spoonfuls of good-quality tomato purée, one by one, stirring constantly.

If the sauce is not boiling, increase the heat: it should boil, uncovered, while you stir every few minutes, for about 30 minutes. Now the carrots should be almost mashable.

Take a similar saucepan but of smaller dimensions and strain the sauce into it through a conical strainer with fairly small holes (wire mesh is not necessary), pressing on the solids to get the juice out, but not trying to push them through. Set the strained sauce on high heat, placing the saucepan so that it boils on only one section of the surface.

Have at hand ¾ cup of good dry white wine, a small saucepan, and a metal spoon. Add a squirt of wine to the sauce and stir it: in a minute or so a reddish scum will come to the surface; skim this with the metal spoon into the small saucepan. Add another squirt of wine, stir, wait for the scum to rise, and skim. Repeat this operation until all the wine is gone, being most careful to scrape the bottom of the pan during the entire process, to prevent the sauce from sticking.

Withdraw the sauce from the heat and add a few drops of vegetable caramel (such as Kitchen Bouquet or Gravymaster) to darken its reddish color to a deep brown. Mix it well, then pour into a jar or other receptacle, preferably not very wide in proportion to its depth to minimize surface exposure, which would cause a skin to form. (As a further precaution, lay on the surface of the sauce little slivers of butter, which will melt to form a film and isolate the surface from the air.)

Do not cover the sauce until it is completely cold, then cover it with a thin sheet of paper and then the lid of the container, to conserve its flavor, and put it away in your refrigerator (not the freezer). It should last in perfect condition for 2 weeks at least.

N.B. Painstaking as the job is, the result is *very* rewarding, as you will need this basic sauce at every turn.

SAUCE MADÈRE
[Madeira Sauce]

To Sauce Espagnole (see above), add Madeira wine to taste. Warm to serve.

SAUCE POIVRADE
[Brown Sauce with Pepper]

To Sauce Espagnole (see above), add chopped shallots that have been boiled for 10 minutes in good white wine vinegar. Add also a pinch of cayenne and black pepper, freshly ground. Warm to serve.

If the sauce is to be served with game that has been marinated, the liquid of the marinade can be added to the sauce, but then the mixture should be strained through fine mesh. Other variants call for the addition of gooseberry or cranberry jelly, and even the blood of the animal.

SAUCE PÉRIGUEUX
[Brown Sauce with Truffles]

To Sauce Espagnole (see above), add finely chopped black truffles and the liquid from the tin in which they came.

SAUCE AUX CHAMPIGNONS
[Mushroom Sauce]

Trim off the root end of mushroom stems, wash the mushrooms thoroughly, and chop them up fairly fine. Sauté in hot butter, stirring until they are brown. Do not let the butter turn black, as it is then very indigestible.

Lift the mushrooms with a skimmer to a saucepan. Add three times their quantity of Sauce Espagnole (see above) and the juice of ½ lemon. Heat and stir well before serving.

SAUCE ROBERT
[Brown Sauce with Mustard]

Chop ½ pound of onions fairly fine and add them to a saucepan containing 2 spoonfuls of melted butter. Set the pan on medium-low heat and cook, stirring from time to time, until the onion has softened and has *begun* to turn yellow. Then add 1 cup of Sauce Espagnole (see above) and stir well. Finish with a spoonful of Dijon prepared mustard.

[*Egg and Cream Sauce*]

This sauce (the second name for which was given during World War I), used for white meats, is a Sauce Espagnole (see above) of yellowish color; so absolutely no browning must be permitted. The beef consommé is replaced by chicken broth (which can be made very successfully with chicken bouillon cubes dissolved in hot water in a proportion to your taste; or you can use tinned). Neither tomato purée nor vegetable coloring is used; in their stead, 1/2 cup of mush-room broth (made by boiling fresh mushrooms in water for 15 minutes) is added.

After "refining"—i.e., skimming the sauce and adding the white wine as in Sauce Espagonle—dilute 3 egg yolks in a cup with a little of the sauce, and then stir the mixture back into it. Immediately remove the sauce from the heat; any boiling would "scramble" the eggs and ruin the sauce. Strain it, pour it into a container if it is to be kept, and butter it as for Sauce Espagnole.

SAUCE POULETTE

Make Sauce Allemande (see above), *but do not refine it with white wine*. Instead, use the cooking liquor of fresh mushrooms (see page 230), and add 4 egg yolks at the end.

SAUCE TOMATE
[*Tomato Sauce*]

Cut 1 pound of ripe, fleshy tomatoes in quarters and with a tea-spoon remove the seeds. Squeeze the water out of the tomatoes by pressing them—not too hard—in your hand.

Melt 2 spoonfuls of unsalted butter and add the same amount of all-purpose flour; stir over medium-high heat, leave it to puff up for a few seconds, stir it again, and when it begins to turn yellow remove it from the heat. Add ⅔ cup of beef consommé, little by little, and stirring just to make a creamy mixture (if you do it too gradually, the consommé will dry out; if too quickly, the mixture will be lumpy). Add the tomatoes, a pinch each of sugar and white pepper, and a teaspoonful of sweet basil. A very small piece of crushed garlic (if not objectionable) is recommended.

Stir and cover well, then set in 325° F. oven for 1 hour.

If the sauce is to be kept for future use, butter it as for Sauce Espagnole (see above) after straining it into a container. Keep in the refrigerator.

SAUCE BÉCHAMEL
[White Sauce and Its Derivatives]

Named after Louis de Béchamel, Marquis de Nointel, supervisor of Louis XIV's table, this sauce was originally much the same as Sauce Allemande, but during the last century and a half it has lost its meat component.

For 3 cups

Peel, core, and chop 2 medium carrots (about 2 ounces of chopped carrot in all) and put in a heavy saucepan, along with the same amount of chopped onion and 2 spoonfuls of butter, over medium heat. Add a bay leaf, a sprig of fresh thyme (or ¼ teaspoon dried), and a few white peppercorns. Do not let the onion turn yellow; stir the mixture often.

After 15 minutes of cooking, just before the onions turn color, add 2 spoonfuls of all-purpose flour, stir well, and remove from the heat, continuing to stir for 30 seconds. Moisten the mixture very gradually with 3 cups of *boiling* milk, stirring and scraping the bottom of the pan, then replace on the heat to boil gently.

After 15 or 20 minutes of boiling and stirring, strain the sauce through fine mesh into the top of a double boiler. Add 2 or 3 spoonfuls of cream (the heaviest you can get). Mix well and, finally, if the sauce is not to be used right away, dot the surface with flakes of butter to prevent a skin from forming. Reheat over simmering water.

A simpler—less flavorful—béchamel is made thus: Melt 2 spoon-fuls of butter and add the same quantity of all-purpose flour. Stir well on medium heat. Let the mixture puff up, then stir again and repeat this process three or four times without letting the mixture (which here may be called a "binding" because it binds liquids and solids together) turn yellow. Wet it down *gradually* with milk (pre-ferably boiling, but cold will do in a hurry), stirring constantly: if you stop or if you pour too much milk at a time, you will have lumps in your sauce.

Finally, season with onion salt and white pepper to taste.

SAUCE MORNAY
[Cheese Sauce]

This is a béchamel to which you add grated Gruyère (or fresh Parmesan) cheese just as you take it off the heat: for 3 cups of sauce, 3 or 4 spoonfuls of grated cheese. Accent on the white pepper.

SAUCE AURORE
[Tomato-Flavored Béchamel]

More than the flavor, what matters in this sauce is the color, for its effect on the eye. To a béchamel enriched with heavy cream, add either tomato puree or paprika and/or vegetable dye. The color should be pink, *aurore* meaning of course "dawn."

SAUCE HOLLANDAISE
[Egg Yolk and Butter Sauce and Its Derivatives]

For 1½ cups of sauce

Melt ½ pound of the best unsalted butter on gentle heat; it must not fry. The casein, or cheesy white element, will separate—remove it and throw it away. Set aside the clear remainder, which is *clarified butter*.

Mix 3 spoonfuls of good white wine vinegar and 2 spoonfuls of water in the top of a double boiler and boil down over direct heat, to 1 spoonful. Let cool to the point where you can put your finger in it without discomfort, then add to the liquid 3 large egg yolks, which you have separated *without leaving any trace of egg white*. Mix well (thus reducing the risk of the heat later "scrambling" the egg yolks). Add a teaspoon of the medium-cool clarified butter.

Place the pan over simmering water on medium heat, and from now on never stop stirring. Add the butter bit by bit as you see the sauce thickening, the heat making an emulsion of egg and butter. For safety's sake you should keep a little cold water near at hand; at the slightest sign of "curdling," add a bit of cold water and remove the pan from over the water, stirring vigorously.

When all the melted butter has been added, remove from the fire altogether and add the juice of half a lemon and salt and pepper to taste. The sauce must not be reheated, and is served lukewarm; *otherwise it "curdles."*

Very experienced cooks thoroughly familiar with their stoves can make hollandaise without a double boiler. This is a challenge worth taking up. But to add flour or any other starch, or cream, and so on, is sacrilegious, unless it is to make a derivative sauce, as explained below.

SAUCE MOUSSELINE; SAUCE MOUTARDE
[Creamy Hollandaise Sauce; Mustard Sauce]

To Sauce Hollandaise (see above), add 3 or 4 spoonfuls of thick (double) cream and mix the two thoroughly—the result is sauce mousseline. If to this you add Dijon prepared mustard, preferably the "nature" kind of a light yellow color, in the proportion to suit your taste, you have sauce moutarde (or sauce mousseline-moutarde).

SAUCE BÉARNAISE
[Hollandaise Sauce with Tarragon]

Proceed as for Sauce Hollandaise (see above), *but* increase the vinegar to 5 spoonfuls and add to it a spoonful of chopped tarragon leaves, which remain in the sauce. Also, reduce the vinegar and water mixture much more slowly in order to make the infusion of the vinegar stronger (good tarragon white wine vinegar comes in useful *also*). Shallot salt or even onion salt is preferable to ordinary salt in the final seasoning.

VINAIGRETTE
["French Dressing"]

The proportion of oil to vinegar is a matter of taste, and so is the kind of oil used (whether olive or some other vegetable oil) and even the use of lemon juice instead of vinegar. If there is a "standard" mixture, it is this: 2 spoonfuls of oil, freshly ground pepper, a spoonful of vinegar, and salt to taste. Adding herbs (chives, tarragon, parsley, chervil, and so on) and rubbing the salad bowl with garlic or with a garlic-impregnated piece of bread are fairly usual.

Wooden bowls are claimed to be better than china or glass salad bowls; but they are apt to go rancid after some time. Mixing the dressing in a glass jar to shake it up or in a cup to stir it is common practice.

The classic manner was to make the mixture in the salad serving spoon, stirring with the serving fork (both implements being of wood at the tip or of ivory or china), and to let the dressing drip over the lettuce, which was then tossed over many times.

SAUCE GRIBICHE
[Vinaigrette with Chopped Egg and Parsley]

To Vinaigrette (see above) add chopped hard-boiled egg and finely chopped parsley, sufficient to make the dressing as thick as cream.

MAYONNAISES

SAUCE MAYONNAISE

Montagné contradicts the great Carême (who argued that the proper name of this sauce should be *magnonaise*, derived from the French verb *manier*, meaning "to handle and work over") and says the name should be *moyeunaise*, derived from the old French word *moyeu*, meaning "egg yolk." Both disdain *mahonnaise* and *bayon-naise*.

The proportions are inviolate—except for such slight deviations as may be necessitated by variation in the size of the eggs.

Measure 2 cups cold-pressed olive oil per 3 egg yolks. (Since cold ingredients mix less easily and thoroughly, warm the eggs in warm water before using them. If the oil is very cold, put it in the top of a double boiler over warm water.) In a bowl that has been rinsed in warm water, put the yolks (from which every last particle of white has been removed), a pinch of fine, dry salt and a pinch of white pepper, and a few drops of lemon juice or white wine vinegar. Mix well.

Add the oil drop by drop, preferably out of a small bottle or even with a dropper, stirring constantly. As the mixture becomes creamy you can be bolder in adding the oil, and if it gets too solid you can add a few more drops of lemon juice or vinegar.

Once all the oil is spent, add, stirring constantly, 1 or 2 spoonfuls of boiling water; this helps solidify the sauce. However, mayonnaise must *not* be *hard*: it should be homogeneous and solid enough to hold its shape but not to require pressure from a spoon.

N.B. Never put mayonnaise away in the refrigerator as it is most likely to decompose in any but mild temperatures.

SAUCE VERTE
[Green Mayonnaise with Herbs]

For every 2 cups of sauce, take 1 ounce each of leaves *only* of the following: spinach, watercress, parsley, chervil, tarragon. Wash the leaves well in cold water and dry them lightly on a clean towel. Throw them into boiling water with a pinch of bicarbonate of soda—to keep them green—in an enameled (*not* aluminum, *not* tin-lined copper) pan and boil them for 6 minutes, then dump them into a fine strainer and run cold water over them to cool.

Dry the cooled leaves completely in a clean towel by twisting it, then strain them through a fine strainer (or, better, through tammy cloth) to obtain a fine purée. Add this to mayonnaise, little by little.

When properly made, the sauce shows no particles of green leaves and is of an even, light-green color.

SAUCE RUSSE
[Mayonnaise with Caviar]

Although we have known for many years a variety of red or pink mayonnaise called in America "Russian dressing," the recipes given by European authors have very little in common with it. Sauce Russe is mayonnaise to which have been added, in the proportion of one-quarter of its volume, caviar and shellfish coral creamed into a fine paste. (The obvious objection is that, if the caviar is not good, it will not improve the mayonnaise and, if it *is* delicious, to use it thus is a waste.)

HARD-BOILED EGG SAUCES

A variety of cold sauces or dressings can be made with hard-boiled eggs, the yolks being creamed into a paste and the whites in some cases chopped up fine. The addition of chopped pickles and other highly spiced preserves and herbs, mustard, cream, etc., is up to the fancy of each palate.

SAUCE RAIFORT
[Horseradish Sauce]

To 1 tablespoon of white bread crumbs soaked in milk, add 2 spoonfuls of grated horseradish and mix well. Finish with *thick* cream.

THIRTEEN LESSER SAUCES

ANDALOUSE: (*Cold.*) Mayonnaise well mixed with tomato and red pimento purée.

BERCY: (*Hot.*) Finely chopped shallots and onions cooked slowly in butter, moistened with dry white wine and fish stock, mixed with chopped chervil and parsley, then thickened with arrowroot.

DIABLE: (*Hot.*) Chopped shallots reduced in half-vinegar–half-white wine, strained and mixed with Sauce Espagnole, plus chopped herbs and hot red pepper.

DIEPPOISE: (*Hot.*) A simple béchamel made with fish stock, plus mussel juice and mushroom cooking liquor.

DUXELLES: (*Hot.*) Chopped shallots and mushrooms sautéed in butter until dry and mixed with Sauce Espagnole, plus one-quarter the amount of Sauce Tomate.

GRAND VENEUR: (*Hot.*) Sauce Espagnole mixed with the marinade of game, plus the blood, and gooseberry jelly, currants, and high seasoning.

MATELOTE: (*Hot.*) Fish stock made with red wine, plus Sauce Espagnole and a touch of anchovy butter.

NANTUA: (*Hot.*) A thick béchamel made with fish stock and cream, plus crayfish butter and chopped tails. Pale pink in color.

RAVIGOTE: (*Hot.*) Shallots and half vinegar–half white wine reduced with tarragon leaves and parsley, plus chicken velouté.

RAVIGOTE: (*Cold.*) Mayonnaise with mustard, pickles, chopped onions, capers, chives, and herbs.

RÉMOULADE: (*Cold.*) Same as Sauce Ravigote (above), plus cayenne pepper and anchovy paste.

SUPRÊME: (*Hot.*) A béchamel made with chicken broth, mushroom cooking liquor, and heavy cream.

TARTARE: (*Cold.*) Same as Sauce Ravigote (above), plus a little mashed garlic and more chopped pickles.

CHAPTER 2

Soups

[For Fish and Shellfish Soups, see Chapter 9]

BOUILLONS
[*Meat Broths*]

Any edible substance properly cooked in water will make a broth, even a palatable one. But broths are generally thought of as the juice of *meats* extracted by cooking in water (these broths have a special name: bouillons), and so they will here be considered, to the exclusion of vegetable broths.

To make a bouillon, one needs time, because quick boiling will not extract the juices and flavor of meats: cooking must proceed slowly and be attended with care.

Beef is, of course, the best meat for broths, especially the portions of the hind quarter, which are tough and cartilaginous, but also the brisket and the tail. There is no better way to procure a good beef broth than by following the recipe for Pot-au-Feu (see page 133), because the flavors of vegetables and aromatic herbs are combined intimately with that of the meat. So the broth of this good dish can serve as the basic beef broth—when well degreased.

For chicken broth, substitute a mature bird for the beef and other-wise proceed as for *pot-au-feu*, shortening the cooking by about half.

N.B. Chicken bouillon cubes plus raw chicken debris and vege-tables (see Le Poulet au Pot, page 169) can make delicious chicken broth.

CONSOMMÉS

BEEF CONSOMMÉ

For 2 quarts

Beat 2 egg whites lightly. Put them into a saucepan of adequate capacity, along with the broken shells from 2 eggs; 2 pounds of lean beef (hind quarter), cut into small dice; and 2½ quarts cold bouillon from Pot-au-Feu (see page 133), taking care not to pour in any sediment from the *pot-au-feu*. Put the saucepan on medium heat.

With a wire whisk, stir the mixture. When the liquid begins to throw up froth, skim it off. Continue stirring with the whisk *to enable the egg whites to absorb matter that would make the consommé muddy*; they can do so only if the heat increases very gradu-ally. After thorough skimming, let boil steadily but moderately for about 1 hour.

Add 2½ ounces of plain gelatin, in small doses. Remove from the heat and strain through a clean, odorless napkin wrung out in cold water, on a wide strainer over a clean saucepan, without pressing the solids.

The consommé should be limpid but of a nice brown color. If you wish a deeper color, add a few drops of vegetable caramel (like Kitchen Bouquet or Gravymaster), *not* burnt onion.

GARNITURES POUR CONSOMMÉS
[Garnishes for Consommés]

By this phrase is meant simply sago, tapioca, and cut-up salt custard.

Sago and tapioca are *dribbled* into salted boiling water and boiled for 20 minutes, then lifted with a skimmer and added to the consommé in the proportion (moderate, please) desired.

SALT CUSTARD

Bring 1 cup of chicken bouillon (may be from can or cube) to a boil. Beat together (don't raise a froth) 2 whole eggs and 3 egg yolks, then add the hot bouillon to the beaten eggs very gradually while stirring; strain this mixture through fine mesh into a buttered pie plate or two. Skim or wipe off any froth. Cover the pie plates with metal foil, set them in an oven dish or roasting pan containing boiling water, and place in 375° F. oven for 30 minutes. Before removing the pie plates from the oven, lift the metal foil and make sure the custard is set. When cooled, cut the custard in parallel crossing lines, either checkerboard or lozenge shaped.

This garnish is called *royale*; hence, *consommé a la royale* or *consommé royale*. A nice fillip can be given to this garnish by adding a little finely chopped chervil to the custard preparation—or, if the garnish is to be used in a fish broth, finely chopped dill. Of course, the dice or lozenges of the salt custard must be no bigger than a (feminine) little finger nail.

SOUPES
[Soups]

There is some disagreement among authorities regarding the difference between *soupes* and *potages*. Here the former will be considered as the lighter form—that is, simpler and less thick—which is in keeping with the very old idea of *potage* as a great meal in itself and not essentially what in English is termed a soup.

SOUPE À L'OIGNON
[Onion Soup]

Again, there is some disagreement on whether the broth should be clear or contain a thickening of flour and even of milk. The following is recommended:

Sauté some onions (sliced medium thin), in clarified butter (see page 10) until they are golden brown. Meanwhile, cut thin slices (about 2 per person at table) of French bread. When the onions are done, remove them from the skillet and put in the bread; let the bread absorb the butter.

Put the bread, with the onions, in a hot soup plate and sprinkle generously with grated Gruyère cheese. Pour over *boiling* beef consommé to the desired level.

(This is not the peasant edition, which often dispenses with broth —not to mention consommé—and concentrates on the onions and the bread, with a little cheese.)

N.B. No mention is made here of seasoning, as it is presumed that the consommé has all that is necessary.

SOUPE AÏGO BOUÏDO
[Garlic Soup]

In its simplest form, this is a garlic soup made with water, a generous amount of crushed garlic cloves, aromatic herbs such as sage and parsley, salt and pepper, and olive oil, all boiled together (sometimes the garlic is sautéed in the oil first) for 30 or 40 minutes and poured on slabs of bread sprinkled with chopped parsley.

It has a fish variant that requires only 20 minutes of boiling. This contains pieces of firm-fleshed fish, garlic, onion, herbs, and potatoes, and is finished with the addition of olive oil well beaten in the liquid, and sometimes with the addition of garlic-and-oil puree (*aïoli*)—the whole served on slabs of bread.

Each Provençal locality—or perhaps each kitchen—has its version.

SOUPE PÉRIGOURDINE AUX MIQUES
[Vegetable Soup with Salt Pork and Dumplings]

The dumplings are made by mixing 1 pound of corn (yes, American corn) meal with wheat flour, in equal proportions, with a spoonful of lard, salt, and water, then kneaded well, formed into dumplings, and poached for several minutes in salted boiling water. These dumplings are added to the soup just before serving.

The soup is made of cabbage, carrots, turnips, celery, onions stuck with cloves, and herbs; and for meat a piece of salt pork (not smoked), such as off the shoulder or picnic. Once the vegetables (excluding the cabbage) are cooked, they are removed to a skillet and sautéed in lard, dusted with all-purpose flour to make a binding, and moistened with the broth into a creamy consistency: this is returned to the soup pot and mixed with the rest of the broth and the cabbage, and then served on two plates—one with the salt pork *on* the cabbage and surrounded by the *miques*, or dumplings, and another (a soup plate, of course) with the broth and the vegetables on slices of bread.

GARBURE PAYSANNE
[Puree of Vegetable Soup]

Fundamentally this is a puree of vegetables—onions, leeks, turnips, carrots, cabbage, celeriac, beans, peas and so on—dissolved in the water or broth in which they have boiled, with or without a piece of pork fat, and seasoned with herbs (especially chervil), crushed garlic, salt, and pepper. It is served thick and on slices of rough country bread on which are piled some of the puree and grated Gruyère cheese.

GARBURE BÉARNAISE
[Puree of Vegetable Soup with Goose Preserve and Bacon]

A variation of Garbure Paysanne (see above), this has in it Confit d'Oie and uncured bacon (pork belly), is cooked for 3 hours (which cannot improve the nourishing values or flavors of the vegetables), and is finally separated into semisolids topped with slices of bread that have been dusted with cheese and browned in the oven, the broth being served on the side.

Rough and repetitious as these soups are, they are nonetheless delicious if executed by a loving hand and with fresh materials.

POTAGES

Should this be translated as "elegant soups"? Of course, that is what they are, especially some of them.

POTAGE À LA REINE
[Cream of Chicken Soup]

Put a 2½-pound chicken, after it has been well wiped inside to clean it of all blood (the soup must be creamy-white), into a saucepan with 2½ quarts of chicken broth, the white part only of 3 leeks, and half a bunch of celery stalks (whitish portion only). Cover and let boil on medium low heat for 1 hour, after skimming carefully at the first boil.

Meanwhile, boil 4 ounces of rice in water (containing 1 teaspoon of salt) to cover by 1 inch for 45 minutes, stirring now and then and regulating the heat so that the water will not evaporate before the rice is mushy—which is what is required. (Before being boiled, the rice should *not* be washed but should be carefully sorted on a white surface to remove the small black beans almost always present in rice.)

Remove the chicken from the broth, carve out the breasts, and, having taken off the skin, cut up the white meat in very small dice, which you will reserve between two warm plates. Cut up rest of the chicken (minus the skin, which you discard) into small, rough pieces, and then reduce these to a fine puree in a mortar with a pestle (if you did this by grinding the meat, a loss of the juices would result).

Mix the rice mush, also reduced to a puree, with the mashed chicken and add the broth. Stir thoroughly and verify the seasoning. Bring to a boil on low heat.

Meanwhile, beat 3 or 4 egg yolks and gradually mix them with ⅔ cup thick cream until they are absolutely homogeneous.

Throw this mixture into the boiling soup and immediately withdraw it from the heat: it must not boil again or the eggs will "scramble" (so-called curdle).

Strain through fine mesh and serve hot, with the little dice of chicken breast floating about in the liquid.

POTAGE SAINT-GERMAIN
[Cream of Fresh Green Pea Soup]

Throw 4 cups of large, freshly shelled green peas into 5 cups of boiling water with ½ teaspoon salt. Add the well-washed leaves of a medium-sized head of lettuce and some parsley and boil for 20 minutes, or until the peas are soft enough to crush.

Meanwhile, in another saucepan put 1 cup of *small* fresh peas in water barely to cover and cook for 35 minutes, starting cold, with a pinch of salt and another of bicarbonate of soda and a bigger pinch of sugar. Set aside.

Lift out the large peas, lettuce, and parsley and force them through a fine mesh strainer to make a puree. Moisten this with the *liquid* from the small peas plus some of the liquid from the larger peas, taking care to keep the mixture thick. Bring the mixture to a boil while stirring. Verify the seasoning, then add 3 or 4 spoonfuls of heavy cream. Remove from heat.

Add 6 spoonfuls of butter and the reserved small peas, stirring carefully so as not to break them. Sprinkle with a spoonful of finely chopped chervil and serve immediately.

N.B. An improvement is to cook the peas, large and small, in chicken bouillon or broth—that made from cubes is quite satisfactory —instead of water. As bouillon or broth contains salt, do not add salt in boiling the peas.

POTAGE CRÉCY
[Cream of Potato and Carrot Soup]

Peel and core 1 pound of carrots (preferably young and tender) and chop them up fairly fine. Stew them in 4 spoonfuls of butter, a good pinch of salt and one of sugar, and a dusting of white pepper. When soft, mash them.

Meanwhile, peel 1/2 pound of potatoes, then boil them in salted water for 25 minutes. Mash them, then combine them with the carrot puree and moisten with 5 cups of boiling chicken bouillon (cubes or tins are fine). Strain through fine mesh into a clean saucepan. Bring to a boil, add 6 spoonfuls of butter, and withdraw immediately from the heat.

Serve with diced, fried toast (see page 28) or small potato dice browned in hot butter and dried.

POTAGE DUBARRY
[Cream of Cauliflower Soup]

Wash a medium-sized cauliflower well, put it into boiling salted water, and cook at a steady boil, uncovered, for 25 minutes.

Meanwhile, make a white binding with 2 spoonfuls butter and 2 spoonfuls all-purpose flour (see page 9). Add enough chicken bouillon to make a creamy liquid, then set the mixture on high heat and skim off the froth that rises to the surface, stirring and adding 1 tablespoon at a time of cold water. Repeat this process three or four times. Withdraw from the heat and cover.

Pick off a few little clusters of the cooked cauliflower to decorate the soup at serving time, and keep them warm. Put the rest of the cauliflower into the white soup and stir it together for a minute of boiling. Strain through fine mesh, then bring to a boil again. Add 3 or 4 egg yolks beaten with 1/2 cup of heavy cream, stir, and immediate remove from the heat. Stir again.

If you have to wait before serving, lay a few bits of fresh butter on the surface to prevent a skin from forming, and keep covered in a double boiler (not boiling). Decorate with the reserved little clusters of cauliflower at the moment of serving.

CRÈME DE RIZ
[Cream of Rice Soup]

This can be prepared with rice grains or rice flour.

If grains are used, boil them in 3 times their amount of water, lightly salted, until very mushy. Strain through fine mesh. Use for thickening vegetable broths.

If rice flour is used, dilute it very gradually with cold boiled milk (powdered milk dissolved in water is recommended) to a thick, creamy consistence, and add it to a vegetable puree made from cooked (25 minutes in salted water) green asparagus tips, artichoke hearts, celery or celeriac, leeks, potato and onions, potato and sorrel, or almost any vegetable leftover.

POTAGE CONDÉ
[Red Bean Soup]

Prepare red beans as on page 250, with 3 parts water to 1 part good red wine, preferably fruity, and dilute it with half consommé and half boiling water. Verify the seasoning, and add a lump of butter off the heat to thicken it.

POTAGES VELOUTÉS
["Velvety" Soups]

The "velvety" quality is obtained by an addition of beaten egg yolks and heavy cream.

For 4 servings

Make a binding of 2 spoonfuls butter and 2 spoonfuls of all-purpose flour on medium heat (see page 9), and dissolve this with a mixture of 2 cups concentrated beef consommé and 2 cups water, or with 4 cups of chicken broth.

Beat 2 egg yolks, stir in ⅓ cup heavy cream, and add the mixture to the soup just before removing the saucepan from the heat. Strain through fine mesh to serve.

N.B. This is classical "hotel soup" when made with a good broth, and it can be very comforting to a cold or tired stomach.

CHAPTER 3

Eggs

OMELETTES

To succeed in making a perfect French omelette probably requires a certain knack; it undoubtedly requires practice. An omelette of more than 10 eggs should not be attempted; indeed, one of 2 eggs is more likely to succeed than one of 10 eggs. A note of caution may be not amiss; break each egg into a cup to make sure it is fresh, then add it to the rest.

Two eggs and a spoonful of butter per person is the normal proportion.

Beat the eggs thoroughly, but without raising a froth, and season them with salt and white pepper.

Meantime, heat the butter over high heat until it *begins* to brown. Throw in the eggs. As soon as they begin to set round the edge of the pan, scrape them toward the center. Repeat this scraping to the center until there is little liquid egg there, then loosen the edge round the pan and shake the pan back and forth without lifting it from the heat.

When, on lifting with the spatula the edge of the forming omelette, you see a deep golden color, fold it forward with the spatula—or, if you are very deft, give the pan a forward jerk and the omelette will half fold itself. The second fold is given with the spatula or by flipping the omelette over on the dish or serving platter. Rub the surface of the omelette lightly with butter to glaze it and serve immediately.

VARIATIONS

From *omelette fines herbes* (finely chopped parsley, chives, tar-ragon, chervil, etc.) to *omelette Rossini* (chopped truffles, foie gras), the range is great.

If vegetables containing liquid, such as spinach or tomatoes, are used, they must be partially dried in very hot butter and added to the omelette once it is ready to fold. (An omelette is said to be *fourrée* when it is folded over something else that was cooked inde-pendently and added at the last minute.) Other ingredients may be added to the beaten eggs before cooking.

FOR OMELETTE ROSSINI: Add chopped black truffles to the eggs, make the omelette, and place on top of it small pats of foie gras that have been rolled in flour and lightly sautéed in butter.

N.B. In speaking of omelettes it is more correct in French to call them *moelleuses*—i.e., creamy soft like cooked bone marrow—than *baveuses*—i.e., like "drool."

OEUFS BROUILLÉS
[*Scrambled Eggs*]

The variety of combinations possible with scrambled eggs is huge, and stimulates the imagination of any cook. Alexandre Dumas, in his famous *Gastronomic Dictionary*, specially recommends mixing the beaten eggs with the juice of veal kidneys that have been sautéed in champagne mixed with chicken broth.

Unlike the omelette, which requires high heat, scrambled eggs should be cooked on medium temperatures; the time-honored French method, in fact, is to cook them in a double boiler.

The proportion is 2 spoonfuls of butter to 2 whole eggs, and a pinch of salt and pepper. (Half the butter *may* be held back and added to the eggs once they are set.) Beating should be a little more thorough than for omelettes but not quite so much as to make the eggs froth.

When cooking in a double boiler, eggs and butter are put in together; when cooking in a pan on direct heat, the butter is *melted* first and the beaten eggs added. Stirring and scraping should start immediately. At the first signs of *drying* at the bottom of the pan, it should be removed from the heat, but without discontinuing stirring. If half the butter has been reserved, add it now, just before serving.

The ideal consistency is *creaminess*; the worst is *hard lumpiness*. Adding cream while the eggs are cooking is not advisable: to do this does not make the eggs more creamy but turns them into a bad sort of custard.

(American "Scrambled eggs, country style"—i.e., added *unbeaten* to the hot butter and stirred only when the whites set—are not in the French repertory, delicious as they are.)

Truffles, shellfish coral or slices, every kind of mushroom, cheese (not the very strong ones), cooked tender vegetables, ham, bacon, miniature sausages, finely minced meat, or smoked fish can be used as a base on which to serve scrambled eggs. But the concoction should invariably be accompanied, either on the side or better under it, by a thin slice of fried bread or leaf pastry.

FOR FRIED BREAD: Cut off the crust of an ordinary loaf of white bread (*pain de mie*); from it cut thin slices, moisten each in sherry or Madeira, and brown it in hot butter. Slices may be cut in round shapes or triangles.

OEUFS BROUILLÉS À L'URIBE
[Scrambled Eggs with Tomato Paste]

Add to the beaten eggs enough tomato paste to give them a reddish tint, and season with salt and paprika.

OEUFS BROUILLÉS ARGENTEUIL
[Scrambled Eggs with Asparagus Tips]

Cook thin asparagus tips in salted water for 15 minutes; then sauté them lightly in butter. Place them all round the scrambled eggs on toast.

OEUFS BROUILLÉS À LA BERCY
[Scrambled Eggs with Sausages]

Garnish scrambled eggs with miniature sausages, and top with a spoonful of Sauce Espagnole (see page 3) mixed with tomato paste.

OEUFS BROUILLÉS ROSSINI
[Scrambled Eggs with Foie Gras and Truffles]

In hot butter, lightly sauté small slices of foie gras and, separately, small slices of truffles. Place these over the scrambled eggs, and top with a spoonful of Sauce Madère (see page 5) in the form of a little ring.

OEUFS BROUILLÉS FINDHORN
[Scrambled Eggs with Finnan Haddie]

Chop as finely as possible 1 or 2 tablespoons of cooked finnan haddie. Mix it with a little Sauce Béchamel (see page 8) or very thick cream, and lay it on fried toast, topping the whole with scrambled eggs on which you pour a little ring of béchamel.

OEUFS BROUILLÉS À LA POULETTE
[Scrambled Eggs with Mushrooms and Sauce Poulette]

Cook fresh mushrooms in butter, water, and lemon juice for 10 minutes. Cut them up in fine slices and mix them with Sauce Poulette (see page 7), then mix with the scrambled eggs and top the whole with a little ring of the sauce.

OEUFS BROUILLÉS AUX CRUSTACÉS
[*Scrambled Eggs with Shellfish*]

In a double boiler, heat small shrimps (cooked, shelled, and cleaned) in Sauce Américaine (see page 59). Spoon the mixture over scrambled eggs on toast. (Leftover bits of lobster, crab, etc., can be used as well; or the *sauce américaine* alone can be spooned over scrambled eggs on toast in a little cordon or ring.)

OEUFS BROUILLÉS À LA FLORENTINE
[*Scrambled Eggs with Spinach*]

Squeeze the water out of cooked spinach and mix with a little hot butter. Spread on buttered toast, then top the whole with scrambled eggs and spoon over them a ring of Sauce Mornay (see page 9).

OEUFS BROUILLÉS AUX FOIES DE VOLAILLES
[*Scrambled Eggs with Chicken Livers*]

Poach chicken livers (do *not* boil them) in Sauce Espagnole (see page 3) for a few minutes, or until they have turned brown. Chop them up coarsely and place them, with a spoonful of the sauce, in a hollow in the middle of your scrambled eggs.

OEUFS POCHÉS
[*Poached Eggs*]

The only practical way to poach eggs is to use a poacher furnished with little shallow cups set in a disc over boiling water. The cups should be well buttered, and the eggs broken into them when the water below is boiling. This method not only saves much care and worry, but also produces a perfectly shaped egg.

Care must be taken to cover the pan (disc and all) with its lid so that the escaping steam will cook the top of the eggs. *Above all, never allow the eggs to overcook—i.e., do not let the yolks harden.* And in removing the eggs from the little cups, care must be taken not to break the yolks: a good method is to loosen the edge of the egg in the cup with a small knife and then to turn it upside down on a napkin.

All the recipes given above for varieties of scrambled eggs may be adapted for poached eggs.

N.B. Eggs Benedict are not in the French repertory, although at *international* restaurants in France they are sometimes obtainable. Gastronomically it would appear that a poached egg on a slice of ham on half an English muffin, the whole covered with hollandaise sauce, is rather gilding the lily!

OEUFS MOLLETS
[Coddled Eggs]

These are not quite hard boiled, not quite soft boiled: the whites must be solid enough to allow removal of the shell without the egg running, but the yolks within must be liquid.

First, the eggs must not be cold out of the refrigerator, or they will split in the cooking. Second, they must be cooked together in a wire basket that fits inside a saucepan with boiling water: this facilitates the immersion of the eggs *simultaneously* into the boiling water and likewise their removal.

Third, the eggs must stay—*all at the same time*—in the boiling water no longer than 6 minutes, and must likewise be removed and plunged all at once into cold water until they are cool enough to be handled to shell. Fourth, shelling must be done delicately to avoid gouging the whites. Finally, the shelled eggs should be kept, until used, in a pan or bowl of *warm* water (not so hot as to solidify their centers).

OEUFS MOLLETS CHATEAUBRIAND
[Coddled Eggs with Artichoke Hearts]

Place coddled eggs on boiled artichoke hearts that have been carefully trimmed and lightly sautéed in butter and are surrounded by
cooked green peas. Pour Sauce Allemande (page 7) over the
whole.

OEUFS MOLLETS ARGENTEUIL
[Coddled Eggs with Puree of Asparagus]

Make a puree of boiled asparagus tips (preferably white). Fry in
butter a slice of white bread 1 inch thick, pared of its crust. Place
the coddled egg in the middle, surround with the asparagus puree,
and cover the whole with Sauce Mousseline (see page 10).

OEUFS MOLLETS À LA BÉARNAISE
[Coddled Eggs with Mashed Potatoes and Sauce Béarnaise]

Make a little patty of mashed potatoes with a hollow middle (made
by pressing with a spoon), brush it with melted butter, and brown
it lightly under the grill. Place a coddled egg in the hollow and cover
with Sauce Béarnaise (see page 11).

OEUFS MOLLETS À LA CHÂTELAINE
[Coddled Eggs with Puree of Chestnuts and Onions]

Set a coddled egg in the hollow center of a thick piece of fried
bread (without crust), surrounded by a mixture of chestnut purée
and onion puree (onion slowly softened in butter without browning). Top the whole with Sauce Allemande (see page 7).

OEUFS MOLLETS À LA CRÉCY
[Coddled Eggs with Puree of Carrots]

Place a coddled egg on a round mound of puree of carrots. Cover the whole with Sauce Mousseline (see page 10).

OEUFS MOLLETS À LA FLAMANDE
[Coddled Eggs with Stewed Endives]

Place coddled eggs on a bed of endives that have been stewed in butter and chopped coarsely. Top the whole with Sauce Allemande (see page 7).

OEUFS MOLLETS CHASSEUR
[Coddled Eggs with Puree of Mushrooms]

Place coddled egg on a fine mushroom puree that has been shaped with a small mold or an inverted glass. Cover the whole with Sauce Espagnole (see page 3) mixed with tomato paste and a few drops of Cognac.

OEUFS FRITS
[Fried Eggs]

Prosper Montagné gives some 280 egg recipes. Only some 15 are for fried eggs. This suggests that the latter are not a favorite preparation in French cookery. They are, moreover, probably less digestible than other egg dishes.

Fried eggs are nevertheless required for certain elaborate preparations, such as Poulet Sauté Marengo (see page 173), and various exotic dishes.

To obtain a properly fried egg, you must fry only one at a time. The pan must be small so the required amount of oil—12 spoonfuls, or ¾ cup—will not spread out too shallow: it should half cover the egg. The oil must be practically odorless and tasteless; the egg must be absolutely fresh.

When the oil in the pan begins to smoke lightly, slip in the egg and add a small pinch of salt to the *yolk* (the white dissolves a bit with salt). With a small skimmer, flip hot oil onto the yolk. When you see the white setting, turn the egg over, then lift it *immediately* with the skimmer and lay it on a clean cloth over a warm plate. Each egg requires just 1 minute to fry.

The oil in the pan must not smoke heavily, and no particle of egg should remain in the oil after frying. This requires removing the pan from the heat as needed, and skimming as well.

A practiced hand can fry a dozen eggs in less than a quarter of an hour.

OEUFS À L'ALSACIENNE
[Fried Eggs with Ham and Sauerkraut]

Fried eggs on a slice of ham over sauerkraut, topped with Sauce Allemande (see page 7).

OEUFS À L'ESPAGNOLE
[Fried Eggs with Tomatoes, Red Peppers, and Onions]

Fried eggs garnished on the side with tomatoes and red peppers sautéed in oil, onions lightly softened (in rings) likewise, and the whole sprinkled with Sauce Espagnole (see page 3) mixed with tomato paste.

OEUFS À LA GENOISE
[Fried Eggs with Macaroni]

Fried eggs on boiled cut macaroni (well drained), topped with Sauce Espagnole (see page 3) mixed with tomato paste and spiced with a pinch or two of saffron. (If saffron threads are used, grind them in a small mortar and dissolve them in a little white wine or even water.)

OEUFS SUR LE PLAT
[Shirred Eggs]

Individual shirring dishes, each containing one or two eggs, are preferable for easier serving.

Only a small amount of butter—just enough to grease the dish, and again as much melted—is required.

The greased dish is heated, the egg is dropped into it, and its yolk is lightly anointed with the melted butter. Then the dish is put in a medium oven (350° F.) for 3 or 4 minutes, or until the white is set. Salt and white pepper are added after the dish is removed from the oven.

When many eggs are cooked simultaneously, it is convenient to place the little dishes in a large roasting pan, thus assuring even cook-ing and easy handling. The slight glaze formed over the yolks in this process has earned for these eggs the alternative name *oeufs miroir* ("mirror eggs").

N.B. Almost any garnishing—meats, vegetables (cooked or raw), shellfish, etc.—will go with shirred eggs.

OEUFS SUR LE PLAT ARCHIDUC
[Shirred Eggs with Onions, Truffles, and Sauce Allemande]

Over the shirred eggs put chopped onions that have been softened gently in butter and seasoned with paprika. Sprinkle with minced truffle and top with Sauce Allemande (see page 7), lightly mixed with paprika.

OEUFS BERCY
[Shirred Eggs with Sausages]

Garnish shirred eggs with small sausages that have been sautéed in butter.

OEUFS YORKSHIRE
[Shirred Eggs with Ham and Sauce Allemande]

Garnish shirred eggs with minced York ham (or Virginia ham) and top with Sauce Allemande (see page 7).

OEUFS AUX WITLOOFS
[Shirred Eggs with Endives and Sauce Allemande]

Flank shirred eggs with braised endives, and cover with Sauce Allemande (see page 7) that has been laced with thick cream.

OEUFS GRATINÉS
[Shirred Eggs with Sauce Mornay]

As the eggs go into the oven, pour over them a little Sauce Mornay (see page 9), and on that put very small pats of butter.

OEUFS À LA MEXICAINE
["Ranch-Style Eggs"—Shirred Eggs with Bacon, Tomatoes, and Chilies]

Cook thin slices of bacon in the shirring dish, add slices of tomatoes and a few chilies, and drop an egg into the sizzling fat.

OEUFS MEYERBEER
[Shirred Eggs with Lamb Kidneys]

Garnish shirred eggs with sautéed lamb kidneys, and top with
Sauce Madère (see page 5) that has been mixed with a little foie
gras and minced truffles.

OEUFS À LA COQUE
[Soft-Boiled Eggs]

Very fresh eggs, soft boiled and sitting in their little egg cups of
fine porcelain, are served at elegant Parisian houses as a first dish.
Small gold or gold-plated spoons (which are not discolored by contact
with the egg) are used to cut the top of the egg and to eat it from
its shell.

Eggs should be washed carefully in lukewarm water before boiling.
If kept in the refrigerator, they should be allowed to warm up to
room temperature; otherwise there is a risk of their bursting in cooking. Also, they should never be kept near strong smells, because egg
shells are porous and absorb them.

The safest and perhaps best method of soft-boiling eggs is to put
them in a saucepan with enough cold water to cover them well. Bring
the water to the boil and withdraw the pan from the heat. One
minute later take the egg out of the water. If you wait until the water
boils furiously and then remove the egg from it, you will, of course,
have a slightly more cooked egg.

Like many other simple preparations, soft-boiled eggs have to be
taken seriously if they are to be good.

OEUFS DURS
[Hard-Boiled Eggs]

Put the raw eggs in cold water to cover. From the time the water
boils, count 8 minutes of cooking. Remove them, put them in cold
water, and shell them. (There is a risk that eggs cooked in this way

will have a lop-sided appearance when shelled; on the other hand, there is always the risk that the eggs will burst if they are cooked by plunging them into boiling water.)

Hard-boiled eggs can be made into attractive and delicious dishes by cutting them in halves or in quarters, then scooping out the yolks and mixing them with anchovy butter, curry sauce, creamed onions, or tomato paste, etc. The egg whites are then refilled with the mixture and topped with Sauce Allemande (see page 7) or Sauce Espagnole (see page 3), with the addition possibly of tomato paste, chopped parsley, or some other herb or condiment.

SOUFFLÉS
SOUFFLÉ MAR'JEANNE
[A Cheese Soufflé]

For 4 persons

Separate carefully the yolks and the whites of 4 eggs into two bowls and set aside. Mix 3 or 4 spoonfuls of powdered milk and $1\frac{1}{2}$ to 2 cups of water, and season with salt and white pepper and a pinch of mace (or nutmeg). Set this seasoned milk aside as well.

In a medium-sized saucepan, melt 4 spoonfuls of unsalted butter. As soon as it melts completely, add 4 spoonfuls of sifted all-purpose flour. Stir on medium heat, scraping the bottom of the pan but stopping now and then for a second or two to let the mixture fluff up. At the first sign of *yellowing*, add a little of the seasoned milk, stirring vigorously, to form a smooth, creamy paste. Add more milk as you go along, stirring and mixing to prevent lumping, removing the pan from the heat when you fear that the mixture is drying, adding milk bit by bit until you have a very thick kind of béchamel—almost as thick as very creamy mashed potatoes. Remove from the heat.

Beat the egg yolks to a froth and add them to the flour and milk mixture once it has cooled enough for you to stick your finger into it without discomfort. Beat the whole vigorously, then gradually add 2 ounces (about $\frac{1}{2}$ cup) grated Gruyère or Emmenthal cheese and mix thoroughly.

Now beat the whites until they are *stiff*—i.e., until a spoonful of beaten whites will stand up at the end of the egg beater when held upside down, and there is no more liquid at the bottom of the bowl. Then, with a wide spatula, cut into the beaten whites, scoop some out, and *thrust* it into the egg yolk–cheese mixture, turning the spatula and lifting it in order to incorporate the beaten whites without mashing them down; the object here is to avoid losing the tiny bubbles of air in the beaten whites. Continue this process until all the whites are incorporated. Pour the whole into a soufflé mold, about 7 inches in diameter and 3 inches deep, that has been well buttered, bottom and sides, and kept in a warm place (perhaps over hot water).

Put the soufflé in an oven preheated to 375° F. and bake for 18 to 20 minutes. The soufflé should be golden yellow on top and runny creamy at the bottom.

SOUFFLÉ AU FROMAGE SURPRISE
[*Cheese Soufflé with Coddled Eggs*]

This is a cheese soufflé containing a surprise: coddled eggs.

Follow the recipe above, but pour only one-third of the mixture into the mold. Then place 1 coddled egg (shelled, of course) per person on this layer and pour the rest of the mixture on top. (For coddled eggs, see page 31.)

SOUFFLÉ FINDHORN
[*Finnan Haddie Soufflé*]

Follow the recipe above for Soufflé Mar'Jeanne, but instead of the milk use the cooking liquor from finnan haddie, and instead of cheese add a cup of flaked, cooked finnan haddie.

FISH AND VEGETABLE SOUFFLÉS

Follow the recipe above, but instead of using the finnan haddie cooking liquor use plain milk, and for the cooked finnan haddie substitute a pureed vegetable that has been dried on a buttered pan (or fish, likewise treated). Any addition of watery substances will keep the soufflé from rising.

SWEET SOUFFLÉS

Follow the recipe above for Soufflé Mar'Jeanne, but omit salt and pepper and add to the milk the flavor desired. Vanilla extract of excellent quality is satisfactory, but the infusion of a real vanilla "bean" in the milk, heated to boiling, is preferable. Sugar should be added to the milk, to taste.

SOUFFLÉ AU CURAÇAO

The best method for this soufflé is to rub sugar lumps on the skin of an orange, turning it this way and that until the lump is well impregnated with the zest, and sweetening the milk (hot) to taste by dissolving the sugar lumps in it. The addition of Curaçao liqueur at the moment of presentation by thrusting a knife into the soufflé and pouring a jigger of the liqueur into the hole is a trick practiced with good effect in some restaurants.

CHAPTER 4

Crêpes

FRENCH PANCAKES are, like soufflés, principally a mixture of flour, egg, and milk. They can be made sweet or salt, for a dessert or for a first dish at lunch.

Crêpes are prepared on the street, on electric griddles, all over Paris during the cold weather, and are generally eaten on the spot by the customers, a piece of paper "protecting" the fingers. Usually the crêpes are lightly sprinkled with a butter and jam mixture. In Brittany the country people make a meal of crêpes prepared on the open hearth and eaten with little garnishing.

CRÊPES MAR'JEANNE

These can be used for a dessert with a sweet filler, flamed or not, or for a lunch dish with a creamy filler of meat, vegetables, or fish.

For about 10 crêpes

Make a mound of 6 heaping spoonfuls of all-purpose flour, then make a hollow in the top. Break an egg into the hollow, add 2 *salt-*

spoonfuls of salt, and mix well with a spoon. Gradually add a wine-glass of milk mixed with 2¾ wineglassfuls of water. This will result in a thin-creamy consistency; the batter must be very well mixed.

Any small frying pan, preferably of plain iron, may be used; but a special, rather heavy pan with a low rim and small diameter (7 inches) is preferable, especially for flipping the pancakes in the air. It must be kept greased constantly by rubbing the inside with a piece of raw pork fat. (After use, it is advisable to put away the pan in a cellophane bag to keep it free from dust.)

Having heated the pan to the point where a drop of the batter cooks instantly, pour into it about one-third of a soup ladle of the mixture and immediately roll it around the pan so it spreads all over. Set the pan on the heat again, and without lifting it move it back and forth so as to loosen the pancake from the pan. If it sticks, loosen it with a spatula.

Lift a corner of the crêpe with the spatula to see if it has browned. If so, grasp the handle of the pan firmly and jerk it upwards with a slight tilt toward yourself: the pancake will turn in the air and land back on the pan, uncooked side down. The first attempt is hardly ever successful, but practice makes perfect.

Crêpes should be thin and of a golden color. They should be put on a warm plate, one on top of another, and covered.

CRÊPES SUZETTE
[Flamed French Pancakes]

The best pans for flaming pancakes are lined with silver or are silver plated with a copper bottom. Tin-lined pans and aluminum pans are unadvisable, because these metals tend to discolor the sauce. An enameled pan, on the other hand, is perfectly acceptable.

Having prepared the pancakes (Crêpes Mar'Jeanne, above), rub 6 large lumps of sugar on an orange or two to get them to absorb the zest. Grind the lumps and mix them with about 6 spoonfuls of un-salted butter (half butter and half sugar, measured in spoonfuls), then put a spoonful of this mixture on each pancake. Either fold the pancake in half and then again in half (making a triangular shape) or roll it up.

Place the pancakes in a buttered flaming-pan and put it on medium heat. Pour over the crêpes about 2 spoonfuls each Curaçao and Cognac. When the liquid in the pan has become hot enough, light it with a match (take care not to drop the head of the match into the pan—and beware of the sudden burst of flame). If you work over an alcohol flame, as with a chafing dish, a slight inclination of the pan will make the flame of the burner leap onto the pan—an amusing trick. The flame can be fanned out with your hand.

Enough of the sugar and butter in the crêpes will ooze out to furnish the sauce, which is then spooned over them. Serve immediately.

CRÊPES AU POISSON À L'ANGEVINE
[Crêpes with Sole and Sorrel]

Having prepared the pancakes (Crêpes Mar'Jeanne, above), melt 4 spoonfuls of butter. Add to it 2 or 3 (depending on size) fillets of sole without any trace of bones or skin. Season with salt and pepper and cook on minimum heat until the fillets turn white, like chalk.

In another pan, melt a spoonful of butter. Add to it a handful of sorrel leaves, pared of all stems. Cook the leaves for 5 minutes, then bind them with a well-beaten yolk of egg. Mix the result into a rough hash with the cooked fish, and fill the pancakes with it, rolling them up. Warm them in a covered pan in a medium oven for a few minutes.

If, at the moment of serving, the pancakes seem too dry, cover them with a little Sauce Béchamel (see page 8) mixed with the butter left in the pan in which the fish was cooked.

N.B. In the United States, the lemon sole (Fr. *limande*) is commonly called "sole."

CRÊPES POULETTE
[Crêpes with Chopped Mushrooms]

Sauté mushrooms in butter for 5 minutes, season them with salt (preferably onion salt) and pepper and a little lemon juice, bind them with a well-beaten egg yolk, add heavy cream, chop them up, and roll up in Crêpes Mar'Jeanne (see above). If dry, cover with Sauce Poulette (see page 7).

CHAPTER 5

Rice, Gnocchi, and Noodles

DRY WHITE RICE

BY THIS IS MEANT cooked rice unseasoned except for salt, dry as opposed to mushy or gummy, with grains separate from one another but soft to chew. It is cooked thus in rice-growing countries.

Butter is anathema in the preparation of such rice, because butter is simply not a cooking fat in such countries. Milk in hot tropical countries contains little butterfat; milk has to be kept from souring by boiling soon after leaving the cow, so the rustics could not separate the cream (if there were any) by the old method of settling pans. In India the liquid butter called *ghee* tastes rancid to a Westerner, and can be tolerated only in curries of such high seasoning that it is hardly perceptible.

Vegetable oils are used in cooking where industrial development has reached the level of machinery for their extraction. This is not the case of the torrid tropical countries where rice is grown; and, if it is in some areas, it is not rooted in the past.

Pork lard, then, is the cooking fat of that part of the world, and, whatever other objections may be raised against its use as a general frying and baking agent, it is unbeatable when it comes to preparing dry white rice. For this there are two principal methods.

METHOD 1: The most widespread method is to wash the rice in cold water three times and to throw away the water, which contains a good portion of the nourishment of the cereal; then, to throw it into a large pot of boiling salted water—not dribbling it as in civilized centers. After 20 to 25 minutes of boiling, a spoonful of pork lard is added with the juice of ½ lemon—sometimes. The pot is removed from the fire and whatever water left in it is drained out; the rice is put back in the pot and left off the fire to "dry." The results, from the hands of a person who has done this a lifetime, are excellent; and it would seem that the rougher the elements, such as in working-camp cooking, the better the results.

METHOD 2: The most reliable method is not to wash the rice, thereby saving a good part of its nourishment, but to throw it dry into very hot lard, give it a stir until the grains lose their slight "pearliness" and turn chalk white, and then cover them with salted boiling water by about ½ inch. Again *one* rapid stir, and immediately clap on the lid—which must fit well (not, however, a pressure-cooker) and let only a wisp of steam escape. After 10 or 15 minutes, lift the lid for one second to see if the water has been absorbed. If it has, there will be on the surface of the rice a ring of little pits. Then remove it from the heat, always with the lid on.

Temper the heat to minimum, and after 10 minutes or so replace the pot on this very mild heat. It is better to let it thus remain for at least ½ hour before serving: it is best to cook it the day before and warm it up in a double boiler. Before serving, fluff it up with a fork. (A heavy enameled cast-iron cocotte is necessary to avoid burning of the rice.) This method is very easily mastered.

The proportions of rice and water are about 1 to 2, respectively. One-half cup (U.S.) of dry rice is enough for two or even three hearty eaters.

A final note: if the rice "catches" a little at the bottom of the pot, forming a yellow (not black) "gratin," do not be distressed, as this is highly appreciated by connoisseurs. It is crisp to the tooth but not offensively so. The rustics of some Spanish-American countries call it *cocolón*, and prize it highly.

GNOCCHI À LA PARISIENNE
[Gnocchi with Mornay Sauce]

Heat 2 cups of milk with 6 spoonfuls of butter and a pinch each of salt, white pepper, and nutmeg. When it boils, remove from the heat and throw in 8 ounces sifted all-purpose flour. Stir furiously with a short wooden spoon to beat the mixture, placing it again on the heat from time to time without ceasing to stir and beat until it comes off the bottom and sides of the pan. *This requires vigorous work.*

The proper condition is attained when the dough (as it should be called) no longer sticks to the pan and can be handled without the hands getting sticky. Then, without letting the pan get cold, *add one by one* 6 whole eggs, beating and mixing strenuously so that each egg is absorbed by the dough before the next one is added. The time necessary for this tense operation depends on the speed and effort put in by the cook. Ordinarily you can count on 30 to 45 minutes.

On a lightly floured board or glazed paper, shape the dough into a long sausage about 1½ inches thick. Cut off 1-inch pieces and throw them into a wide pan containing *boiling* salted water. The pieces go to the bottom and then they float—which is the moment to remove them from the water with a skimmer. Put them on a large, flat drainer, such as a bread-cooling rack.

Arrange the *gnocchi* in one layer on a heatproof dish that has been well buttered. Pour over them thick Sauce Mornay (see page 9). Dot small pats of butter over the whole, and brown lightly in the oven.

NOUILLES
[Noodles]

For 4 persons:

Sift 4 ounces of all-purpose flour into a solid bowl (to resist the beating). Make a hollow in the center of the flour, and into it pour

1 whole egg that has been beaten with a pinch of salt and 1 egg yolk. Beat flour and egg vigorously. (If the dough becomes flaky, add another egg yolk; but you must not aim for a soft dough or an elastic or "pully" one.) Roll the dough into a ball and wrap it up in a clean cloth. Let it "rest" for at least 1 hour, in a cool place if possible but *not* in the refrigerator: this helps to eliminate elasticity.

Break the ball, if necessary, and spread it with a rolling pin into a very thin sheet. Roll this up, like a roll of paper, and cut across in strips. These strips are noodles, so, in spreading out the ball of dough, you must calculate a length of at least 8 inches for them. If they seem sticky, dust them very lightly with flour. Finally, if possible, hang them over a cord stretched out to dry for about an hour, or lay them stretched out on a clean, dry cloth for that time.

NOUILLES À LA CRÈME
[Noodles in Fresh Cream]

Boil the noodles in salted water, uncovered, for 8 minutes, then drain them and put them, with a spoonful of butter in an enameled frying pan on medium heat. Add heavy cream to make a sauce, and a pinch of salt and another of nutmeg. Stir delicately and serve on hot plates.

This delicious dish is very attractive when finished in a chafing dish at table, and does very well as a first course at luncheon.

NOUILLES AU BEURRE MAÎTRE D'HÔTEL
[Noodles with Butter]

Boil the noodles in salted water, uncovered, for 8 minutes, then drain them and put them in a serving dish. Add small portions of Beurre Maître d'Hôtel (see page 59) and turn them over and over with two forks.

Shrimp, lobster, or crayfish butter can be used in the same way; so can beef marrow cut in small pieces, put in boiling water for a few seconds and then kept in that water, off the heat, for 1 minute.

CHAPTER 6

Fish

ALTHOUGH THE HUGE United States, with frontage on two oceans, the Great Lakes, and the Gulf of Mexico, can boast of a much greater variety of seafood, freshwater fish, and shellfish than France, French fishmongers, especially in Paris, usually offer much more to choose from than do their American counterparts. And while it is true that the real fish lover prefers simple preparations that bring out the flavor of each kind, the French have carried the art of fish cuisine to incomparable heights.

You can tell if the fish you select is fresh if the eyes are shining bright, the gills are rosy and *not* brown-red, and the flesh is firm to the touch. Soles and their ilk resist skinning when fresh; if the fishmonger skins them without effort, they are not fresh. If these conditions are not met, do not take the fish.

Generally speaking, shellfish should be purchased alive; however, there are reliable fishmongers who sell cooked shrimps and lobsters that are irreproachable.

Smoked fish, especially the delicious French cod bathed in pyroligneous acid and partially dried, is difficult to judge as to freshness, the best guide being the nose.

Only exceptional fishmongers scale fishes properly, and the fish has to be washed at home. It is best to run the back of the knife from the tail to the head, holding it away from you to avoid the spatter of scales. Cold water from the tap should be run through the fish to remove traces of blood and entrails. The tail should be cut off with scissors almost down to the flesh; the head should be kept on.

A fish that is to be grilled, such as a sole or a similar flat fish, should be skinned; and the fillets should be very slightly raised, with the point of a small sharp knife, on both sides: this allows the heat to penetrate more readily. To skin the fish, cut the skin across at the root of the head and pull down with your fingers toward the tail.

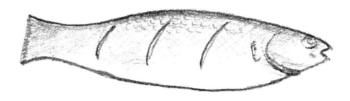

A fish readied for the oven

For roasting or braising, fish should be *scored*, i.e., diagonal gashes should be cut not too deep from head to tail, three or four according to the size of the fish.

POACHING

Boiling is not a proper way to cook fish—you might say "Fish boiled is fish spoiled" (excepting shellfish). But poaching is an excellent way.

Whatever liquid you use to poach fish, it must be cold when you put the fish in it, and it should almost cover the fish. The heat should be turned on after the utensil, which should not be covered, has been put on the stove. *As soon as the first signs of boiling appear, reduce the heat to minimum, where the liquid cannot possibly boil, and cover the utensil with aluminum foil.*

Fat fishes weighing 1½ pounds should simmer for about 15 minutes. The smaller the fish, the longer the time required *per weight.* A practical test is the change in the color of the flesh (which can be seen by scraping a bit of skin where it is scored) from bluish opalescent to white. The longer fish is cooked, the *fishier* it gets: this must be remembered especially in making fish soups and stock.

For poaching as well as for baking fish, enameled cast-iron dishes that follow roughly the shape of "round" fishes are advisable: they heat slowly and cool off equally slowly. For large turbots there are special tin-lined copper kettles the shape of this fish; but these are hardly practical for home cookery.

A court-bouillon is generally the preferred liquid for poaching fish, excepting trout to be *cooked blue* (*truite au bleu*) and milk-cooked fish such as finnan haddie.

COURT-BOUILLON FOR POACHING

To 2 cups of cold water, add ½ cup good white wine vinegar (tarragon vinegar will do), ½ spoonful salt, 2 onions (each peeled and stuck with a clove), a sprig of fresh thyme (or ¼ teaspoon dried), a bay leaf, several stalks of parsley, and (if you do not object) garlic.

Cover and boil for 45 minutes to 1 hour, then withdraw from the heat and let cool, covered. (If you are in a hurry, put the covered saucepan in a larger one with cold water.)

A more delicate court-bouillon can be made by replacing the vinegar with dry white wine: use 2 cups with 1 cup water (*no vinegar*). Or *red* wine may be used; if the quality is good and the wine light in body, use 2½ cups (*no* vinegar, *no* water).

N.B. Court-bouillon made with vinegar is of little use after the fish is poached, but if made with wine can be used for certain sauces.

FRYING

By this of course is meant *deep frying* in oil or lard. Obviously, unless the kitchen is equipped with a powerful ventilating system, frying fish will fill the atmosphere with a strong, penetrating odor.

Oil that has not already been used sometimes froths dangerously when the fish is added; so let it cook first by itself for some 25 minutes. Carefully strained and cooled, it can be used two or three times.

Large fishes weighing over 1½ pounds should not be fried, except in the form of fillets or "steaks," and those under this weight, if "round," should be scored. All fishes, fillets, or "steaks" to be fried either should be moistened with milk (easily done on a plate) and rolled in all-purpose flour sprinkled with salt, or they should be dipped in a batter prepared thus:

PÂTE À FRIRE POUR POISSONS
[Batter for Frying Fish]

Mix thoroughly 4 ounces sifted all-purpose flour, a good pinch of salt, 2 spoonfuls cooking oil, and ⅔ cup lukewarm water. At the moment of using, add 2 egg whites, beaten *stiff*.

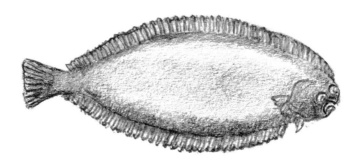

True sole

Season the fish with salt and white pepper, and dredge lightly in flour; then pick up with a fork and dip in the batter for a few seconds, lift to let drip a little, and plunge in hot fat. As soon as golden, lift it with a skimmer to a piece of brown wrapping paper. Do not let it cool.

The oil should be sufficient to cover the fish amply, and very hot (lightly smoking). *The smaller the fish the hotter the oil.* Thus the heat will penetrate the thicker fish without forming a crust on the surface that would leave the flesh inside raw. If you raise the temperature while the fish is frying, so much the better because the inner flesh will then be cooked; but a drop in temperature while frying will give you an oily, limp fish. *From the moment you put the fish in the lightly smoking oil until you take it out with a skimmer, allow 10 minutes for the bigger fishes and half this time for the smaller ones, bearing in mind that if you fry several smaller fishes at the same time you must count almost as much time as for a big one.* All this applies of course to fillets and steaks (and to "scrod" in New England), as well as to whole fish.

N.B. Fried parsley is practically always served with fried fish (and even with sautéed ones). A small frying basket is very useful here. The parsley, well dried to prevent dangerous spattering when it is immersed in the hot oil, remains in it just an instant: it is immediately removed and drained on brown paper. It should be bright green and crisp.

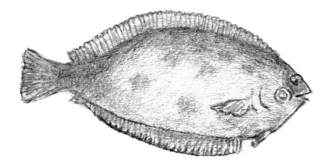

Lemon sole

SAUTÉING

The French verb *sauter*, meaning "to jump," is now recognized by the *Oxford English Dictionary* as a cookery term. It means in both languages cooking in a shallow pan in shallow fat (usually in butter and for a short time). The "jump" is hazily conveyed when the pan is moved back and forth over the heat: very far fetched it seems!

Flat fishes such as sole (the true sole is not found in American waters but is shipped frozen from Europe and is very acceptable), lemon sole, flounder, and perhaps very small "chicken" halibuts are appropriate for sautéing whole. Scrod and fillets or slices of other fishes, if they are thin, may be sautéed.

To sauté properly, the butter in the pan should be enough to cover its entire bottom, even when slightly tilted, and sizzling hot. It must not turn black: burnt butter is very indigestible. A good way to avoid the burning of butter is to use it clarified (see page 10). Indeed, if you have several fishes or pieces of fish to sauté, it is best to do it in clarified butter. According to the size of the fish, the time will be 10 to 20 minutes, the butter being very hot.

First, season the fish with salt and white pepper, and dredge it in all-purpose flour. Shake off the excess flour by picking the fish up with a fork under the head, or with the fingers by the tail, and set it in the hot clarified butter. After 5 minutes turn it—a slight push-and-pull motion of the pan (in French, *va-et-vient*) is advisable—and, when the fish is golden yellow, lift it to a serving platter (hot) and pour over it hot unclarified butter that, in another utensil, you have melted but *not* allowed to brown. Sprinkle chopped parsley over all and serve immediately.

N.B. Lemon in halves or quarters is usually served with fried, sautéed, or grilled fish.

GRILLING

Flat fishes and slices of other fishes are appropriate for grilling. (A nonflat fish that is to be grilled whole or in halves must be split from head to tail and opened up like a book in order to make it, in effect, like a flat fish.) One-inch cubes of swordfish, fresh tuna, or salmon on a brochette are equally suitable.

After washing, the fish must be dried thoroughly, brushed with melted butter, and then seasoned with salt and pepper; onion salt and dill weed (dried) are excellent complements.

Grilling must be done as much *in the open* as possible, preferably over coals in the hearth (rare today) or under an electric caloroid in an appliance with front and sides entirely open. When you have an enclosed space, even with one side open—such as in an oven, portable or not—you will have surrounding heat, in other words *baking*. Grilling sears food quickly; baking cooks by enveloping food in heat. If an open electric grill is not available, use a so-called barbecue gadget burning charcoal or coke.

As fish cooks very quickly, it is advisable to set it on a grill for the first 5 minutes about 5 inches below the red-hot caloroid; this should turn it brownish yellow. Then raise the fish to about half that distance from the heat for 2 minutes. Lower it again to turn it around with two spatulas, and repeat the performance, but shortening the process by half ($2\frac{1}{2}$ minutes at 5 inches, 1 minute at $2\frac{1}{2}$).

N.B. Melted butter and halved or quartered lemon are customary with grilled fish.

In Mediterranean France a kind of striped bass, called there *loup de mer* ("seawolf"), is grilled over a fire made of wild fennel twigs, which impart a decided flavor to the fish. However, restaurants are apt to roast the fish on an open wood fire or even in an oven and then serve it on burning fennel twigs after appropriate seasoning with powdered fennel. The latter version can be copied at home, with striped bass, if the twigs are procurable.

OPEN-FIRE ROASTING

This process, erroneously called "barbecuing," is excellent if well handled. (Barbecuing is a rough, Spanish-American method of cooking meat.)

After washing, fish should be well dried and seasoned with salt and pepper, then wrapped in oiled paper, spitted, and secured to the spit by metal string or wire—unless the spit is equipped with proper clamps. The fire should be bright but not hot enough to burn the paper. The time of roasting may be estimated at 15 minutes to the pound—very roughly, as so much depends on the heat and nearness of the fire. Here only experience can rule.

BAKING

Baking in the oven is the convenient way of cooking fishes that are not flat and that weigh $1\frac{1}{2}$ or more pounds. The oven should be preheated to 250°–300° F. As in all fish cooking, the temperature should be higher for the smaller fish.

A bed of rather thickly (so that they will not burn easily) sliced onions and diced or sliced carrots, chopped up mushrooms, and herbs should line the baking dish, which should be about the shape and size of the fish and of enameled cast iron. The fish should be scored, and several spoonfuls of clarified butter (see page 10) poured over it; then it should be seasoned with salt and white pepper. (The seasoning should be added *after* the butter, which otherwise would cause the seasoning to run off the fish.)

Basting is not necessary except in the case of a very large fish requiring more than half an hour in the oven.

BRAISING

As this is a combination of sautéing and baking, the remarks regarding both processes apply.

FONDS (or BOUILLON or FUMET) DE POISSON
[Fish Stock]

Put into a thick enameled iron cocotte or stewpan 3 or 4 spoonfuls of clarified butter (see page 10), 4 or 5 spoonfuls of chopped onion, a bay leaf, a sprig of fresh thyme (or $1/4$ teaspoon dried), several stalks of parsley (crushed), and some mushroom peelings (if handy). Set on low heat, covered.

After 20 minutes, during which you stir from time to time to prevent discoloring or sticking at the bottom, add approximately 1 pound of raw fish heads and tails (what fishmongers throw away when filleting). Mix well, and increase the heat to medium. After 5 minutes, add 1 cup of dry white wine and 2 cups of cold water (or enough wine and water in the proportion of 1 to 2 to cover the solid contents by about 2 inches). Bring to a boil, cover, and set the heat to keep boiling gently 30 minutes. (*More boiling than this may make the broth turbid, which is undesirable.*) Season with salt and white pepper.

BEURRES ASSAISONÉS POUR POISSONS
[Seasoned Butters for Fish]

BEURRE D'AIL
[Garlic Butter]

Boil peeled garlic cloves in water for 2 minutes. Grind in a mortar and mix well with twice their amount of butter. Strain through fine mesh.

BEURRE D'ANCHOIS
[Anchovy Butter]

Strip off the flesh of salted anchovies with a small knife, and grind into a paste. Mix with twice its amount of butter, then strain through fine mesh.

BEURRE DE CHAMPIGNONS
[Mushroom Butter]

Chop up well-washed and dried mushrooms (minus the tip of the stems), and sauté them lightly in butter. Season with salt and white pepper and add a drop of lemon juice. Grind in a mortar; mix well with an equal amount of butter. Strain through fine mesh.

BEURRE D'ÉCREVISSES, CREVETTES, OU HOMARD
[Crayfish, Shrimp, or Lobster Butter]

Peel and finely dice 6 medium carrots and 6 medium onions (the quantity of carrots and of onions should be about the same) and put in a cocotte with finely diced celeriac (about half the quantity of the carrots and onions, or 2 thin slices) and the heads, shells, and other debris of 6 to 8 crayfish or shrimp, or of 1 lobster. Add to the cocotte enough good cooking oil or clarified butter (see page 10) to spread all over the bottom (about ⅓ cup) and add a dash each of powdered fennel, salt, and pepper. Stir to mix. Cook on medium heat for 30 minutes, then remove the shells, heads, and other shellfish debris. Pound into a paste in a mortar, then add to this the strained juice from the cocotte.

Once cooled, add a few drops of red vegetable dye and fresh butter, enough to make the mixture orange-red. Strain this through fine mesh to clear it of particles of shell, then cool to solidify.

N.B. The coral of crustaceans, if not otherwise used, should be added to this paste.

BEURRE MAÎTRE D'HÔTEL
[Parsley Butter]

Wrap butter in a clean cloth, and let soften at room temperature (do not melt). Mix it well, *without mashing excessively,* with chopped parsley leaves, salt and white pepper, and a few drops of lemon juice.

BEURRE NOIR
[Black or "Burnt" Butter]

This is really neither *noir* ("black") nor burnt: burnt fats are practically poisonous.

In a small saucepan, reduce 2 tablespoons good wine vinegar to 1 tablespoon on moderately high heat. At the same time, in another saucepan, heat 4 spoonfuls of unsalted butter until it is deep brown. Withdraw from the heat for a minute or two, then add the reduced vinegar to the brown butter.

N.B. Care must be taken *not* to add the vinegar to the brown butter while it is very hot *or you risk dangerous spattering.* A precaution worth considering is to pour the hot brown butter into a sauceboat and *then* add the reduced vinegar.

FISH SAUCES

SAUCE AMÉRICAINE
[Tomato and Lobster Sauce]

This is sometimes erroneously called *Sauce Armoricaine* (from Armorica, the Roman name for Brittany, which is *not* a country for tomatoes, an essential ingredient).

(continued)

For about 1 cup

This sauce is made best with the cooking liquor of Lobster à l'Américaine (see page 100). Lacking that, take the shell and other waste portions of a lobster and, unless boiled very red, cook them in clarified butter (see page 10) to obtain that color, then crush them and pound them in a stone mortar to obtain a paste. Add the paste to ½ cup finely diced, cored carrots, ½ cup chopped shallots, and a bay leaf, and cook over medium heat for half an hour.

Pour over the pan contents a small glass of good Cognac, and set a match to it to flame for an instant. If necessary, put the flame out by covering the saucepan with its lid. Add 2 spoonfuls of tomato paste, ½ cup dry white wine (such as Pouilly-Fuissé, Pouilly-Fumé, or Graves Sec) and ½ cup concentrated beef consommé. Stir and boil gently for half an hour, then strain through fine mesh.

Just before serving, to thicken the sauce, add, off the heat, ¼ pound of unsalted butter that has been thoroughly mixed with 2 ounces of all-purpose flour. (If the sauce is not a nice red color, add 2 or 3 drops of red vegetable dye.)

SAUCE GENEVOISE
[*Properly, Sauce Genoise*]

Proceed exactly as for Sauce Espagnole (see page 3) *except* substitute a broth made of fish heads, tails, and bones (cooked about 45 minutes) for the beef consommé, and a good Bordeaux *red* wine for the white wine. And, when all the wine has been used, add ½ teaspoon of anchovy butter (made by mixing butter and boned, mashed, tinned anchovies and then straining the mixture).

SAUCE BEURRE BLANC
[*White Butter Sauce*]

Cook 2 spoonfuls finely chopped shallots slowly in ½ cup white wine vinegar (or very dry white wine, such as Muscadet) until only 1 spoonful of liquid is left. Gradually add ½ pound of unsalted butter, whipping it continuously with an egg beater so that it froths up, then season with salt and white pepper to taste. Strain.

FISH DISHES

ALOSE
[Shad]

ALOSE GRILLÉ À L'OSEILLE
[Grilled Shad with Sorrel]

For 4 persons

Score a 2½′ to 3-pound shad deeply and marinate it for 1 hour, in a *cool* place, in 3 spoonfuls each of olive oil, white wine vinegar or lemon juice, enough thin onion rings to cover the fish, salt and white pepper (dill weed is also recommended), then brush off these components and brush on clarified butter (see page 10). Put the fish under a hot grill and, after 10 minutes, turn it over. Brush again with clarified butter and season with onion salt and white pepper. Turn it over again after 10 minutes, and cook under reduced heat for 15 minutes. (Cooking times given total 35 minutes, which is right for a shad of 2½ to 3 pounds. For quicker grilling—i.e., 20 to 30 minutes—take a shad that has been split in half its entire length.)

Serve the fish on a bed of sorrel leaves (minus stems) melted in butter and then whipped together into a cream with raw egg yolk.

ALOSE POCHÉ, BEURRE BLANC
[Poached Shad with Butter]

Poach the whole fish in a white wine or vinegar court-bouillon (see page 51), then drain it on a rack. Over it pour Sauce Beurre Blanc (see page 60).

ALOSE ARÊTES FONDANTES
[Shad with "Melted" Bones]

For 4 persons

To 1 or 2 cups (depending on the size of the fish) Sauce Alle-mande (see page 7), add 3 or 4 finely chopped shallots and I clove garlic (crushed). Cut the flesh of a shad in strips 1½ inches thick and lay them in a thick saucepan that has a good lid and has been well buttered.

Mix 1 spoonful of white wine vinegar with the sauce and pour it over the fish. Spread 2 thin slices of raw ham, cut into strips, over all, and a few sorrel leaves. Bring to a boil, cover well, and cook in a very moderate oven (200° F.) for 6 or 7 hours.

Add a small glass of Cognac or applejack or marc an hour or so before serving. (The bones will be softened so that you can chew and swallow them).

ANGUILLE
[Eel]

The eel *must* be alive.

After killing the eel with a sharp blow on the head, grasp it in a clean cloth (it is very slippery) and cut the skin just below the head. Tie a string around the head above this cut and fasten it to a hook or nail on the wall; then, gripping the skin with the cloth, pull down to strip the fish—like peeling off a glove inside out. Cut off the beard, fins, and tail and remove the entrails by slitting open the belly. Wash the eel well, taking care that no blood is left in or on it. Dry it with paper toweling.

MATELOTE D'ANGUILLE
[Eel Stew]

For 2 or 3 persons

Chop up 2 medium onions (about 5 ounces in all), half a clove of garlic, and 3 shallots. Soften them gently in 4 spoonfuls of butter over medium-low heat, then turn them out into a wide, shallow pan (enameled iron) with a good lid.

Add a skinned, cleaned eel (see above), cut in sections of 2 inches, a bay leaf, and 1 teaspoon powdered fennel (or small twigs). Stir well, then add enough good white wine (or ends of good bottles, white *and* red) just to cover and bring to a boil on high heat. Add a small glass of Cognac and ignite immediately. Cover and let simmer for 15 minutes.

Meanwhile, lightly brown 12 small pearl onions and 12 small mushrooms (minus tail tips). Set aside. And, in a saucer, mix thoroughly about 6 spoonfuls cold fresh butter and 2 ounces all-purpose flour.

Season the stew with salt and white pepper. Remove from the heat and add the flour and butter mixture to thicken the sauce, stirring well. Lift the pieces of eel to a serving platter, and combine them with the little onions and mushrooms. Pour the sauce through a strainer over the whole and garnish all around with fried toast cut in triangles or heart shapes.

ANGUILLE À LA POULETTE
[Eel with Sauce Poulette]

Over medium low heat, sauté in butter for 15 minutes a fresh eel that has been skinned and cleaned (see above) and cut into sections of 2 or 3 inches. Add good white wine to barely cover and bring to a boil, then remove the eel sections and keep them warm. Reduce the liquid to a spoonful. Add this liquid to the eel and pour Sauce Poulette (see page 7) over the whole. Cover and *simmer* (inspecting and stirring once or twice to prevent "curdling") for 10 minutes. *If the sauce boils, the dish is spoiled.*

ANGUILLE MEUNIÈRE
[Eel Sautéed in Butter]

Sauté 2- or 3-inch sections of skinned, cleaned fresh eel (see above) as described under sautéing for fish (see page 53).

BAR
[Saltwater Bass]

Names of fishes in French almost never have exact equivalents in English, mainly because the creatures in widely separated seas differ from one another. Fishes zoologically akin may not be gastronomically the same. Then there are regional and local nomenclatures, which further confuse the issue. In New England there is the striped (pronounced by the local fishmongers "stri-ped") bass, which is almost identical with the French *bar*; but there is also the "sea bass," which has stripes much more distinctly marked and is in appearance quite unlike the *bar*. However, both fishes can be cooked successfully like *bar*.

BAR RÔTI AU FOUR
[Baked Saltwater Bass]

Score a 2-pound saltwater bass on both sides after shortening the tail and washing off blood, etc.

Take an enameled cast-iron fish dish of the proper dimensions to lodge the fish quite exactly and spread on it 2 or 3 rather thickly sliced onions (hold some back for later) and (if not objectionable) half a clove of garlic, crushed or sliced. Pour into the dish enough melted butter to cover the bottom (hold some melted butter in reserve), and break into it a handful of small wild fennel twigs (if not available, dust the fish with fennel powder).

Lay the fish in the dish, and season it with salt and white pepper. Cover it with the reserved sliced onions, and douse it with the remaining melted butter. Put it in a preheated (300° F.) oven for 30 to 40 minutes, according to the size of the fish, basting every 10 minutes.

Serve the bass with the juice in the dish, with or without its skin, after squeezing lemon juice generously from head to tail.

N.B. If the juice, or sauce, is too liquid, thicken it with arrowroot, thus: Dissolve 1 teaspoon of powdered arrowroot in 1 teaspoon of cold water and add it to the boiling sauce; stir quickly and withdraw from the heat.

BAR POCHÉ
[Poached Saltwater Bass]

Score the fish, poach for 30 to 40 minutes in white wine court-bouillon (see page 51), skin, and serve with Sauce Hollandaise (see page 9) or Sauce Moutarde (page 10).

BROCHET
[Pike]

QUENELLES DE BROCHET
[Pike Quenelles]

A quenelle is vaguely similar to a dumpling, but no dumpling was ever made as delicate as a quenelle must be.

First prepare a panade: to 4 ounces stale, white, crustless bread (broken up in small pieces), add about ½ cup of *boiling* milk and a pinch of salt. Once softened, mash the crumbs with a spoon into a paste, and then dry it out on medium-high heat, stirring with a wooden spoon until the mixture does not cling to it. Turn out on a plate that has been lightly buttered and let cool.

Meanwhile, cut up 1 fresh, cleaned pike (about ½ pound), removing every bit of skin, bones, and blood. Grind the flesh in a mortar with a pestle, seasoning with salt and white pepper and a pinch of mace, and working it until it is a very fine paste.

Add to it the panade, 4 spoonfuls fresh butter, and 2 egg yolks well mixed with 1 egg white. Mix thoroughly and strain through fine mesh.

The resulting paste should be rather soft than hard. (To test it, drop a pellet of it the size of a small egg into boiling, salted water: if it bursts, it is too soft and requires the addition of another egg white, beaten just enough to turn white but not to froth.) Then add 2 spoonfuls of *thick* cream, beating the whole vigorously to assure a perfect amalgam. Roll up in a clean cloth and put away in the least cold portion of the refrigerator for 2 hours.

Quenelles are shaped roughly between two spoons, put into boiling water, and removed from it as soon as they float (in about 10 minutes) to a flat, wide-meshed strainer to drain. It is best not to have them touching.

Quenelles de brochet are served to great advantage in individual ovenproof china timbales, rubbed with butter inside, covered with Sauce Mornay (see page 9), dotted with butter on top, and lightly browned in a warm oven. (Sauce Américaine, on page 59), is also an excellent complement.) You must watch the oven warming carefully, preferably protecting the timbales with aluminum foil spread on the oven grill or shelf above.

N.B. If a fresh pike (*brochet*) is not available for making quenelles, you may substitute *merlan* (whiting).

BROCHET POCHÉ
[Poached Pike]

After being scored, pike is poached in vinegar court-bouillon (see page 51). It is served with any white sauce, but preferably with Sauce Mousseline-Moutarde (see page 10) to make its flavor more interesting.

CABILLAUD
[Fresh Cod]

TRONÇONS À LA DIEPPOISE
[Scrod with Mussels and Shrimps]

Select 2 handfuls of mussels. (Throw away those that are wide open; on the working table, rap those that are slightly open—if they close, they are alive, but if they remain slightly open, they are dead and must be thrown away.) Wash and clean the live ones thoroughly and put them in a saucepan with ½ glass of good dry white wine. Cover the pan and place on high heat. In about 5 minutes the mussels will open, and their juice will ooze out. Withdraw the pan from heat and set aside, covered.

Score 4 pieces of cod (each weighing 5 or 6 ounces) lightly with a sharp knife, and season them with salt and white pepper. Put them in an enameled cast-iron dish of appropriate size in which you have put chopped mushrooms and parsley. Pour over the fish enough (half of each) dry white wine and fish stock (see page 57) to barely cover, dot with small pats of fresh butter, and bring the liquid to a boil on top of the stove. Put the dish in the oven (300° F.) and cook for 15 to 20 minutes, basting often.

Just before removing to serve, strain through very fine mesh or cheesecloth the cooking liquor or juice of the mussels, and pour it over the scrod. Then pour into a saucepan all the liquid from the dish holding the fish. Add to this liquid a handful of cooked, cleaned shrimps and the mussels (removed from their shells). Bind the liquid with egg yolk (1 or 2 yolks according to the size of the pieces of fish), pour over the fish, on its dish, and serve.

CABILLAUD À LA PORTUGAISE
[Fresh Cod, Portuguese Style]

Examine 1 to 1½ pounds scrod (about 1 inch thick) for bones and remove them. Cut in half lengthwise, season with salt and white pepper, and set aside. Heat 1 or 2 medium onions, sliced not too thin, in 2 or 3 spoonfuls of oil. Stir and let soften without browning.

Dredge the scrod in white flour and add it to the onion. (If several pieces of fish are cooked, the pan must be large enough to accommodate them flat without piling up.) Moisten with ¾ cup dry white wine, then add 3 skinned red peppers (tinned Spanish pimentos are satisfactory), 2 or 3 spoonfuls of tomato purée or paste (according to the number of pieces of scrod); ¼ clove of garlic (if unobjectionable) and cook on medium heat for 15 minutes, covered.

N.B. White rice (see page 45) is served with this.

CABILLAUD MORNAY
[Fresh Cod with Mornay Sauce]

Divide 1 to 1½ pounds of scrod (about 1 inch thick) in two lengthwise, and cook it for 10 minutes in 2 spoonfuls of butter and 1 cup white wine, seasoned with salt and white pepper. Remove the fish to a warm plate and cover it while you reduce the cooking liquor to 1 spoonful. Mix this with about 6 spoonfuls of Sauce Mornay (see page 9) and put it in an enameled cast-iron dish to fit the scrod. Lay the fish on the sauce, cover with 6 additional spoonfuls of Sauce Mornay, and dot it with fresh butter. Brown it in the oven or under the grill.

MORUE
[Salt Cod]

Ordinarily, before using salt cod, soak it in cold water in a large basin for 24 hours, renewing the water several times.

BRANDADE DE MORUE
[Puree of Salt Cod]

After 24 hours of soaking, put 1 to 1½ pounds salt cod in cold water, uncovered, on high heat. As it begins to boil, skim well, then cover and cook on very low heat for 15 minutes.

Drain the fish and tear it apart with knife and fork, removing all traces of bones, skin, or discolored pieces. Put it back on medium heat, along with ½ cup fine olive oil and cook for 30 minutes, stirring often.

Add a dash of garlic powder (if unobjectionable), then put the mixture in a stone mortar. Grind it with the pestle into a paste, adding ¾ cup boiled whole milk (or diluted powdered milk) to make it slightly fluffy. The *brandade* should be very white.

Serve on a hot platter, piled up in a conical shape and surrounded by triangles of fried bread.

SOUFFLÉ DE MORUE
[Salt Cod Soufflé]

After 24 hours of soaking, put some salt cod (enough to make ¾ cup when cooked and shredded) in cold water, uncovered, on high heat. As it begins to boil, skim well, then cover and cook on very low heat for 15 minutes.

Drain the fish and tear it into small pieces with knife and fork. Mash lightly and moisten with ¼ to ½ cup hot milk to a creamy consistency; then combine with *very thick* Sauce Béchamel (see page 8)—as thick as creamy mashed potatoes. Mix well with 4 eggs whites that have been beaten stiff, and 4 beaten egg yolks (see Soufflés, page 38).

Put into a warm, buttered soufflé mold and bake in a 375° F. oven for 20 minutes.

MORUE À LA PARISIENNE
[Salt Cod with Bread Sauce]

After 24 hours of soaking, put 1 to 1½ pounds salt cod (cut like fish fillets) in cold water over high heat, uncovered. As it comes to a boil, skim carefully. Cover and cook on very low heat for 15 minutes.

Meanwhile, hard-boil 4 eggs, chop some parsley leaves very fine, and cook 2 finely sliced onions in approximately 2 spoonfuls of butter until *yellow*. Strain the onions off and work the butter in which they cooked with ¾ cup soft white bread crumbs (no crusts) into a cream. Put this over the fish on a serving platter, and decorate with the hard-boiled eggs (sliced), the chopped parsley, 2 spoonfuls of capers, and, of course, lemon quarters.

N.B. The quantity of butter depends on the quantity of fish.

CARPE
[Carp]

CARPE AU VIN ROUGE
[Carp in Red Wine]

Put into a suitable utensil the fish, scored lightly on both sides, and all the elements for a court-bouillon (see page 51), except for the water and the vinegar substitute about 2½ cups of red wine—enough to cover the fish. Bring to a boil and immediately place on low heat to simmer, covered, for 25 minutes.

Melt 2 spoonfuls of butter and add to it 2 spoonfuls of all-purpose flour; mix well. Stir to keep from burning and, when the mixture begins to turn yellow, moisten gradually with the cooking liquid of the fish, stirring it into a sauce of the consistency of syrup.

Verify the salt and pepper seasoning. To this sauce may be added a little Beurre d'Anchois (see page 58) to taste.

This preparation may be called Carpe à la Chambord if you decorate the carp with truffles and *quenelles* (see page 65) and carp milt. No matter how elaborate the present-day recipes may be, they are poor approximations to the classical recipe, which called for a variety of meats to make a huge dish.

Carp milt may be cooked like roe: wrapped in a well-buttered paper, in the oven for 10 minutes, seasoned with salt and white pepper. Or it may be poached in salted water for 5 or 10 minutes, dried, and served on a bed of cooked spinach, the whole having been covered with Sauce Mornay (see page 9) and lightly browned in the oven. Or it can be finished with Sauce Béchamel (see page 8) under it, without the spinach, and Sauce Mornay over it, lightly browned in the oven and sprinkled with chopped truffles.

CARPE À L'ALSACIENNE
[Stuffed Carp with Sauerkraut]

Stuff the carp with fish forcemeat(see page 65) mixed with heavy cream. Poach it for 25 minutes in white Alsatian wine, (enough to half cover it), turning the fish from time to time. Serve it on a bed of braised sauerkraut with the cooking liquor seasoned with salt and white pepper and thickened with arrowroot poured over.

CARPE RÔTIE AU FOUR
[Baked Carp]

Deeply scored on both sides, the carp is laid on onion rings that have been softened in butter for 15 minutes without browning. The fish is basted generously with melted butter, seasoned lightly with salt and white pepper, and cooked in the oven for 40 minutes (300° F). Or it may be put on a roasting rack, belly side down.

CARRELET
[Flounder]

This equivalent is given in *Madame Prunier's Fish Cookery Book*. There is a fish akin to the halibut in northern European waters called *flandre* or *flondre*.

CARRELET À LA DUGLÉRÉ
[Flounder with Tomatoes and White Wine]

Dugléré was the great chef of the old Café Anglais, long since vanished. Although his manner of preparing fish, which now carries his name, was originally invented for the humble flounder, other and choicer fishes are cooked in this way—e.g., bass, small turbot, brill, etc.

Rub a gutted 1-pound flounder with coarse salt to firm its flesh, then wipe and cut across into 1½-inch steaks.

In an enameled cast-iron dish to suit the size of the fish, melt 5 or 6 spoonfuls of butter. Add 1 medium onion (sliced), half a clove of garlic (chopped), 4 tomatoes (peeled and seeded), a sprig of fresh thyme (or ¼ teaspoon dried), a bay leaf, and a few stalks of parsley. Heat to sizzling, then add the fish steaks. Turn them over after 1 minute, moisten with ¾ cup dry white wine, season with white pepper, and cover with aluminum foil. Put in a 350° F. oven for 15 minutes, then remove the steaks to a hot plate and cover.

Strain the contents of the cooking dish into a saucepan and correct the seasoning. Thicken the resulting sauce with 1 teaspoon arrow-root (see page 65).

CARRELET FLAMBÉ
[Flamed Flounder]

Humorous as the name in English sounds, the result is respectable. Dredge flounder fillets or steaks in flour, and season them with salt and white pepper. Heat butter in a frying pan (preferably of enameled cast iron and *not* black iron) until it begins to turn yellow. Put in the flounder fillets or steaks and sauté for a minute or two, then turn them. Pour in a small glass of dry London gin and set it ablaze, then remove the pan from the fire. Baste the fish with the sauce, which you thicken with fresh butter, bit by bit, while beating it.

Serve with lemon quarters.

CARRELET SAUTÉ MEUNIÈRE
[Flounder Sautéed in Butter]

First, rub flounder fillets (it is best not to sauté the fish whole) in coarse salt to firm up the flesh. Then sauté them (see page 53).

CARRELET FRIT
[Fried Flounder]

Cut the fish across into 1-inch-thick steaks, dry them well with a paper towel, season them with salt and white pepper, soak them well in Pâte à Frire pour Poissons (see page 52) and fry them in very hot, tasteless oil or clarified butter (see page 10) until the batter turns golden. Drain on brown paper for a few seconds and serve with lemon quarters.

ÉPERLANS
[Smelts]

Smelts are a saltwater fish, but some authors class them among freshwater fishes because they come from the sea into brackish waters.

ÉPERLANS EN BUISSON
[Smelts in a Cluster]

Clean the smelts through the gills with minimum amount of handling: if they are dirty, rinse them lightly in cold water; these delicate
little fishes spoil easily. Thrust a wire through their eyes, making
a sort of ring of several smelts. Moisten them with salted milk, dredge
them in flour, and fry them in deep, tasteless oil—very hot—for 5
minutes. Drain on brown paper and serve with lemon quarters and
fried parsley (see page 53).

FLÉTAN
[Halibut]

The French halibut is not nearly so delicious as the halibut of
New England, especially the "chicken" halibut, and is not usually
found at Paris fishmongers.

BAKED HALIBUT STEAKS

Choose steaks—i.e., pieces cut across or sectionally through the
fish near the tail—about 1½ inches thick. Put sliced onions and
butter in an ovenproof pan, then add the steaks. Season them with
salt and pepper and dill weed or powder, and on top put more sliced
onions and butter. Bake in a 350° F. oven for 20 to 25 minutes.

N.B. The quantity of butter and of onions depends on the amount
of fish.

HADDOCK
[Smoked Haddock—Finnan Haddie]

The English name "haddock," pronounced without the *h*, is used
in France to designate smoked haddock and even smoked unsalted

cod, treated also with pyroligneous acid, of excellent flavor. The proper French name for haddock is *aiglefin* or *égrefin*. Paris fishmongers sell quantities of British smoked haddock. The name "finnan haddie" is a corruption of "Findhorn haddock," Findhorn being a fishing village approximately twenty-five miles as the crow flies from Inverness, on the Moray Firth, in Scotland.

HADDOCK À L'ÉCOSSAISE
[Finnan Haddie in Milk]

Choose one or more pieces of the thick part of the fish (or cut in two, lengthwise, the imported British fish). Lay the fish in an enameled cast-iron pan deep enough to contain it, plus enough cold milk to cover it. The milk should have been boiled or, better, should be dissolved powdered milk (3 or 4 spoonfuls to a cup of water). Add several pats of butter on top of the fish, some white peppercorns, and several spoonfuls of heavy cream. Do not add salt.

Bring to a boil on high heat, and at the first signs of boiling— when a white froth rises from the bottom—lower the heat to minimum, and cover the pan with aluminum foil. Do not let it boil again.

After 30 minutes or so, lift the pieces of fish out with a skimmer. Spoon the sauce, from the surface where the butter floats, over the fish.

N.B. If you prefer more butter, melt some and add it. The excellence of the dish is accentuated by the milk-cream-butter cooking liquor.

SOUFFLÉ FINDHORN
[Finnan Haddie Soufflé]

See page 39.

HARENG
[Herring]

This delicious fish is at its optimum during the spawning season, October to the end of the year, in Northern Europe: after that it is very ordinary.

HARENGS GRILLÉS
[Grilled Herrings]

Clean the herrings through the gills, then rinse in cold water and dry with paper toweling. Brush with melted butter well mixed with finely chopped parsley leaves and season with salt and white pepper.

Place on a grill about 4 inches under a red-hot caloroid (or gas flame, which is less good—best of all, of course, is to grill over hot embers) and turn after 3 minutes. The other side requires about the same time, but an inch or so farther from the heat.

Serve with lemon quarters.

N.B. When herring is grilled in this way, any milt in the male or roe in the female is perfectly cooked *in the fish*.

LAITANCE DE HARENG
[Herring Milt]

This is more delicate than the roe (eggs). If preferred, it can be lightly sautéed in butter, seasoned with salt and white pepper and a few drops of lemon juice, and spread on a piece of fried bread or a slice of *brioche*.

MAQUEREAU
[Mackerel]

A very small mackerel is sold in Paris, sometimes under the name of *lisette de Dieppe*, which is not at all as fat as the regular mackerel:

it is excellent grilled after the regulation brushing with butter, etc., and served as a light first dish, 2 per person.

MAQUEREAU GRILLÉ
[Grilled Mackerel]

Cut off the tail, then clip off the end of the mouth in order to make possible the opening up of the fish. Run a knife along the back from mouth to tail. Then nip the bone at the middle, thus enabling you to unfold the two halves without separating them—like opening up a book.

Brush with melted butter on both sides but with moderation, this fish being rather greasy, and season with salt and white pepper. Place on a grill, skin side up, about 4 inches from a red-hot caloroid or gas flame. After 5 minutes, turn skin side down to cook for another 5 minutes.

Place on a hot serving platter, skin side down. Spread Beurre Maître d'Hôtel (see page 59) on one inside half, and fold the other half over it, thus restoring the fish to its original shape.

Serve with lemon.

MAQUEREAU POCHÉ
[Poached Mackerel]

Poach for 30 minutes either whole mackerel, or mackerel in sections, in vinegar court-bouillon (see page 51) after scoring both sides. Serve with Sauce Hollandaise (see page 9) or Sauce Moutarde (see page 10).

MAQUEREAU À LA FLAMANDE
[Mackerel, Flemish Style]

Score the fish on both sides. Poach in vinegar court-bouillon (see page 51), with a sprinkling of dill, for 30 to 40 minutes, then drain and wipe dry with paper toweling.

Cover with Sauce Béchamel (see page 8) mixed with gooseberry jelly (or, better, fresh gooseberries lightly sautéed in very little butter).

MERLAN
[*Whiting*]

Do not scorn this fish: it can be delicious whole, or mashed for stuffing other fish or used, in place of *brochet* (pike), for making quenelles (see page 65).

MERLAN À LA COLBERT
[*Fried Whiting*]

Run the knife down the back of the fish and remove the backbone, then dip the fish in salted milk, dredge in flour, roll in beaten whole egg, and then in fine bread crumbs. Fry in hot oil until golden, then lift with a skimmer and serve with Beurre Maître d'Hôtel (see page 59).

MERLAN BERCY
[*Baked Whiting*]

Butter well a narrow oven dish, and sprinkle it with a little chopped shallot. Run the knife down the back to the bone, but do not open up the fish. Put the fish in the dish, moisten with white wine, and season with salt and white pepper and a little lemon juice. Bake in a 350° F. oven, basting every minute, until done. (The fish is done when only a little sauce remains in the dish.) Serve with chopped parsley leaves.

MERLAN À LA DIEPPOISE
[Poached Whiting with Mussels]

Select a handful of live mussels (see page 67). Wash them well, and put into a small saucepan with ½ glass of dry white wine. Cover. Place on high heat for about 5 minutes: the mussels will open and their juice will ooze out. Withdraw the pan from the heat and put aside, covered.

Cut the whiting down the back and put it in an oven dish to fit. Dot the fish with a little butter and pour the juice of the mussels over it. Season with salt and white pepper. Bring to a boil and immediately lower the heat, then cover and let poach on minimum heat for 20 minutes. Thicken the sauce with fresh butter, *without letting it boil.*

MOUSSE DE MERLAN
[Whiting Mousse]

Take 1 pound of whiting, carefully boned and without a trace of skin, and pound it in a mortar into a paste. Season with salt and white pepper.

In a mold or a very light saucepan sitting in a bowl of ice cubes or cracked ice, mix the fish paste carefully with 2 well-beaten egg whites and 1 pint of heavy cream. The mixture should be firm but very light. Turn it into a buttered tin mold about as deep as it is wide, with ears. (The mold must have ears to keep it from resting on the bottom of the pan when it is cooked.) Place the mold in a saucepan sitting on medium-high heat and containing boiling water to reach up to half the height of the mold. Lower the heat under the pan immediately and keep on *minimum* heat for 30 minutes.

Unmold on a hot dish and serve with Sauce Américaine (see page 59) spooned over.

MULET
[Gray Mullet]

Mullet may be cooked also according to recipes given for *bar* (salt-water bass) (see pages 64–65).

MULET RÔTI AU FOUR
[Baked Mullet]

After washing well, scoring, and drying the fish, lay it on a bed of sliced onions in a well-buttered dish (enameled cast iron, preferably) to fit its size and shape. Cover with more sliced onions and season with salt and white pepper. Pour several spoonfuls of melted butter over and sprinkle with dill weed, then bake in a 300° F. oven for 30 minutes, basting after 15 minutes.

Serve with the pan juice and quartered lemons. The pan juice may be thickened with prepared Dijon mustard (*nature*).

MULET POCHÉ
[Poached Mullet]

Poach the fish in salted water for 30 minutes (see page 50), drain it, skin it, and serve it with Sauce Beurre Blanc (see page 60).

PERCHE
[Perch]

Always have the fishmonger cut away the dorsal fin, which is needle sharp.

PERCHE SAUTÉE MEUNIÈRE,
PERCHE POCHÉE AU COURT BOUILLON,
PERCHE FRITE
[Sautéed Perch, Poached Perch, Fried Perch]

As this very delicate fish must have its own flavor respected, these are the methods of cooking (see pages 50–53) that are recommended.

When poached, the skin and scales may be removed *after* cooking, and the fish rinsed in the court-bouillon to make sure no skin or scale adheres to it. Sauce Hollandaise (page 9) or just melted butter is served with it.

RAIE
[Skate]

The skate that has little pimples on its skin (called *raie bouclée* in French) is the finest and therefore the kind that should be bought. It is the only fish that should not be eaten absolutely fresh: its flesh is then tough and insipid. It should be a few days old, though kept cold; but if the "gooey" slime that covers it has dried out, it is stale —i.e., uneatable.

RAIE AU BEURRE NOIR
[Skate with "Black" Butter]

Cut the skate down the middle, avoiding the eyes, from mouth to tail, and the insides into halves. Wash well, then put the pieces (called *ailes* in French, meaning "wings") into water and vinegar (4 to 1) to cover, with 1 spoonful of coarse salt. Bring to a boil and skim well. Lower the heat to minimum and poach for 25 minutes, covered.

Remove skate with a skimmer to a dish and *scrape off* the skin on both sides with the back of a knife or any other handy implement.

Then put the pieces back into the cooking liquor to keep warm until serving.

Serve with Beurre Noir (see page 59), after sprinkling with chopped parsley leaves. Serve very hot.

ROUGET
[Red Mullet]

The best of this tribe is the very small *barbet de roche*, which is grilled without removing the insides, which are minute and delicious (in this respect, a comparison has been made with woodcock, which is also cooked without drawing).

ROUGET GRILLÉ
[Grilled Red Mullet]

Brush the fish with melted butter and season with salt and white pepper. Place fairly close to a red-hot caloroid or gas flame, on a grill, for 5 minutes each side. Serve with melted butter or lemon quarters.

SAINT-PIERRE
[John Dory]

This exceedingly ugly fish is rarely found in American waters. Pity. It is delicious; so, just in case, here is a recipe:

FILETS DE SAINT-PIERRE À LA MAZATLÁN
[John Dory Fillets à la Mazatlán]

Wash the fillets and dry with paper toweling, then lay them in a fireproof dish. Cover with cold water and add 1 spoonful of coarse salt, 1 or 2 garlic cloves, a few white peppercorns, and a sprinkling of dill weed. Bring to boil, then lower the heat to minimum. Cover. If using several fillets, turn the bottom ones topside.

After 30 minutes, drain well, and serve on hot plates with plenty of lemon juice and very fruity olive oil.

SARDINES [fresh]

The best way to cook fresh sardines, after scaling, emptying, and washing them, is to grill them.

Brush them with melted butter, season with salt and white pepper, and put on a grill, some 3 inches under a red-hot caloroid or gas flame, for 3 minutes each side.

Serve with lemon quarters and melted butter.

N.B. Where sardines are fished, the beach people grill them without scaling or washing, just as they come out of the sea, sometimes roughly oiled (olive oil)—nothing better.

SAUMON
[Salmon]

SAUMON POCHÉ
[Poached Salmon]

For a large fish, it is best to have a salmon kettle of ample dimensions, with a sleeve, and preferably of tin-lined copper. Purists insist that salmon should be poached only in salted water and not in a court-bouillon, especially not in one containing vinegar. Also, the fish should be gutted and washed of all blood but not scaled, for the scales protect the fish from bursting. Finally, it is advisable to wrap the fish in a single piece of cheesecloth that has been well washed in hot water (no soap).

The salted water must be just sufficient to cover the fish and be cold when the latter is immersed in it. After it is brought to a boil, it should be set where it will simmer. The time is reckoned at 6 to 8 minutes the pound, except that there is a minimum time of 30 minutes for even a very small salmon.

After removal from the kettle, the fish is skinned carefully, and melted butter is poured very "lightly" over it. It should be served with hot drawn or melted butter and very finely sliced cucumbers.

N.B. This way of cooking and serving may be criticized as being too much *à l'anglaise* ("in the English fashion"), but no other method will ensure more effectively the proper appreciation of a fine salmon.

SAUMON GRILLÉ
[Grilled Salmon]

Cut the fish across through the backbone into sections (steaks) of 1½ inches. Brush with melted butter, then season with salt and white pepper. Put under the grill (see page 55) until browned, then turn, butter again, and brown again. Serve with Beurre Maître d'Hôtel (see page 59) and with a quarter lemon for each serving.

BROCHETTES DE SAUMON
[Skewered Salmon]

Cut the raw fish in large dice, roll them in melted butter, season with salt and white pepper, and skewer them with alternating slices of cucumber or tiny tomatoes that have also been rolled in melted butter. Grill them until golden, turning as needed.

SAUMON FROID, SAUCE VERTE
[Cold Salmon with Green Sauce]

After being cooked and skinned (see above), the cold fish is decorated with tarragon and watercress leaves, very thin slices of peeled tomato, and hard-boiled egg quarters, the whole resting on crisp lettuce leaves. The Sauce Verte (see page 13) is served in a sauceboat.

N.B. A whole fish should be served with individual portions marked at intervals of $1\frac{1}{2}$ to 2 inches with a sharp knife down to the bone; and helpings should be gouged out from the back to the front with a fish serving fork, then spooned onto the plate.

SOLE

Although the true sole is not found in American waters, and some purists insist that it exists only in Northern European seas, it is now flown frozen to the United States and is very acceptable.

SOLE GRILLÉ
[Grilled Sole]

Skin the fish on both sides by cutting the skin across just below the head, lifting a little flap of it to grasp with your fingers and then pulling it toward the tail—like taking off a rubber glove.

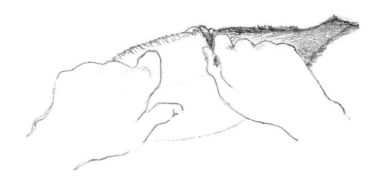

Position of hands while skinning sole

With a sharp small knife, lift the fillets slightly by running the edge down the middle of the fish along its backbone and then on both sides from the center outwards—this to allow the heat to penetrate more quickly.

Brush with melted butter on both sides, season with salt and white pepper, and dredge lightly with all-purpose flour. Put on a grill, about 4 inches from a red-hot caloroid or gas flame, for 4 minutes a side.

Serve with melted butter and lemon quarters. (If you want the crisscross markings of the grill, get the grill very hot before laying the fish on it.)

SOLE À LA MEUNIÈRE
[Sole Sautéed in Butter]

Sauté in butter (see page 53). The whole fish or the fillets can be prepared this way.

SOLE BONNE FEMME

Put 3 shallots (chopped), a few stalks of parsley (chopped), and 4 to 6 mushrooms (chopped) in an oven-proof dish, then lay on your skinned sole (see above). Season with salt and white pepper. Add 4 or 5 spoonfuls of white wine and the same amount of water and bring to a boil. Withdraw from the heat, cover with aluminum foil, and put in a 350° F. oven for 20 minutes, basting after 10 minutes.

Remove the foil and pour out the sauce. Mix it with 1 or 2 beaten egg yolks, *adding the hot liquid to the yolks* while you stir quickly. Add a spoonful of butter and beat it into the sauce. Pour the sauce over the fish and brown it all under the grill.

SOLE CANCALAISE
[Poached Sole with Shellfish, Mushrooms, and Béchamel Sauce]

Open a few oysters, carefully saving their juice. Mix this juice with mushroom cooking liquor (see page 230) and poach the skinned sole (see above) in this mixture.

Transfer the sole to an ovenproof dish. Add to it the oysters and the mushrooms, and (if handy) shelled, cleaned shrimps. Over it all spoon thick Sauce Béchamel (see page 8) mixed with a little white wine, dot the surface with small pats of butter, and brown in the oven under gas flame or caloroid.

SOLE À LA BRETONNE
[Poached Sole in Cream Sauce]

In a flameproof dish of the right size and shape for the sole, put a spoonful of butter, 2 onions (chopped), 2 slices celeriac (chopped) (or ½ cup chopped celery). Cook on medium heat until brown, stirring a few times.

Season the sole with salt and white pepper. Lay it in the dish, pour over ½ cup fish stock (see page 57), and poach, covered, for 25 minutes.

Pour off the sauce into a small saucepan and boil it down to one-half. Mix it with 2 spoonfuls of heavy cream, pour over the fish, and serve.

FILETS DE SOLE
[Sole Fillets]

Sole fillets lend themselves to preparations with vegetables: there are no bones to get mixed up with the vegetables, and service is greatly facilitated.

The basic procedure is simple: cooked fillets are laid on cooked vegetables, the whole is covered with a sauce, and the dish (oven-proof) is put in the oven for browning.

The name of the dish often indicates what vegetable is used: "Florentine" for spinach, "Portugaise" for tomato, "Argenteuil" for asparagus tips, "Carmen" for pimentos, etc. There are more than a hundred ways of preparing fillets of sole. Basically, however, they are usually either poached or sautéed, then cooked with vegetables and/or shellfish or garnished with them. Here is an example:

FILETS DE SOLE PORTUGAISE
[Fillets of Sole with Tomatoes and Onions]

Make a puree of tomatoes and onions by "melting" the onions in oil, and the tomatoes likewise, separately, then mashing them to-gether. Strain, then cook this puree down, if too liquid, to the con-sistency of creamed spinach. Salt and pepper it, and add a pinch of sugar, mixing well.

Make Sauce Béchamel (see page 8), about twice as much as the puree, and lace it with dry white wine.

Poach whole soles in dry white wine, and remove the fillets with a small, sharp knife. Drain the fillets well and lay them in an oven-proof dish, side by side. Pour over the béchamel, then carefully spoon the tomato-onion puree between *every other* fillet so that each fillet will have its portion of puree at serving time.

Sprinkle finely chopped parsley over all the fillets, warm in the oven, and serve.

THON FRAIS ET ESPADON
[Fresh Tuna and Swordfish]

Although quite different fishes, these lend themselves to the same preparations.

THON FRAIS (OU ESPADON) GRILLÉ
[Grilled Fresh Tuna or Swordfish]

Marinate the slice of fish (the slice should be about 1½ inches thick) in oil with sliced onion, white pepper, and salt for 1 hour. Then run your knife over it to remove the onion and excess oil (the fish being fat).

Put on a grill, about 4 inches below a red-hot caloroid or gas flame, for 10 minutes, then turn over and cook for 15 or 20 minutes longer, if necessary lowering the grill to insure penetration of the heat. Remove the skin and serve with Beurre d'Anchois (see page 58) or with Sauce Béchamel (see page 8) generously mixed with capers.

THON FRAIS (OU ESPADON) EN BROCHETTES
[Fresh Tuna or Swordfish on Skewers]

Cut the fish into 1½-inch cubes. Marinate these in oil with white pepper, chopped parsley, and salt for 45 minutes, turning them from time to time.

Meantime, cut a cucumber into slices ⅛ inch thick. Put the slices around the rim of a plate and sprinkle them with salt to get the water out of them. When the fish is ready, wipe the cucumber slices roughly with paper. Then skewer fish cubes and cucumber slices alternately, beginning and ending with fish, and grill at 4 inches from a caloroid or gas flame, turning over once.

Serve "as is" or with Beurre d'Anchois (see page 58), and with white rice (see page 45) on the side.

THON EN CHARTREUSE
[Braised Tuna]

In a thick, enameled cast-iron cocotte, put ½ pound carrots (peeled, cored, and cut in cubes), 6 ounces of bacon (cubed), and 4 ounces of onions, coarsely chopped. Add a heaping spoonful of butter and a bay leaf. Put on high heat and, as soon as the butter fries, add 1 pound of tuna, sliced about ¾ inch thick. Season with salt and pepper. (Omit salt if the beef broth or consommé to be added later is salted.) Moisten with ½ cup dry white wine.

As soon as the wine boils away to a tablespoon or so, add ¾ cup beef broth (bouillon) or consommé just to cover. Put on the lid with a piece of aluminum foil under it. Reduce the heat to low—just enough to keep the liquid boiling very gently for 1 hour.

After an hour, add 2 *small* blanched heads of lettuce (see page 229), squeezed quite dry. Cook covered, for 15 minutes more; then remove from the heat. Take out the vegetables—very carefully so as not to smash the lettuce—to a hot plate, and cover. Skim off the fat from the sauce and bind it with arrowroot (see page 65).

Lift the fish to serving platter with a skimmer, and carefully remove the skin. Surround the fish with the vegetables and pour the thick-ened sauce over the fish. Serve.

TRUITE DE RIVIÈRE
[Brook Trout]

TRUITE AU BLEU
[Poached "Blue" Trout]

Brook or river trout has on its skin a coating of clay that turns bluish when placed in contact with boiling salted water mixed with vinegar: hence the name of this dish. In order to obtain this coloring, obviously, the fish must be handled as little as possible and therefore *not* scraped.

Trout should be alive until the moment they are to be poached. They should then be killed by a sharp blow on the head and cleaned by thrusting the point of sharp scissors into their belly, making as small a hole as possible to remove their insides.

To cook the trout (a special trout kettle with "sleeve" is recom-mended) plunge the fish immediately into boiling court-bouillon well laced with vinegar. Immediately withdraw the kettle from the heat, cover, let stand 5 minutes. Lift carefully from the court-bouillon with two wide-tined forks to let the cooking liquid run out, and serve on a hot plate. Spoon melted butter over the fish and lay next to it a quarter of a lemon.

TRUITE AMANDINE
[Sautéed Trout with Almonds]

You do not have to handle the fish so daintily as for Truite au Bleu (above). Sauté it in hot butter, with almonds, sliced very fine, which you lift with a skimmer when lightly browned and use at the moment of serving to dress the fish.

TRUITE À LA MEUNIÈRE
[Trout Sautéed in Butter]

Proceed as indicated under sautéing (see page 53).

TRUITE BONNE FEMME
[Trout Braised in White Wine]

Cut into small strips peeled and cored carrots, celeriac, and onions, and stew them, with water to cover and butter, in a cocotte or pan on gentle heat for 30 minutes, covered.

Add the fish, scored lightly on both sides, with enough dry white wine to just cover it. Add also a bay leaf and a few stalks of parsley. Put the covered cocotte or pan in a 300° F. oven for 20 minutes, then remove the fish to a hot plate. Reduce the cooking liquid to half, season with salt and pepper, and thicken (strained or not) with arrowroot (see page 53).

Pour over the fish to serve.

TRUITE SAUMONÉE
[Salmon Trout]

Salmon trout such as are fished from the Great Lakes of North America, where they attain the size of a medium-large salmon (in New England they are called "lake trout"), are seldom obtainable in France. They can be poached in a strong wine court-bouillon to bring out their flavor and served with Sauce Beurre Blanc (see page 60), or Beurre Nantaise.

CHAPTER 7

Shellfish

COQUILLES SAINT-JACQUES
[*Scallops*]

The origin of the French name, which means literally "Saint James's shells," is attributed to the legend of a horseman who on his steed plunged into the sea on the coast of Galicia, northwestern Spain, at the spot where a barge carrying the body of Saint James the Apostle ran ashore: lo! when he came out of the water, he and his horse were covered with scallop shells. It makes very little sense—or no more than a great many other old legends.

The small Cape scallops of New England, which are fried in deep fat, are very rare in France. French scallops are almost always cooked with their coral, which is not usual in America, but certainly adds to the flavor and the beauty of the presentation.

If you are going to prepare scallops in their shells, choose large scallop shells that are tightly closed. If they gape, rap them on the kitchen table or sink. If they close, they are alive; if they do not, they are dead and must be thrown away. Put tightly closed ones in a pan on very low heat, flat side of the shell up. They will open up if they are alive. With a small knife, remove the flat top shell (which you throw away) and then the contents of the shell, which you put on a plate. Rinse in cold water, and then scrub the lower shells clean; reserve the shells. Slice the white portion (what fishmongers in the United States sell as "scallops") into thin discs and the coral less fine. Chop up the beards. Poach all in a little white wine court-bouillon (see page 51) for 5 minutes; drain them, but keep the cooking liquor. Dry them with paper toweling.

COQUILLES SAINT-JACQUES À LA PARISIENNE
[Scallops with Mushrooms and Béchamel Sauce]

Lightly sauté 2 onions (chopped), 4 shallots (chopped) and 6 mushrooms (chopped) in 2 spoonfuls butter. Add the chopped beards (if available) of 6 scallops cooked as in recipe above, some chopped parsley, and ½ cup white bread crumbs. Moisten with ½ cup fish stock (see page 57), then cook down while stirring until you have a sort of creamy purée.

Spread this on lightly buttered scallop shells, and on it distribute the scallop whites and coral from the 6 scallops. Over all pour enough Sauce Béchamel (see page 8) or Mornay (see page 9) to fill the shell. Sprinkle with about 2 spoonfuls bread crumbs and dot with butter. Brown lightly in 350° F. oven.

N.B. If the shells are inclined to tip over in the pan in which you put them in the oven, a little bed of rock salt will prop them up.

COQUILLES SAINT-JACQUES À LA DIEPPOISE
[Scallops with Mussels and Shrimps]

Open 20 mussels in white wine (see page 67), saving the juice carefully. Remove the mussels from the shells, which you throw away. Poach 1½ pounds scallops in white wine court-bouillon (see page 50) for 5 minutes. Reserve the cooking liquor.

Cook together 2 spoonfuls each of flour and butter, stirring until pale yellow, and dissolve this with $1/2$ cup fish stock (see page 57). Add the reserved scallop cooking liquor and the juice from the mussels to make a creamy sauce. Add 10 cooked, cleaned shrimps, the mussels, and the scallop meats.

Pour into scallop shells, cover with thin layer of very fine white bread crumbs (called *chapelure* in French). Dot with butter and brown lightly in a 350° F. oven.

COQUILLES SAINT-JACQUES À LA POULETTE
[Scallops with Sauce Poulette]

Spread on scallop shells finely chopped—even mashed—mush-rooms that have been cooked in butter and then seasoned with salt, white pepper, and lemon juice and mixed with fine white bread crumbs to make a paste. Put poached scallop meats (see page 93) on this, and cover them with Sauce Poulette (see page 7).

Cover with aluminum foil and warm in a 350° F. oven for 5 minutes.

COQUILLES SAINT-JACQUES FRITES
[Fried Scallops]

Start with *raw scallops* well dried with paper. Roll them in beaten egg with salt and pepper, and then in fine white bread crumbs. Fry till golden in hot, deep fat, and serve with fried parsley and lemon quarters.

A VARIATION: Skewer the breaded scallops with alternating very thin pieces of smoked bacon, and fry them in deep fat.

N.B. In either recipe, if you use the coral, fry it *very slightly*.

CRABE
[Crab]

The delicious soft-shell crab of North America is unobtainable in Europe.

As with all shellfish, it is indispensable that crabs should be alive.

Choose medium-sized crabs that feel heavy when picked up: light-weight crabs are watery.

CRABE À L'ANGLAISE
[Crab with Mustard Sauce]

Brush 2 medium-sized crabs with a stiff brush to clean them, and run the cold water tap on them. Plunge them into boiling salted water with 2 spoonfuls of white wine vinegar and boil them for 25 minutes.

When cool, pry open the apron of each crab and cut it away with scissors. Take out all the meat (carefully removing any particles of shell) and the creamy substance next to the liver, also the meat in the claws and legs, which you can break with a nutcracker or mallet.

The top shell, cleaned out, is then filled with the crab meat mixed with the creamy contents and the liver and the following dressing: 2 teaspoonfuls of dry mustard, salt and white pepper, and ⅓ cup fine olive oil dripped on the crabmeat mixture as if making a *sauce mayonnaise*, stirring constantly, and finally a spoonful of white wine vinegar.

Hard-boiled egg, finely chopped, and chopped parsley may also be added—even boned anchovy fillets.

N.B. The legs are not served.

CRABE À LA SAUCE AMÉRICAINE
[Crab with Sauce Américaine]

Proceed as for Crabe à l'Anglaise (see above) except use Sauce Américaine for dressing.

May be served hot or cold.

CRABE À LA DIABLE
[Deviled Crab]

Proceed as for Crabe à l'Anglaise (see above), except prepare the dressing as follows:

Chop a small onion and a shallot fine and "melt" them in butter. Strain the hot butter, pressing the cooked onion and shallot, which you discard. Add a teaspoon of brandy to the butter and then some Sauce Moutarde (see page 10). Mix this with crabmeat mixture, seasoning with a pinch of cayenne pepper.

CRABE À LA BÉATRIX
[Crab with Sherry]

Proceed as for Crabe à l'Anglaise (see above), except for dressing use a little good dry Spanish sherry (Fino), salt, and white pepper. (This preparation is especially good for sea spiders, a variety of huge crabs found in Brittany.)

CREVETTES
[Shrimps and Prawns]

These are sometimes marketed alive in France. The large prawns of the British Isles, of Spain (gambas), and of Italy (scampi) are generally unobtainable in the United States, in spite of the fact that perhaps the largest, some as big as small lobsters, are found in the West Indies. French bouquets are small shrimps (red when cooked) and *grises* ("gray over," gray-brown when cooked) : both are served as hors d'oeuvres.

COQUILLES DE CREVETTES
[Shrimps in Scallop Shells]

The tails of cooked shrimps are pulled away from the body— also, if you are meticulous, you run a sharp knife down the middle of the top and scrape off the black *foeces*—and the shrimps are warmed in a double boiler with Sauce Américaine (see page 59) then laid on a scallop shell that has been filled with Potatoes Duchesse (see page 240) mixed with Sauce Béchamel (see page 8) and warmed in the oven.

To cook live shrimps, throw them into enough salted water to cover them, then bring them to a boil and boil them for 3 minutes.

ÉCREVISSES
[Crayfish]

This fresh-water miniature lobster is found in the United States, but is seldom seen on any menu there, private or public, except in Louisiana.

ÉCREVISSES À LA NAGE
[Crayfish Boiled in Court-Bouillon]

Choose the larger kind weighing about 3 ounces and dark color: like lobsters, they turn deep red in cooking. They can be kept alive in a basket with a lid for 5 or 6 days, with some weeds such as those which grow near brooks.

Prepare a wine court-bouillon (three-fourths wine) with 4 spoon-fuls of butter, some dill weed, and carrots, onions, and shallots (all chopped) in a wide pan, to just cover the crayfish. Cook for 30 to 45 minutes.

While the court-bouillon is boiling, prepare the crayfish by thrust-ing a knife into the middle of the underside of the tail to make a small incision. Through this seize the insides and draw them out carefully, so as not to tear them (if left in the crayfish they would give it a bitter taste). Plunge the cleaned crayfish in the boiling court-bouillon, cover, and cook for 9 minutes. Remove the pan from the heat, but leave the crayfish in it, covered.

Serve hot, with the pan juices.

ÉCREVISSES À LA BORDELAISE
[Crayfish in White Wine Sauce]

After degutting the crayfish (see above), sauté them in hot butter on high heat, covered, for 8 minutes, shaking the pan now and then. Add Cognac, which you have burned in a small saucepan (to avoid the possible scorching of the tails if you burn it directly in the pan, which would ruin the sauce); white Bordeaux wine, dry or sweet; carrots (peeled, cored and *finely* chopped); onions (chopped); a shallot (chopped); a bay leaf; dried thyme; a speck of garlic; salt; a pinch of cayenne; and tomato paste. Cover and bring to a boil, then lower the heat and cook very gently for 15 minutes, shaking the pan now and then. Remove the crayfish to a warm serving platter.

Stir the sauce while reducing it on high heat to half its volume, and add some concentrated beef consommé—or (better) some Sauce Espagnole (see page 3). Mix well and thicken if necessary with fresh butter off the heat. Pour the sauce over the crayfish and serve.

N.B. Quantities are not given because they depend on the num-ber of crayfish.

HOMARD
[Lobster]

The American article—i.e., the Maine lobster grilled plain with butter—is superior to the French. A curious note on French gastronomy is the fact that its early and mid-eighteenth-century authors seem to have been ignorant of the existence of the lobster.

Killing the lobster (as of course it must be brought to the kitchen alive) not only arouses humane consideration but actual gastronomic argumentation. It would seem to an impartial—if somewhat hard-hearted—observer that plunging the creature into boiling water is no more nor less cruel than driving a sharp knife into it and cutting it in two. Advocates of each method insist that the flesh is rendered firmer by it. But those who favor the knife have a point: the lobster is less likely to lose its juice than by the boiling-water demise.

If boiling is chosen for execution, tie the legs of the lobster with string wound around so it will not splash boiling water all over the stove. Have the water boiling, salted, and plentiful; and plunge the living lobster into it for 3 minutes. That will kill it.

If the knife is preferred, lay the lobster on a clean dish and thrust a big, sharp knife down and diagonally toward the head, into the middle of the joint between head and tail. Cut down right through toward the middle of the legs and then backward, severing the tail in two halves lengthwise. Now sever, also lengthwise, the forward portion. Be careful to collect the juice that oozes out of the lobster: it adds greatly to the flavor of the finished dish.

Near the head you will find a sac that contains gravel: remove and throw it away.

If the lobster is a female, the roe will be found in the curl of the tail: remove and keep it. In the forward part of the body the sub-stance called the "coral" is found: remove and keep it as well. Cut away the legs and crack open the claws and dig the meat out. Gather the coral, the roe (if there), and the juice from the dish; mash them together with a large pat of butter and set aside.

HOMARD À L'AMÉRICAINE

Among gastronomical authorities there is considerable disagree-ment, spiced with chauvinism, on the authenticity of this label versus *homard à l'armoricaine* (meaning "lobster in the Breton fashion,"

Armorica being the Roman name of Brittany). There is a report that a cook-innkeeper in the South of France was stumped as to what to offer a party of American travelers who suddenly arrived at his establishment: he had only a few lobsters and, of course, the usual vegetables and herbs of the country; but he managed to concoct a dish that his guests enthusiastically celebrated. Answering their query as to its name, he christened it in their honor *homard à l'Américaine.* Supporting its authenticity is the fact that tomatoes, olive oil, and garlic are typical of South of France cooking. Furthermore, the entire preparation has none of the characteristics of Breton cooking, but does have the hallmark of Provence.

In an enameled cast-iron skillet, heat 4 to 5 spoonfuls of fruity olive oil and half as much butter. Add the lobster tail cut in 6 pieces across (3 to each half), and sauté them until the shell turns a vivid red (about 5 minutes). Add the claw meat. Moisten with 5 spoonfuls of Cognac and then ⅔ cup dry white wine. Stir well, then cover and withdraw from the heat.

Finely chop 2 shallots, ½ clove garlic, some parsley leaves, and tomatoes that you have peeled, seeded, and squeezed to rid them of their water. Add all these to the lobster, then put the pan back on high heat, mix and stir well, and add ¼ cup Sauce Espagnole (see page 3). Cover and continue to cook on medium heat for 15 minutes.

Just before serving, mash the coral, etc., with 1 spoonful of butter and mix with the sauce, whipping it up. Cook a few seconds. (If the sauce is too liquid, thicken it with fresh butter off the heat.)

Serve the sections of lobster on a plate, with the shell down and the sauce poured over the meat. Sprinkle with a few drops of lemon juice and finely chopped parsley.

N.B. Rice (see page 45) is often served with this dish. Many pieces of fried toast (see page 28) are recommended.

HOMARD THERMIDOR
[Lobster Thermidor]

Having cut the lobster in half lengthwise, cut off the tail portions, season them with salt and pepper, brush them with butter, and grill them at a distance of 6 inches from a red-hot caloroid or gas flame, for some 10 minutes. Remove the meat from the shells and cut into 1-inch slices.

Pour into the shell a few spoonfuls of Sauce Moutarde (see page 10) with a strong mustard accent. Put back into the shells the meat slices, well stacked together, then pour over more Sauce Moutarde and then over all a little melted butter.

Brown very lightly under the grill.

HOMARD À LA NEWBURG
[Lobster Newburg]

Kill a lobster and cut it up, etc., as described on page 100. Sauté the pieces in 2 spoonfuls of hot butter and season them with salt and pepper. When the shells turn bright red, moisten with a small glass of Cognac, and then ⅔ cup Oloroso or Fino sherry and reduce by a third on high heat. Turn the heat down to medium and add 1 cup of thick cream. Stir well, cover, and cook on medium-low heat for 15 minutes, then lift the lobster pieces out to a warm plate and cover.

Bind the sauce with 3 egg yolks beaten with ½ cup thick cream and quickly mix with it the reserved portions of the inside of the lobster (creamy substance, coral, juice, and butter, as described on page 100). Do not let boil again. Remove the lobster meat from the shell and pour the hot sauce over the pieces of meat.

N.B. A recommended accompaniment is triangles of bread that have been moistened in wine (or sherry) and fried in butter.

HOMARD VICTORIA
[*Lobster Victoria*]

The same as Lobster Newburg (see above), with the addition of sliced black truffles and Sauce Allemande (see page 7) instead of the last addition of cream.

LANGOUSTE
[*Crawfish*]

The English name "crawfish" is sometimes derided as an "Americanism," and no less an authority than the *Oxford English Dictionary* makes it and "crayfish" identical in meaning. The *Encyclopaedia Britannica* (14th edition) identifies *langouste* as "Rock Lobster, Spiny Lobster, or Sea-Crawfish (*Palinus vulgaris*) without claws," under the authority of W. T. Calman, D.Sc., F.R.S., Keeper of the Department of Zoology in the British Museum.

If the *langouste* is to be served as a cold dish (this is usually the case), kill it, after securing legs and feelers back with string, by boiling it in a wine court-bouillon (see page 51). If you should want it hot, kill it with a knife and prepare it like regular lobster, following the recipes for lobster given above. A crawfish weighing $1\frac{1}{2}$ to 2 pounds should be boiled for 35 minutes; one of $2\frac{1}{2}$ to 4 pounds, 40 minutes.

MOULES
[*Mussels*]

Mussels must be alive. Those partially open should be rapped on the edge of the kitchen table or sink and, if they do not close, should be thrown away. The live ones are *tightly shut*. Bits of seaweed, etc., clinging to the shell must be scraped carefully away with the mud, sand, etc. After cleaning and washing, they should *not* be submerged in fresh water, which kills them.

MOULES MARINIÈRE
[Mussels with Bread Crumb, Herb, and Wine Sauce]

Per person, calculate 1 to 2 cups of mussels in their shell if they are medium-sized, which are best.

For 4 persons

Spread over an ordinary (agateware) roasting pan a layer of fresh white bread crumbs without crust, using a whole loaf of white baker's bread. Chop 12 shallots and a large bouquet of parsley, mix them, and distribute over the bread crumbs. Lay 6 cups of medium-sized mussels (in their shells) on top, and pour over a bottle of dry white wine. Dot generously with butter (using a quarter pound) and season with salt and white pepper.

Cover with aluminum foil, tucking it under the rim so as practically to seal the pan. Put the pan in a hot 400° F. oven for 10 minutes, then take out the mussels, beat the other contents of the pan together, and pour over the mussels.

Serve in soup plates with spoons and forks—and finger bowls.

MOULES À LA POULETTE
[Mussels with Sauce Poulette]

After verifying, cleaning, and washing the mussels (see page 103), put them in a pan with a well-fitting lid and add a glass of dry white wine. Cover and cook on high heat for 5 minutes. (If on lifting the lid some mussels have not opened, cover and continue cooking for 2 or 3 minutes more *only*. If you cook them too long, they get tough.)

Turn the mussels out into a pan containing an appropriate amount of Sauce Poulette (see page 7), very hot, and let them simmer in it for a couple of minutes. (If the sauce is very thick, the cooking liquor should be added to it.)

Serve with finely chopped parsley.

BROCHETTES DE MOULES
[Mussels on Skewers]

Open the mussels in a little white wine, as described above for Moules à la Poulette. Drain them well, keeping the pan juice. Separate the mussels from their shells, which you throw away.

Skewer the mussels with alternate squares of thinly cut bacon. Dip the dressed skewers in beaten egg seasoned with salt and pepper, then roll them in fine bread crumbs and grill, 4 inches under a red-hot caloroid or gas flame, until golden-brown, turning them so as to cook all sides.

Mix the little juice left in the pan with butter and pour a little streak of this on the mussels. Serve with lemon quarters.

CHAPTER 8

Land Snails
and Frogs' Legs

ESCARGOTS
[Snails]

Although French cookery books generally include snails in the fish chapter, this book will be so tiresome as to insist that only sea snails should be so considered, and that those are quite different from the *escargots de Bourgogne* or the *petits gris* ("little gray ones") that will be dealt with here. Sea snails, by which is not meant the tiny *bigorneau* that is eaten with a pin, are very rarely seen on French menus, and are not prepared like their distant land relatives. (In support of this separate heading for snails, here is a quotation, given by Alexandre Dumas in his famous *Grand Dictionnaire de Cuisine*, from a poem by J. Rouyer:

> *Les anciens Romains faisaient leurs délices*
> *De ces Escargots [ni chairs ni poissons]*
> *Qu'hommes de science appellent "hélices,"*
> *Et qu'il ne faut pas croire Limaçons ...*

The ancient Romans delighted
In these snails [neither meat nor fish]
That scientists call "helices"
And must not be mistaken for common cockles . . .

According to the Larousse dictionary, *limaçons* is the common name for *escargots* [snails].)

The edible land snails feed on green plants and are seldom car-nivores: this remark is intended for those who have the prejudice that snails are disgusting. Remember that the filthiest feeder of all edible creatures is the chicken.

ESCARGOTS À LA BOURGUIGNONNE
[Snails with Herbs and White Wine]

Choose only live snails (24 to 32 of them). Put them in a metal box (the snails will chew their way through one of cardboard) with a secure lid, or something similar, and keep them there in a cool place —e.g., the cellar—for a week. The right time comes when they are sealed—i.e., they develop a covering over their holes like a glazed seal. During this process they have "purged" themselves of what they have eaten before, supposedly plants that might be harmful to human digestions.

Put them in a large pan—e.g., a roasting pan—with water to cover, 1 cup common strong vinegar, wood ashes (from the fire-place), and a spoonful or so of quicklime. Within a short time the snails will start out of their shells; they should be removed to a basin of clean water, where they can be extracted altogether from the shells with any pointed tool. *Care must be taken not to put one's hands in the quicklime water:* the snails should be removed from it with a skimmer. They should be thoroughly washed, likewise their shells, which should be wiped inside carefully.

Cut away the small black portion at one end of each snail, then put the snails into a saucepan with cold water to cover and bring this gradually to a boil. Boil for 10 minutes, skimming off the muck that rises to the surface, then drain and rinse well in cold water.

Put the snails in a saucepan with a large onion stuck with 2 whole cloves, a large carrot (cut in pieces), a clove of garlic, a handful of shallots (3 or 4), half a spoonful of white peppercorns, a sprig of fresh thyme (or ¼ teaspoon dried), a bay leaf, some parsley leaves and stems, a stalk of celery, 3 spoonfuls of coarse salt, and 2 cups white wine cut by 1 cup water—all enough to cover the snails. Bring to a boil, skimming, then cover and boil *gently* for 3 or 4 hours.

Lift the snails on to a wide strainer to drain. Sauté them in 4 spoonfuls of butter with 2 or 3 shallots (chopped) for 5 minutes without letting them harden.

Now prepare the *beurre d'escargots* (snail butter):

Cream 6 spoonfuls of butter with 12 to 16 shallots (finely chopped), some parsley leaves (finely chopped), salt, and pepper. Stuff a little of this mixture into each of the clean, dry shells. Follow it up with a snail, and finish with more of the mixed butter. Arrange the snails on plates made for this purpose—called *escargotières*—dust with very fine bread crumbs, and bake in a hot (400° F.) oven for 8 minutes. (When the snails are ready for the oven, they can be kept in the refrigerator for as long as the butter will keep).

Serve piping hot.

N.B. The reader will notice that garlic is not mentioned in the recipe above. Snails are served as a first dish; if one's tasting organs are saturated with garlic, the rest of the meal will taste of nothing else. If this argument is found specious, it is quite simple to add to the butter stuffed into the shells the desired proportion of garlic.

CUISSES DE GRENOUILLES
[*Frogs' Thighs—Frogs' Legs*]

There are no better frogs' legs than those found in the United States. Yet Americans as a rule do not like to eat them. Is it an atavistic repulsion from the British aversion to this tasty food?

In France, frogs' legs are sold 12 to a stick, on which they are clamped after having been cleaned of the upper body and entrails and skin.

CUISSES DE GRENOUILLES SAUTÉES FINES HERBES
[Frogs' Legs Sautéed with Herbs]

Rinse frogs' legs under the cold water tap, then dry them. Clip off the claws, if any (in France they are sold with them on to certify the real article). Throw the legs into sizzling butter with finely chopped shallots and parsley, salt, and white pepper. (If you want to thicken the sauce, roll the legs in flour before sautéing).

When you see the meat separating from the bones, remove and serve with a few drops of lemon and a sprinkling of finely chopped parsley.

N.B. You may add a little Cognac or whisky to the pan and light it while it is hot: this makes the sauce more interesting. You may also add thick cream at the last minute.

CUISSES DE GRENOUILLES, SAUCE POULETTE
[Frogs' Legs with Sauce Poulette]

After washing and drying the legs and, if necessary, clipping off the claws, sauté them in very little butter to the point where the meat begins to part from the bones, then lift with a skimmer and serve with hot Sauce Poulette (see page 7). (Or sauté for one or two minutes, and then simmer in a little Sauce Poulette.)

CUISSES DE GRENOUILLES, SAUCE AMÉRICAINE
[Frogs' Legs with Sauce Américaine]

After washing and drying the legs and, if necessary, clipping off the claws, season them with salt and white pepper and dredge them in flour. Sauté in hot butter to the point where the meat begins to part from the bones, lift with a skimmer, and serve with hot Sauce Américaine (see page 59).

CHAPTER 9

Fish and Shellfish
Soups and Stews

BOUILLABAISSE

As this is a soup of the Marseilles region, only the fish and shellfish native there can be used if one is to make the real thing, which is to say that away from those waters one should probably not attempt it. However, cooks must be daring.

The prime ingredient that cannot be found elsewhere in its fresh state is an ugly fish called, commonly, *rascasse*, or *diable*, *scorpion*, or *crapaud de mer* ("sea devil," "sea scorpion," or "sea toad"). This is a tough creature fit only for highly flavored soups, to which it gives a particular unctuousness without being greasy. The American redfish looks like a *rascasse*—somewhat—but it is not tough enough. To try to compensate somewhat for the lack of it, one can be heavyhanded with the *bones* of such fish as conger eel or even halibut.

Like all fish soups, *bouillabaisse* should be cooked quickly: long cooking would make it unpleasantly "fishy." Also, the broth must not be thick—i.e., it must not have the consistency of cream soups. Finally, the bread eaten with it should not be toasted or fried: it should be an ordinary kind of French loaf cut in diagonal slices not very thin—or, better, cut lengthwise in halves and then across in sections 4 or 5 inches long. It should be needless to mention the most fundamental requisite, but here it is: absolute freshness of all fish ingredients.

So, let us be brave and take—

For 8 persons

About 5 pounds of fish and shellfish, consisting of 1 live lobster (about 1½ pounds); 1 red snapper (about 1 pound), cleaned and cut in 3-inch pieces; ½ fresh cod (about 1 pound), cleaned and cut in 3-inch pieces; 1 redfish (about 1 pound), cleaned and cut in 3-inch pieces; and ½ conger eel (about 1 pound), cleaned and cut in 3-inch pieces.

Kill the lobster with a knife (see page 100) and save the juice. Cut the lobster in half, remove and discard the gravel sac, and then gut it.

Put ⅔ cup excellent *fruity* (highly scented) olive oil and about 6 ounces of chopped onion in a large, heavy pan on medium-low heat to "melt" the onion for 15 minutes. Then add 2 cloves of garlic (finely chopped) and stir for 2 or 3 minutes.

Put the lobster in the hot oil and turn the heat to high. Remove the lobster once it turns vivid red, cut up into 8 pieces, and set aside.

To the pan add the pieces of fresh cod, conger eel, and redfish. Stir carefully, so as not to break the pieces of fish, and in 1 or 2 minutes add 2 large tomatoes (peeled and seeded). Now pour in about 2 quarts of boiling water, and add the peel of ¼ orange (grated), 2 bay leaves, a good pinch of thyme and another of fennel powder (or several fennel twigs), and ½ teaspoon powdered saffron, plus salt and pepper to taste. Add the red snapper and lobster pieces and the lobster juices. Cover, but watch not to let boil over. Cook 12 to 15 minutes longer and remove from the heat.

Cut up a loaf of French bread as directed above. Put the bread on one dish, pour some broth over, and sprinkle with chopped parsley. Arrange the pieces of fish and lobster (cut in the desired number of pieces) on another dish to display the variety. Pour the remaining broth through a strainer into soup plates, and let each person take his choice of fish and bread.

LA BOURRIDE
[Fish Soup with Aïoli]

For 8 persons

Put the same fish ingredients as for Bouillabaisse (see above) in a saucepan with some chopped onion, a good pinch each of thyme and fennel powder, a bay leaf, and some grated orange peel. Pour in boiling water to cover, add salt and pepper, and boil on high heat for 10 minutes.

Meanwhile, with a pestle in a mortar, grind into a paste several peeled garlic cloves. Mix the paste with 1 egg yolk and drip on this mixture some olive oil (say, 1 cup), stirring constantly to make an emulsion like Sauce Mayonnaise (see page 12). If it thickens ex'cessively, add a little lemon juice. (This garlic cream is called *aïoli*.)

Now place slices of French bread in a saucepan and moisten them with some of the fish broth. In another saucepan—preferably a heavy one, to avoid breaking down of the *aïoli*—put 1 egg yolk and 2 spoonfuls of *aïoli* per person at table. On this, through a strainer, drip the remaining hot fish broth, stirring the while. As the mixture thickens, add more broth less cautiously until all of it is spent.

Put the bread into soup plates (or a tureen) and pour the thickened fish soup on top, with the fish sections served apart or in the soup.

N.B. Besides *aïoli,* another complement for the fish soups of the Marseilles region is *rouille* (in English, "rust"), made with hot red peppers soaked (mercifully) in cold water for several hours, then pounded into a paste with garlic and fish *livers*, all mixed with the fish broth and served hot.

LA PAUCHOUSE
[*Burgundian Fish Soup*]

For 4 persons

Cook 3 or 4 ounces bacon (diced) with a spoonful of butter for 5 minutes on medium high heat. Throw in a spoonful of all-purpose flour, stir, and cook until the mixture begins to turn yellow. Gradually wet down with 1 pint of water and 1 quart of very dry white wine to make a light, creamy liquid. Add 4 or 5 garlic cloves, 6 or 7 small onions, salt to taste, and several white peppercorns. Cook on medium heat, covered, stirring from time to time to prevent sticking.

Meanwhile, cut 1½ pounds of any freshwater fish in sections, and wash them well. Add them to the mixture in the saucepan and simmer, stirring from time to time but without breaking up the fish, for 15 minutes.

Fry in butter (or toast and butter) 8 slices of bread and rub them with garlic—i.e., crush garlic cloves on a plate and rub the bread on them with a fork, to save your fingers. Put these slices of bread on a hot plate, and lift the sections of fish onto them.

Thicken the broth (or sauce) with arrowroot (see page 65) or kneaded butter (see page 63) and pour over all.

VELOUTÉ DE POISSONS
[*"Velvety" Fish Soup*]

Make a blond *roux* (the French term for this preparation): Melt a spoonful of butter on medium high heat and add a spoonful of all-purpose flour, mixing and stirring well to make a thick creamy paste tinged with yellow. Add very gradually, while stirring, 2 cups of fish stock (see page 57); the mixture should have the consistency of thin cream. If you have a few mushrooms handy, add them, chopped up (after washing them and clipping off the root ends), then boil gently for 10 or 15 minutes, stirring often. Withdraw from the fire.

Take a spoonful or so of the soup to mix with 1 or 2 egg yolks (according to size) in a bowl. After thorough mixing, pour this back into the hot soup and stir well. Add 4 or 5 spoonfuls of thick cream, then verify the salt and pepper seasoning to taste. The fish flavor should be subtle, especially because the seasoning is delicate.

N.B. This fish cream soup or velouté ("velvety" soup) is used as a base for other, more elaborate soups, such as bisques.

BISQUE DE CRUSTACÉS
[Shellfish Bisque]

Put 4 or 5 spoonfuls of raw rice (*not* the prepared or tricked-up kind but just plain Carolina rice) in a large saucepan (must be big enough to hold also 20 crayfish or 2 or 3 small lobsters). Pour in 1 cup of boiling water, add a teaspoon of salt, and stir. Set on medium-high heat to boil for 10 minutes, tightly covered, then reduce the heat to medium low and lift the lid to see that there is 1 inch or so of water over the rice. If there is not, pour in the necessary amount of boiling water. In 30 or 40 minutes the rice should be soft enough to mash into a puree: it must be watched and stirred to avoid burning at the bottom. Once the rice is soft and ready to mash, pass it through a strainer to obtain a thick cream, with which you are going to thicken your bisque.

Put 3 medium carrots (peeled, cored, and chopped), 2 medium onions (chopped), and 2 shallots (chopped) in a pan with 4 spoonfuls of butter, a bay leaf, a sprig of fresh thyme, ($\frac{1}{4}$ teaspoon dried), and a parsley stem. Stir on medium-high heat until the carrot, onions, and shallots begin to brown and soften.

Meantime, gut and wash the crayfish (page 99) and reserve their juice. Or kill the lobsters with a knife (see page 100) and slice them across, shell and all. Sauté the shellfish in the hot cooking vegetables until the shells get vivid red, then add a good squirt of Cognac, light it, and quickly cover the saucepan to put out the flame. Add about 1 cup of dry white wine, stir, and cover tightly. Set on minimum heat for 15 minutes, stirring and shaking the pan now and then.

Remove about one-fourth of the shellfish, and make with it Beurre d'Écrevisses, Crevettes, ou Homard (see page 58).

Now separate the shell from the meat of the rest of the shellfish (including the meat of the lobster claws, if used). Drain the meat over the saucepan to save all the liquid.

Cut the meat up in small pieces, and grind them very fine. Also, with mortar and pestle, pound the shells into a paste. Combine this paste with the ground meat, strain the mixture, and wet it down with concentrated beef consommé, little by little, to obtain a fine purée. Mix this purée with the cream of rice you made earlier, adding consommé until you obtain a thick soup. Bring it to a boil while stirring. Add the Beurre d'Écrevisses, Crevettes, ou Homard and season with ½ teaspoon sweet red pepper (paprika), salt, and a small glass of Cognac.

On serving, add a dollop of very thick cream per person at table.

N.B. Most authors prescribe that the meat not used for the Beurre d'Écrevisses, Crevettes, ou Homard should be cut in small dice and served as garnishing in the soup. However, the bisques of shellfish actually served in top Paris restaurants, such as Drouant, are totally liquid, with a thick-cream consistence.

CHAPTER 10

Special Meats

A COOK WAS ONCE TOLD by a lady that she could not bear the thought of eating "innards." "Madame," he replied, "do you eat nothing but the hide?"

ANIMELLES DE MOUTON
[Lamb Fries]

Prepare a vinegar court-bouillon (see page 51).

Meanwhile wash the lamb fries *without breaking their outer casing*, not leaving any trace of blood.

Once the court-bouillon has cooled off, put the lamb fries in it and cook on medium-high heat for 20 minutes, covered, then drain them and skin them carefully. Slice about ¾ inch thick.

Mixed with calf's brains similarly prepared (see below) and stewed mushrooms, and covered with Sauce Poulette (see page 7) or Sauce Allemande (see page 7), these are an excellent filling for a *vol-au-vent*, or, served on fried toast, a good first dish at lunch.

CERVELLES DE VEAU OU DE MOUTON
[Calf's or Lamb's Brains]

These require soaking in cold water, which must be changed several times to remove all traces of blood. Also, the little veins have to be picked off by hand *without tearing off the very delicate membrane that covers the brains.*

Boil them in vinegar court-bouillon as for *animelles* (see above), but more gently to prevent the membrane from bursting.

CERVELLES EN VOL-AU-VENT
[Brains in a Pastry Shell]

After boiling in vinegar court-bouillon (see above), drain the brains and put in a pastry patty shell. Cover with Sauce Allemande (see page 7), or Sauce Poulette (see page 7), with or without stewed mushrooms.

CERVELLES AU BEURRE NOIR
[Brains with "Black" Butter]

After boiling in a vinegar *court-bouillon* (see above), drain and cover with 4 spoonfuls of butter that has been heated until it turned dark brown (*never black*), and then with a tablespoon of hot wine vinegar that has been reduced by boiling to half its original volume. (*Do not add the vinegar to the hot butter in the pan, as this results in a dangerous spatter.*)

Serve on fried toast (moistened in wine before frying).

FOIE DE VEAU
[Calf's Liver]

When fresh, calf's liver is yellowish rather than red, and the imprint of your finger does not remain on its surface. The membrane that envelops the liver must be removed.

FOIE DE VEAU GRILLÉ
[Grilled Calf's Liver]

With paper toweling, dry both sides of a slice ½ inch thick. Season with onion salt and white pepper, and dredge in all-purpose flour, then put the liver on the grill, with 2 thin rashers of smoked bacon under it and 2 more on top, about 3 inches below a red-hot caloroid or gas flame, until the top bacon begins to burn. Withdraw this bacon.

As soon as the top surface of the liver gets brown, which is a matter of 1 or 2 minutes, turn the liver and the underside bacon over, with the latter on top. Lift to a plate as soon as the bacon curls up.

Served with boiled or mashed potatoes.

FOIE DE VEAU EN BROCHETTES
[Calf's Liver on Skewers]

Have the liver sliced 1½ inches thick.

Season with salt and white pepper, then dredge in all-purpose flour and sauté in butter just long enough to firm it slightly

Remove the liver to a board and cut it across into 1½-inch cubes. Skewer these with alternating bits of thinly sliced bacon and roll in flour. Grill, about 3 inches under a red-hot caloroid or gas flame, turning once, for 10 to 12 minutes.

Serve sprinkled lightly with melted butter and chopped parsley.

FOIE DE VEAU SAUTÉ
[Sautéed Calf's Liver]

Sliced ½ inch thick and as evenly as possible in order to make cooking even, the calf's liver is seasoned with salt and pepper, dredged lightly in all-purpose flour, and sautéed in hot butter, 4 minutes to each side.

Serve immediately on hot plates or a dish, topped with the sauce of your choice and garnished with vegetables that are not watery, potatoes, etc.

TERRINE DE FOIE DE VEAU
[Terrine of Calf's Liver—Calf's Liver Loaf]

Cut the raw liver in small pieces and remove any hard bits. Put it through the meat grinder.

Line a cocotte or any other appropriate dish (having its own lid) with thin slices of smoked bacon, letting them hang over the sides in sufficient length to fold over the dish once it is filled. Fill it with the ground liver, adding a pinch of pepper, onion salt, and nutmeg to each layer of liver as you press it down.

When the cocotte or dish has been filled, sprinkle a spoonful of port wine and another of Cognac, and fold over the hanging pieces of bacon to cover it all. Put on the lid, and set the cocotte inside another one containing boiling water up to three-quarters its depth. Bake in a 350° F. oven for 1 hour.

Remove both vessels from the oven, and the smaller one from the larger one, and let the former partially cool for 30 minutes. Cut a piece of cardboard the size of the inside of the container and, having pushed it down on the liver, put weights on top of it (2 or 3 pounds) to act as a press. (This should be done on a plate, as fat, etc., generally spills over.) Leave the loaf to cool thus, under press, until it is completely cold.

N.B. The flavor improves after 2 or 3 days.

GRAS-DOUBLE
[Tripe]

TRIPES À LA MODE DE CAEN
[Tripe Cooked in Cider with Bacon and Calf's Foot]

A certain amount of mystery is made by practically all the great authors on this subject. Yet it is not a difficult dish, even when one has to start with the offal fresh from the carcass (as the author once had to do). In Paris all reputable *tripiers* sell tripe well blanched and rolled up. Honeycomb tripe is easily distinguished by what looks in effect like a honeycomb somewhat magnified, but other bits are usually thrown in that are also good components of the dish. As Caen is a Normandy town and the Normans are rather finicky about what they eat (and so are the Scots, who relish haggis, a dish largely of sheeps' offal), people of northern races should not turn up their noses at this excellent preparation.

For 6 persons

Cut up tripe (well cleaned and parboiled, and again washed and scraped) in about 2-inch squares and set aside.

Take a pot that is deep rather than wide and made of thick, enameled iron. Line its bottom with 2 or 3 fairly thin rashers of smoked bacon, and then with several carrots (peeled, cored, and sliced). Put in a peeled onion stuck with a whole clove, then pieces of tripe and, alternately, pieces of fresh calf's foot cut about the same size as the tripe. At the top, leaving some room for expansion from boiling, place more rashers of bacon.

Fill the pot with hard cider of the best quality obtainable, to about an inch or so from the top, and set on high heat, covered. As soon as the first bubbles rise to the surface, lower the heat so that steady good boiling—not furious—continues *for 4 hours*. The heat must be carefully regulated so that boiling over does not occur.

After 4 hours the tripe and the calf's foot should be well cooked:

you can test by a bite. Then put in a saucepan enough of the liquor to make a sufficient sauce, and reduce it to half its volume. Add sweet pimento powder or paprika (yes, not very Norman but very good) and a spoonful of Sauce Espagnole (see page 3).

Serve with boiled potatoes and in *very hot* plates, as the dish is gelatinous (or gummy).

LANGUE DE BOEUF OU DE VEAU
[Beef or Calf's Tongue]

Smoked tongues are not so easily obtainable in Paris as in the United States. The smoked article should be put in cold water, without skinning, and boiled on medium heat for 20 to 25 minutes to the pound; then skinned from the root to the tip, sliced diagonally, and covered with Sauce Madère (see page 5) or even Sauce Moutarde (see page 10). Vegetables that give off water should not be served as garnishing.

LANGUE DE VEAU BRAISÉE
[Braised Calf's Tongue]

Put a 1½-pound calf's tongue, after washing and brushing well, in a cold vinegar court-bouillon (see page 51). Bring to a boil gradually and boil for 10 minutes, then let the tongue cool in the *court-bouillon* for 15 minutes. Run the hot water tap over it quickly, to rid of any scum.

Put the tongue in a cocotte with peeled and cored carrots, onions, butter, a bay leaf, and thyme (add some chopped-up bacon if handy), and put on the lid. Let it *sweat* over medium heat for 20 minutes, then pour in enough dry white wine to half cover the tongue, increase the heat to high, and boil the wine down to a spoonful's worth.

Cover the tongue with concentrated beef consommé (best out of a tin) or your best homemade beef stock, to three-quarters its depth, and reduce this on medium high heat, (uncovered), to one-third. Put on the lid and bake in a 350° F. oven for 30 minutes, then remove and skin. Strain the liquor and mix it with Sauce Espagnole (see page 3). Slice the tongue, skin side up, diagonally and cover it with the sauce.

PIEDS DE MOUTON
[Lamb's Feet]

In Paris these are sold by choice butchers and *tripiers* ready blanched: all that is needed is to singe off bits of wool and to bone the feet (really the shanks).

Cook them in a vinegar or wine court-bouillon (see page 26) with slices of white bread spread over the surface of the bouillon to prevent the feet from rising to the surface and being exposed to the air—which would darken them. Boil them gently for 2 hours, then drain them, and serve them very hot, bathed in Sauce Poulette (see page 7), with boiled potatoes on the side.

N.B. For those who relish gelatinous food, this is one of the finest dishes.

RIS DE VEAU
[Sweetbreads]

The thymus of the calf is the most delicate of all its "innards." It is a ductless gland that is absorbed by the growing animal in its natural development. There are two portions to a sweetbread: one is roundish and smooth in outline, and the other is "knobbly," with many convolutions. The former is by far the choice bit, so, if possible, buy only the former—if not, take both.

Whatever the preparation ultimately chosen, sweetbreads should first be soaked in cold water for at least 1 hour, then drained with the least possible amount of handling and put in a large saucepan with ample cold water to cover.

Turn on the heat gently so as to get it to the boil as gradually as possible—usually 30 to 40 minutes. Skim the scum that rises before it boils, then let boil just 6 minutes and withdraw from the heat.

With a skimmer, remove the sweetbreads to a large bowl full of cold water, and run the cold water tap into the bowl until they are thoroughly cold to the touch. Drain them on a strainer and wrap them up in a *perfectly clean* napkin or dish towel (this is important, as sweetbreads absorb any odor they come in contact with), then set them on a small grill or trivet on a dish, put a small board (or a plate) on them with 2 or 3 pounds of weight on top—to act as a press—and leave them thus all night in a cool place (*not* the refrigerator). In the morning you will find that they have lost most of their sponginess, which is the desired result.

RIS DE VEAU BRAISÉS
[Braised Sweetbreads]

After the initial preparation (see above), take the pressed sweetbreads from their wrapping, *without touching them with your hands*, and lay them on a clean, dry napkin or towel. Lard them with 1-inch-long strips of pork fatback, just on the surface, using the long *tin*

Surface larding needle

surface-larding needle. Braise them by sweating for 10 minutes and then cooking in the oven, covered, for 35 minutes at 300° F. Remove the lid and baste the sweetbreads with the liquor (sauce) in the pan and expose them to this oven heat for 5 minutes to "glaze" them— i.e., to give their surface a sheen.

RIS DE VEAU À LA GRENELLE
[Sweetbread Tart with Mushrooms and Truffles]

Slice pressed sweetbreads (see above) 1½ inches thick diagonally (of course the round bits will be irregular). Season the pieces with onion salt and white pepper, and dredge them lightly in all-purpose flour. Slip them into a skillet with very hot butter and turn them over as soon as the underside is light brown. Pour a good squirt of Cognac over them, light it, and withdraw the pan from the heat. Put the flame out by waving your hand quickly over it.

Sauté some sliced mushrooms and put them, along with 2 sliced truffles and the sweetbreads, into an ovenproof china tart dish or pie plate. Top lightly with Sauce Madère (see page 5) and cover the dish or plate with Pâte Feuilletée (see page 273), well stuck around the sides and with a hole in the middle to let the steam out. Brush the whole with beaten egg and bake for 35 minutes in a 375° F. oven.

Have enough Sauce Madère to spoon over each helping.

N.B. Two sweetbreads should be enough for 4 or 5 people, and so should 1½ pounds of *pâte feuilletée.*

RIS DE VEAU RÉGENCE
[Braised Sweetbreads with Two Sauces]

Proceed as above, but do not let any coloring take place—i.e., cook more slowly and on gentler heat—and, after the liquor has been reduced, moisten with white (chicken) broth. Serve topped with a thick Sauce Allemande (see page 7) and then Sauce Madère (see page 5) poured carefully out of a pitcher with a lip, so as to form a thin ribbon curling over the surface.

VOL-AU-VENT FINANCIÈRE
[Sweetbreads and Brains in Patty Shells]

The classical recipe for this dish demands cocks' crests and kidneys! Though they can be found in tins in France, they are hardly worth the trouble.

Prepare 2 pressed sweetbreads (see above) and prepare 2 calf's or lamb's brains by boiling in a vinegar court-bouillon as indicated for Cervelles de Veau ou de Mouton (see page 117). Remove the pressed sweetbreads from their wrapping, *without touching them with your hands*, and slice them diagonally. Carefully cut the brains into portions.

Sauté the sweetbreads and brains gently in 2 spoonfuls of butter, then simmer them in 1 cup Sauce Allemande (see page 7) or Sauce Madère (page 5) mixed with 8 sautéed mushroom tops and 2 truffles (sliced).

Fill an 8-inch-wide patty shell (*vol-au-vent*) with the mixture, and heat in a 375° F. oven for 10 minutes before serving.

ROGNONS DE VEAU OU DE MOUTON
[*Veal or Lamb Kidneys*]

Veal kidneys are best when they are pale pink or russet color, *not* when they are deep red. They should be embedded in their ball of suet. In Paris the butcher removes the suet and the fine membrane under it that clings to the kidney. In any case, it must be peeled off carefully. The fat that remains in the convolutions of the veal kidney (there is little of it in the lamb organ) need not be removed before cooking—it can easily be cut away at the moment of slicing.

Lamb kidneys are cut in half from the round face to the B-shaped side, or almost cut through thus, opening like a book for skewering.

ROGNONS DE VEAU OU DE MOUTON SAUTÉS
[*Sautéed Veal or Lamb Kidneys*]

Cut the kidneys diagonally across (lamb kidneys are opened up as described above), then season them, dredge them in all-purpose flour, and sauté them lightly in hot butter. Turn them over as soon as they change color.

Throw in a squirt of Cognac (or whisky) and light it; then shake the pan and remove it from the heat (lamb kidneys take 1 or 2 minutes to sauté). Scrape the pan with a blunt-edged spoon and add a little port, Madeira, or sherry to make a sauce; or, better still, add

Sauce Espagnole (see page 3) to the pan off the heat.

Serve on fried toast (see page 28), or with white rice (see page 45), mashed potatoes, etc.

ROGNONS DE VEAU OU DE MOUTON EN BROCHETTES
[Veal or Lamb Kidneys on Skewers]

Veal kidneys cut straight across, sectionally, or lamb kidneys, opened up as described above, are skewered with alternating squares of smoked bacon, seasoned with salt and pepper, and grilled at a distance of 3 to 4 inches from a red-hot caloroid or gas flame.

Veal kidneys are turned once and are grilled a total of about 10 minutes.

Lamb kidneys are turned once and are grilled a total of about 5 or 6 minutes (they require less time because the skewer is threaded through the *opened* kidney, exposing its cut surface).

TÊTE DE VEAU
[Calf's Head]

Paris butchers and *tripiers* sell this well blanched and rolled up. Otherwise, it must be put in ample cold water to cover it *completely* and brought to a boil *very gradually*. Remove the scum that rises and boil for 6 minutes, then put the head in a large bowl under the cold water tap until cold to the touch. Cut it up in 3-inch squares, roughly.

Meanwhile, prepare a vinegar court-bouillon (see page 51) and, when cold, put the calf's head in it—again, it must be *completely* submerged. Spread on top of the water some slices of bread to prevent exposure to the air, which would make the head an ugly dark gray: it should be as white as possible when served. Boil gently for 3 hours.

Prepare a calf's brain (see page 117), and serve it with the head, accompanied with Sauce Gribiche (see page 11), boiled potatoes, and any vegetable with no very pronounced flavor.

N.B. Calf's head is also served with Sauce Poulette (see page 7).

TÊTE DE VEAU EN TORTUE
[Mock Turtle]

After cooking as above, cut calf's head up in 1½ inch squares, roughly. Serve in a mound on a hot dish, surrounded by veal quenelles, stewed mushrooms, stuffed olives, sour pickles, and sliced truffles—sometimes even with fried eggs on toast and boiled crayfish —and sauced with Sauce Madère (see page 5) mixed with a little tomato puree.

CHAPTER 11

Beef

FRENCH BEEF is excellent when of the Charolais, Normand, and Limousin breeds of cattle. It is not as fat as American beef.

CÔTE DE BOEUF RÔTIE
[Roast Ribs of Beef]

In Paris home cooking, this roast is cooked without the bone, well pared and rolled, and tied with several turns of string. In restaurants it is sometimes served on the bone, which in the case of large joints is certainly better. In both cases the preference seems to be for under-done meat—i.e., oven or spit roasted, at the rate of 15 minutes to the pound in an oven of 400° F. for the first 20 minutes and 350° F. thereafter. The joints rests on a short-legged trivet or grill, or in a roasting rack, after having been rubbed with all-purpose flour mixed with a *little* fine salt and freshly ground pepper. If you omit the salt, you will have less juice in the roasting pan; if you put too much salt, the meat will bleed and be dry on serving. No flour should be added to the pan, but a little hot water at the time of serving is permissible to increase the amount of gravy.

CONTREFILET (FAUX FILET) RÔTI
[Roast Sirloin of Beef]

Same preparation as for Côte de Boeuf Rôtie (see above). And the same applies to rump roast (in Anglo-French, *romsteck*), which at good butchers is sold wrapped up in a thin sheet of pork fat, and is preferred by those who like very lean meat.

FILET DE BOEUF
[Beef Tenderloin]

This is the inside muscle—under the spinal cord—and the tenderest cut of all. It is not, however, the most flavorful.

Paris butchers like to wrap it up in sheets of pork fat, all done up with a string; and as this is the most expensive cut and they weigh the finished package, the method has great advantage to *them*. But a tenderloin should be bought in its splendid nudity, pared of all fat and membranes, and especially of the side muscle called in French *la chainette* ("little chain").

If the tenderloin has been bought in the rough—i.e., without having been trimmed or pared—this operation can be carried out at home: a sharp knife will take care of the removal of fat and membranes, and the fingers can easily detach the *chainette* (which can be used for brochettes with alternate slivers of bacon, for a light lunch or supper).

The tenderloin or *filet de boeuf* narrows down to a point toward the tail of the carcass: this portion can be cut across in slices 1 inch to 1½ inches thick to make little *tournedos de filet mignon*, hence the American term "filets mignons." The opposite end is thick and can best be utilized as a small roast or, sliced 1 inch thick, as a delicate grilled steak. These two "ends" make up about one-half of the total filet. The center, which makes up the other half, is the portion that is best for the usual-sized tournedos, 1½ inches thick, or a roast: here it will be called the "center filet."

TOURNEDOS

These are slices, 1 to 1½ inches thick, cut squarely across the tenderloin and sautéed in butter.

Each tournedos must be carefully dried with paper and very delicately seasoned with salt and ground pepper. The butter must be just turning yellow with the heat.

When you lift the underside, in contact with the pan, and it shows brown-blackish, turn it over. Shake the pan over the heat without lifting it. When the other side shows brown-blackish, the meat is done, and the tournedos should be lifted to a hot plate.

TOURNEDOS ROSSINI
[Tournedos with Truffles and Foie Gras]

Serve on fried toast that has been covered with a little Sauce Espagnole (see page 3). Place on top a slice of foie gras with truffles, and bathe the whole with Sauce Madère (see page 5).

TOURNEDOS À LA LOUIS
[Tournedos with Port Wine and Jam Sauce]

A minute after turning over, pour a tablespoon of port wine over the tournedos. Squeeze the tournedos lightly with a spoon, add 1 or 2 tablespoons of raspberry or blackberry jam to the juice, and mix well. Serve on fried toast (see page 28) with braised celery on the side.

The recipes for various manners of "dressing" tournedos are practically innumerable. Any imaginative cook can invent one. To satisfy readers who like to recognize names on a restaurant menu, here are some other well-known preparations of tournedos:

ANDALOUSE: With sliced, (ham and tomato) stuffed eggplant and little glazed onions.

CHASSEUR: Chopped mushrooms plus Sauce Madère (see page 5).

CHEVREUIL: Marinated, sautéed, served on chestnut purée, topped with Sauce Poivrade (see page 5).

CLAMART: Garnished with artichoke hearts topped with fresh peas.

CLERMONT: Garnished with stuffed onions and artichoke hearts, topped with Sauce Tomate (see page 7).

DUBARRY: Garnished with artichoke hearts, topped with small cauliflower bouquets plus Sauce Mornay (see page 9).

MAJORDOME: Marinated, Sauce Espagnole (see page 3) mixed with marinade, puree of lentils.

MARIE-LOUISE: Artichoke hearts topped with mushroom puree.

PORTUGAISE: Sauce Tomate, garnished with stuffed tomatoes.

SOUBISE: Topped with Purée d'Oignons Soubise (see page 235).

CHÂTEAUBRIANT or CHÂTEAUBRIAND

Escoffier spells it with a final t and Prosper Montagné with a final d—what is more, the latter scolds those who spell it as Escoffier does, because its originator was Montmireil, *chef de cuisine* of the great Châteaubriand.

This is nothing but a thick tournedos weighing 1¼ to 1½ pounds and that has, according to time-honored principles, been flattened somewhat with the cleaver and then grilled.

For the beef lover who relishes a tender cut without much "saucing" or fancy dressing, this cut is excellent: well brushed with melted butter, very delicately salted and peppered, it should be grilled without the least charring of the surface.

In other words, *it cannot be timed: it must be watched.*

FILET DE BOEUF RÔTI
[Roast Tenderloin]

Taken from the center of the tenderloin, it should weigh 2 to 2½ pounds and will serve 6 persons generously. It should be pared as explained above. It thus presents approximately the same thickness throughout.

To wrap it up in a *crépine* (very thin slice of pork fat, or the peritoneum of the pig) is a mistake. Suffice it to brush the surface with melted butter and repeat this during roasting once or twice to prevent the surface from drying out.

If oven roasted, the tenderloin should rest on a rack off the surface of the roasting pan, and the temperature should be 375° F. for the first 15 minutes and 350° F. thereafter, the total time being reckoned at 12 minutes the pound.

The same timing applies to roasting on the spit—in an electrically operated roaster with the caloroid above and *with front and two sides completely open*, thus approaching as nearly as possible the conditions of a real wood fire in the chimney. The caloroid should be red hot before the spit with the meat is placed in rotation, and the distance should be about 4 inches from meat to caloroid.

(*Perhaps this is the place to call attention to the fact that oven-roasting can never take the place of spit roasting, as in the oven there is always a certain amount of humidity that envelops what is cooked in it—hence, even spits that turn in the oven are of no real value.* Nothing quite equals the open wood fire with the complete circulation of air around the meat, plus sniffs of smoke that impart their flavor to it.)

In England, the classical companion of roast beef is Yorkshire pudding. Boiled or roast potatoes come next. Boiled cabbage is the preferred vegetable, the next choice being boiled cauliflower (the cabbage or cauliflower served well drained and freshly buttered). Any green vegetable, presented the same way, is suitable, secondarily. Green salads, especially watercress, are always acceptable. Dry English mustard worked into a creamy paste with water, and Sauce Raifort (see page 14), are usual but actually do not improve the fine flavor of top-quality roast beef.

LE BOEUF BOUILLI or POT-AU-FEU
[Boiled Beef with Vegetables]

This appetizing dish may be eaten freshly cooked and hot, or may be served cold on the morrow (having been kept dry and *not* in its broth). There are those who love it and those who turn up their noses at it.

As it is intended to be both a soup and a meat dish, both lean and fat are needed: lean beef to be presented with the vegetables, and fat for the necessary unctuous substance of the broth. Also, some bones and cartilage (for gelatin) and some marrow are indispensable.

For 4 persons

For the lean: 1 pound of round and ½ pound of chuck. For the fat: 1 pound of brisket, ½ pound of flank, and ½ pound of plate. Besides, add a piece of marrow bone, with the marrow inside, of course. Do *not* wash the meat: examine it and if necessary wipe it, but to wash it would diminish flavor. The pound of round should be well tied with string. Block each end of marrow bone with a bit of coarse salt, and then wrap the bone in a piece of cheesecloth and tie it up securely with string.

Use a large pot that is rather deep than wide (to make skimming easier). It should be of heavy material (such as enameled cast iron) to insure steady cooking. Into the pot put cold water: 3 or 3½ pints per pound of meat and bones (about 6 quarts). Add the meat (round, chuck, brisket, flank, plate) and the marrow bone, and a good tea-spoon of coarse salt. Put the pot on high heat, uncovered. As soon as dark scum rises to the surface, remove it with a skimmer; and repeat this operation as long as the scum comes up.

When boiling begins, add a peeled onion stuck with a whole clove, ½ pound leeks (minus root ends and half their leaf ends), ½ pound carrots (peeled and cored), ½ pound turnips (peeled), a handful of celery leaves (or celeriac), a bay leaf, and 1 sprig of fresh thyme (or ¼ teaspoon dried).

As soon as boiling begins again, reduce heat so that when covered the pot will boil gently. Put the lid on so that a little chink remains open to let a wisp of steam rise: *this keeps the broth from getting turbid*. Boil thus for about 4 hours. (Longer boiling is not only useless but likely to spoil both meats and broth.)

Obviously, the vegetables will be overcooked at the end of 4 hours, but a new lot, including cabbage and potatoes, can be boiled apart, with or without some of the broth, 30 to 45 minutes before serving the meat.

N.B. Some authorities recommend the addition of a fowl to the *pot-au-feu*, especially the giblets: this, of course, would change the dish.

ESTOUFFADE DE BOEUF À LA PROVENÇALE
[*Beef Stew with Red Wine and Mushrooms*]

For 4 persons

Dredge 2 pounds of beef (pieces of chuck, neck, and plate) in flour and set aside. Cut ½ pound lean bacon in rough dice and rinse lightly in boiling water, then drain and sauté in clarified butter (see page 10). Lift the bacon with a skimmer to a plate, and reserve it.

In the fat left in the pan, sauté the well-dredged pieces of beef and 4 medium-large onions (peeled and cut in quarters). When they are well browned, add 1 clove of garlic (minced), and transfer to a larger saucepan. Pour in a bottle of very good red wine, then put on high heat, uncovered, and reduce to half, stirring frequently. Add 3 cups of water, 3 cups of concentrated beef consommé, a bay leaf, 1 sprig of fresh thyme (or ¼ teaspoon dried), and a few stalks of parsley. Bring to a boil on high heat, then cover and set in 350° F. oven to boil gently for 2½ hours.

Meanwhile, sauté 2 cups of mushrooms (sliced) in 2 spoonfuls of butter. Take the pan containing the meat from the oven, and pour its contents into a colander over a saucepan. To the liquor thus strained add the pieces of meat, the mushrooms, and the diced bacon. Add also a spoonful of tomato paste and stir thoroughly. If the sauce is too liquid, melt a spoonful of butter in a saucepan, add a spoonful of flour, stir, and cook until deep yellow or light brown; wet this down with some of the sauce, stirring, and again some more until you have a thick sauce—mix this with the rest.

Verify the salt and pepper seasoning.

N.B. Noodles are an excellent accompaniment.

BOEUF À LA MODE
[Beef Braised in Red Wine]

It is hardly worthwhile to make this dish using less than 3 pounds of beef. For one thing, there will be a reduction in the cooking. Also, the beef should be kept juicy inside, which requires a sizable piece. Finally, *boeuf à la mode* keeps well—and served cold it is excellent.

For 6 to 8 persons

Cut 4 ounces of fresh pork fat in pencil-thin strips and lard a 3-pound piece of beef round through, from end to end, with a deep-

End-to-end larding needle

larding needle at four or five places. A good trick is to thrust the needle through the meat *empty*, withdraw it, dust it lightly with onion salt and pepper and a pinch of powdered thyme, and then place a strip of fat on the needle and draw it gently through the hole (if the strip of fat does not come through, push and pull the needle several times through the meat to enlarge the hole). Then withdraw the needle slowly, leaving the lardoon in the meat.

Put on high heat 3 spoonfuls of clarified butter (see page 10). When it begins to turn yellow, brown the meat in it, turning it only when one side is nicely browned—*not* blackened—so that it will be like a nicely grilled steak all over, including the ends. Then lift the meat to a heavy saucepan that has a well-fitting lid and pour ½ bottle of good red wine and a glass of Cognac over it. Set the pan on high heat, uncovered, and reduce this liquor to about one-third its volume.

Add a boned calf's foot and a 4-inch piece of bacon rind—both will yield a desired gelatinous substance. Add also 3 or 4 medium onions (each peeled and stuck with a clove), 2 or 3 bay leaves, 1 sprig of fresh thyme (or ¼ teaspoon dried), a few peppercorns, a few stalks of parsley, and enough half beef consommé–half water (tinned concentrated consommé cut with an equal amount of water) to just cover the meat. Bring to a boil and skim, then cover tightly with the pot's own well-fitting lid. Put in a 300° F. oven for 3 hours to simmer or boil very gently, examining the meat from time to time and turning it over with two wooden spoons.

Add ½ pound of carrots (peeled, cored, and cut in 3-inch pieces) and verify the salt seasoning. Continue to cook for about 40 minutes. Meanwhile, brown 12 to 18 tiny onions in a spoonful of clarified butter.

At the moment of serving, surround the meat with the tiny onions, the carrots, and the cup-up calf's foot (also boiled potatoes, if desired), and pour over the meat the juice of the pot—lightly skimmed.

If there is more liquor in the pot than would ordinarily constitute a sauce, put the meat on a platter (ovenproof), pour a few spoonfuls of the liquor over the meat, set the platter in the hot but turned-off oven (to *glaze* the meat), and reduce by boiling the rest of the liquor to the desired quantity. If, still, there is too much liquor or it is too liquid, thicken or bind with a dessert spoonful of arrowroot dissolved in a little cold water (the liquor should be boiling when the arrowroot is added, and a few seconds later should be removed from the heat).

Boeuf à la mode not consumed hot is put away covered with its liquor and surrounded by its vegetables and pieces of calf's foot to be served later cold: the liquor should jell in cooling.

BOEUF À LA BOURGUIGNONNE
[Beef Stewed in Red Wine]

This name is really a misnomer, as it implies a Burgundian dish, which this is not. It should be called boeuf au Bourgogne or, more precisely, boeuf au vin de Bourgogne, because that is what it is: beef in Burgundy wine. There are two ways of preparing it:

CULOTTE DE BOEUF BRAISÉE AU VIN DE BOURGOGNE
[Braised Beef in Burgundy Wine]

For 4 or 5 persons

Cut 4 ounces fresh pork fatback in pencil-thin strips, and lard a 2-pound piece of beef top of the round (cut, if possible, parallel to the line of the leg) through, from end to end (the long way), with a deep-larding needle (see illustration page 135) at three or four places; put onion salt, pepper, and thyme on the needle, using the technique described under Boeuf à la Mode (see above).

On the bottom of a large, heavy enameled cast-iron cocotte, spread a spoonful of tasteless cooking oil and half a sliced onion. Place the beef on this, and then on the beef spread the other half of the onion, sliced. Pour over the beef a small glass of Cognac and then ⅔ bottle of a very good red Burgundy wine. Season with onion salt and freshly ground pepper, thyme, and 2 bay leaves (broken in quarters). Cover and let the beef marinate for 3 hours in a reasonably cool place (not the refrigerator). Every hour, turn the meat over with two spoons—not your hands.

After the marinating, remove the meat from the cocotte, set it on a plate—again with two spoons and not your hands, which would sour it—and wipe it with paper toweling: sort of mopping. Strain the other contents of the marinade into another pan and reserve.

Rinse the cocotte, dry it, and pour 2 spoonfuls of clarified butter (see page 10) into it. Set on high heat and, when the butter begins to turn yellow, brown the meat on all sides in it, then remove the meat to a plate. Add 2 spoonfuls of all-purpose flour to the cocotte and stir well. If the mixture turns dark brown, remove briefly from the heat. Then, on very gentle heat, dissolve the mixture with the strained marinade liquid you reserved earlier, and with ½ cup concentrated beef consommé cut with ½ cup water.

Raise the heat again to high and bring to a boil. Add the meat with whatever juice has oozed out on its plate, along with a cup of well-washed, chopped mushrooms and half a clove of garlic (finely chopped). When it boils again, cover, put in a 350° F. oven, and let it boil there for 3½ hours, examining the liquor from time to time to see that it is boiling.

Meanwhile, cut in small dice 4 ounces of lean bacon; put the dice in cold water, bring to a boil, and boil for 5 minutes, then drain and dry them, and sauté them in butter for 2 or 3 minutes. Also sauté in butter 1½ cups of small, whole mushrooms, and about 18 tiny onions.

Remove the cocotte from the oven and skim off the fat with great care. Again put the meat on a plate, and strain the cooking liquor into another pan. Rinse the cocotte, put the meat back into it, and surround with the little onions, sautéed mushrooms, and bacon dice; pour the strained liquor over the whole.

RAGOÛT DE BOEUF AU VIN DE BOURGOGNE
[Beef Stew with Burgundy Wine]

Take the same amount of beef round as for Culotte de Boeuf Braisée (see above). Cut it into cubes of about 2 inches and marinate as above.

Exactly as for Culotte de Boeuf Braisée, blanch (boil) bacon dice, and sauté them in clarified butter (see page 10). Sauté small whole mushrooms and then the little onions in the same clarified butter—bacon fat. After removing them to a plate, brown the pieces of beef in the same fat, turning them over as they brown well.

Drain off the fat entirely and dust the beef with all-purpose flour. On gentle heat, roll the pieces of beef about and brown the flour, then gradually add the marinating liquid, stirring thoroughly to make a sauce. Bring to a boil, cover, and cook on gentle heat for $1\frac{1}{2}$ to 2 hours. Add the little onions, mushrooms, and bacon dice. Cover and simmer for 20 minutes longer.

Serve with the onions, mushrooms, and bacon round the meat, with some of the sauce poured on it and some served apart in a sauce-boat.

QUEUE DE BOEUF
[Oxtail]

QUEUE DE BOEUF FARCIE
[Stuffed Oxtail]

Some expert and obliging Paris butchers remove the bones from the tail without piercing the skin (obviously not the *hide*), and the boned tail resembles a wind indicator sock at an airfield. This makes stuffing very easy. Otherwise the cook has to slit one side of the tail to remove the vertebrae with the meat, and then to sew the tail up for filling. Of course, in any case, *after* stuffing the tail, one will have to sew (or tie) up both *ends*.

Set the boned tail aside while you remove the oxtail meat from the bones; set the bones aside. Mince the meat fine with a knife, and mix it with an equal amount of pork sausage meat ($\frac{1}{2}$ pound) and with 4 ounces of bread (without crust), soaked in milk, and 2 whole eggs (well beaten). If you have a truffle handy, add it, chopped up. Season this mixture, which should be perfectly homogeneous, with salt, pepper, a pinch of grated nutmeg and another of powdered thyme.

Tie the narrow end of the reserved boned tail securely, and stuff the rest of it with the meat mixture, finishing up by tying the wide or top end to form a sort of conical sausage. Put it in a cocotte with enough cold water to cover, add the reserved bones, and set on high heat. As soon as it boils, reduce the heat to gentle so it boils steadily —just above simmering—for 1¼ hours.

Meanwhile, peel, core, and coarsely dice 4 or 5 carrots and chop up 2 medium-large onions. Lay these, with 2 or 3 slices of bacon, at the bottom of another cocotte. Lay the stuffed tail on this (reserve the broth in which it cooked), and pour in enough dry white wine to *nearly* cover the meat. Cover and let boil gently for 45 minutes, then remove the tail to a plate, cover and keep warm.

Reduce the wine on high heat to the desired amount of sauce, adding some of the broth that you reserved from the first boiling. If the sauce is too liquid, thicken it with arrowroot (see page 65). Put the meat in the sauce, cover, and let it get hot for a few minutes before serving with a vegetable and potatoes, rice, or noodles. It is carved across, of course, and the sauce is poured over the slices.

QUEUE DE BOEUF EN HOCHEPOT
[Oxtail Stew]

The *Oxford English Dictionary* gives *hocher* (meaning "to shake") plus *pot* as the origin of the French word. However, there is the old Lancashire "hot pot" which suggests paternity.

For 4 to 6 persons

Skin the tail and throw away the skin, then cut the tail in good-sized pieces across. Do likewise with 2 pigs' feet and 1 pig's ear. (If you are lucky, the butcher will do all this for you.) Put the tail, feet, and ear in a saucepan big enough to hold cold water to cover them and permit skimming. Set on high heat and skim as boiling begins. After a few minutes reduce the heat, cover, and boil gently for 2 hours.

Add 12 small, peeled turnips (or their equivalent in pieces from larger ones), cover, and cook 1 hour, then add twice as many carrots (peeled and cored) cut like the turnips and a good handful of little onions (peeled). Season with salt, pepper, several stalks of parsley, a bay leaf, and a pinch of thyme. Continue cooking for 1 hour—gentle, steady boiling.

Before serving, skim off the grease. If the sauce is too liquid, thicken it with arrowroot (see page 65).

Serve with boiled potatoes and boiled cabbage.

CARBONNADES DE BOEUF À LA FLAMANDE
[Beef and Onions in Beer]

Cut 2 pounds of beef round into thin slices. Brown them on both sides in 2 spoonfuls of very hot lard, then remove to a warm plate. In the same fat, brown ¾ pound of onions (finely chopped); do not let them burn. Remove the onions with a skimmer and set the pan aside, off the heat, leaving the contents untouched.

In a cocotte of appropriate size, lay the slices of beef, seasoned with salt and pepper, and the browned onions, in alternate layers. In another small pan, make a binder for the sauce: stir a spoonful of butter and a spoonful of flour over medium heat until the mixture is deep brown (not black). Withdraw from the heat.

Set the pan in which the beef and onions were browned on medium heat—unless you let this pan blacken, in which case use still another pan into which you have put 2 tablespoons clarified butter (see page 10). Pour in ½ cup lager beer and 1 cup beef consommé (½ concentrated consommé and ½ water) and add this liquid to the binder gradually, while stirring. Add a teaspoon of brown sugar (or caramel) and stir well.

Strain this sauce on top of the meat, add a bay leaf and a pinch of thyme, and bring to a boil. Cover and cook in a 350° F. oven for 2 hours.

DAUBE DE BOEUF
[Potted Beef]

Cut 2 pounds of lower beef round in cubes, each weighing about 1/4 pound. Lard these with 4 ounces of fresh pork fat (see page 135), then season with salt and pepper, thyme, and 1 clove garlic (crushed). Add 3 carrots and 3 onions (both coarsely chopped) and 1 bay leaf. Add red wine to cover (about 2 cups) laced with a small glass of Cognac. Marinate for 4 hours.

Dice 2 spoonfuls of fresh pork fat. Cook these very gently with 2 spoonfuls of olive oil, and, when the fat has melted (or almost), add an onion (quartered) and let it brown lightly. Add the pieces of beef and the drained vegetables of the marinade (reserve the marinade liquid). Brown them all while stirring, and season with the peel of 1/4 orange (grated), a pinch of thyme, a bay leaf, a clove of garlic, several stalks of parsley, and a pinch of grated nutmeg.

Put on high heat, and add the marinade liquor. Reduce it to about one-half, and then add 1 cup boiling water. Cover and remove to medium-low heat to simmer for 4 hours.

There should be little sauce and the meat should be very soft. Serve with macaroni *au gratin*.

CHAPTER 12

Veal

FRENCH VEAL is the best in the world *if* it is not the result of artificial pen feeding—i.e., "scientific" cramming of feed, which produces large calves but tasteless meat. Calves that have grazed do not yield the creamy-pink meat that, when cooked, becomes the color of turkey breast. For this they have to be milk fed.

The best cuts of veal come from the hind quarter, especially the hind portion of it midway between the tail and the hock. Under the muscle known as the *noix* in French (sometimes called the "cushion" in the United States) there is a delicate muscle called in France *la noix pâtissière*, and a portion of this is called *le rond* or "the round" (not to be confused with the round of beef). It is from this portion that the best *escalopes* (French) or collops (proper English)—slices for sautéing—are cut: it is juicy and even in texture, without interwoven nerves or membranes. For roasts to be served to more than 4 people, the *noix* or "cushion" and the saddle, including the rump, are preferable; but the chops, too, make an excellent roast.

RÔTI DE VEAU
[*Veal Roast*]

Veal must be cooked thoroughly, but of course not to the point of drying it up. The oven should be 300° to 325° F., and the time of cooking 25 minutes per pound.

The meat can be placed on an oven dish or roasting pan (preferably a dish just large enough to contain the piece and to permit basting with a spoon) or in a cocotte of like dimensions.

It is advisable to lay the meat on a bed of peeled and chopped carrots and onions with its own fat trimmings or bits of *fresh* pork fat (bacon is likely to affect the color of the meat). Melted butter should be generously poured over it; and salt, pepper (white), a bay leaf, thyme, and stalks of parsley should be sprinkled over it.

Larding through and through from end to end with fresh pork fat (see page 135), and the addition of peeled and cored carrots and shelled pistachio nuts improve the flavor and especially the appearance of the piece when carved. Melted butter should be kept at hand, and the meat basted with it every 15 or 20 minutes.

A veal roast larded end-to-end

At the moment of serving, the pan should be "deglazed" by pouring a few spoonfuls of boiling water in it and scraping it with a spoon over medium heat. If meat glaze is available, or some Sauce Espagnole (see page 3) or Sauce Madère (see page 5)—all the better, of course.

If in doubt as to whether a veal roast has been thoroughly cooked: stick a thin, pointed utensil into it—the juice that comes out should be colorless.

ROGNONNADE DE VEAU RÔTIE
[Roast Loin of Veal with Kidney]

Half the saddle is cut straight across, including the kidneys, thus giving two loins. The loin is boned, the kidney fat is partially cut away, and the flap toward the belly is rolled over the whole piece after seasoning with salt and pepper. The surface is skinned, and the piece is fastened with several turns of string. Thus the roast is quite an affair, fit for a large party. It can be roasted as in the preceding recipe, or braised as in the one below.

PIÈCE DE VEAU BRAISÉE
[Braised Veal]

For 6 persons

In a heavy cocotte with a tightly fitting lid, lay a bed of chopped onions and carrots, a bay leaf, a sprig of fresh thyme (or ¼ teaspoon dried), several stalks of parsley, 2 spoonfuls of butter (in slivers), and a few trimmings or snippets of fresh pork fat. Put a 2-pound piece of tied-up boneless veal on this, and cover the cocotte tightly with its own lid. Place on medium low heat and let *sweat* for 15 minutes. (During this time there should be no browning of the vegetables.) Wet down with enough dry white wine to almost cover the meat (about 1½ cups), then raise the heat to high and, with cocotte uncovered, reduce the wine to a few spoonfuls. Add beef consommé almost to cover the meat (about 1 cup). If needed, add salt. Put a well-buttered piece of aluminum foil over the cocotte and then the lid. Set in a 350° F. oven and cook for 1 hour (30 minutes per pound of meat, weighed when raw), inspecting the contents of the cocotte from time to time to prevent possible burning.

FRICANDEAU DE VEAU

Take 2 pounds veal "cushion" (underside of the upper leg) cut with the grain—that is, parallel to main bone—and slice about 1½ inches thick. Surface lard (with a long thin needle) the slices with 4 ounces of pork fat (in snippets) and then braise them as in the preceding recipe, and using the same ingredients, except as follows:

After adding beef consommé and (if needed) salt, again reduce the cooking liquid to a few spoonfuls. Then add another cup of beef consommé, cover as in the preceding recipe (buttered aluminum foil, lid), set the cocotte in a 325°F. oven, and cook for 40 minutes per pound of meat, inspecting and basting with cooking liquor every 20 minutes.

This slow, long cooking practically melts the meat, hence the other name for this dish: *veau à la cuiller* ("veal-to-be-eaten-with-a-spoon").

VEAU EN CASSEROLE
[Casserole of Veal]

Take the desired number of veal chops (1 per person as a rule), season with salt and pepper, and put in a cocotte rather shallow than deep where they fit snugly.

Moisten generously with clarified butter (see page 10). Add some diced pork fat (fresh), cover, and set on medium low heat to *sweat* for 20 minutes, then lower the heat to *low* and turn the meat over. Cover again and cook at this temperature for about an hour.

A quarter hour before serving, inspect the contents of your casserole. If you find them on the dry side, add a little boiling water, stir carefully without mashing the meat, and baste it. (A little wine would not do it any harm.)

Just before serving, add any cooked vegetable you prefer—so long as its flavor will not predominate. Preferably, add more than one vegetable so as to present a truly mixed dish.

SAUTÉS DE VEAU
[Veal Sautés]

Surprisingly enough, there is considerable error and dispute regarding this term. Many so-called sautés are actually stews because, after an initial sautéing in the pan, the meat is put in the oven, in a covered utensil, to finish cooking. Here only the real veal sautés will be considered.

SAUTÉ DE VEAU À LA BORDELAISE
[Sauté of Veal in Wine Sauce]

Bone veal chops and sauté them in butter, turning them over once one side is light brown, then reducing the heat to finish cooking. Moisten the pan with red or white Bordeaux (dry) wine, enough to make a sauce. Add, if necessary, a little Sauce Allemande (see page 7).

Serve with the sauce poured over the chops and with little browned onions all around, plus (if available) boiled artichoke hearts warmed in butter.

SAUTÉ DE VEAU À LA MILANAISE
[Sauté of Veal with Tomato Sauce and Macaroni]

Have the backbone pared so that the chop lies flat on the pan, like a collop. Dip it in egg beaten with a teaspoon of olive oil, then in bread crumbs seasoned with salt and white pepper, and sauté it in hot clarified butter (see page 10), browning both sides.

Serve with Sauce Tomate (see page 7) over it and, on the side, boiled macaroni well buttered after draining and then generously dusted with grated Parmesan cheese.

SAUTÉ DE VEAU ORLOFF
[Sauté of Veal "Smothered" in Onions]

Have the backbone pared so that the chop lies flat on the pan, like a collop. Sauté in clarified butter (see page 10), browning both sides, then season with salt and white pepper. Cover with Purée d'Oignons Soubise (see page 235) heaped like an inverted bowl and truffle slices shaped like little crescents.

SAUTÉ DE VEAU MARQUISE
[Sauté of Veal with Madeira Sauce and Foie Gras]

Sauté a veal chop as in the preceding recipe, and remove it to a warm plate. Cover. Deglaze the pan with Madeira wine, and add to it little strips of truffle, a tablespoon of Sauce Madère (see page 5), 2 spoonfuls of thick cream, and a spoonful of foie gras puree (the kind that comes in pottery jars). Stir well to make a sauce and pour over the chop.

Serve with asparagus tips lightly covered with butter.

CÒTES DE VEAU
[Veal Rib Chops]

CÔTES DE VEAU FOYOT
[Veal Rib Chops with Cheese, Madeira Sauce, and Truffles]

For 6 persons

Trim off the backbone of 2 pounds of rib veal chops and shorten the rib bones to the edge of the meat. Season with salt and pepper, then brown lightly in hot butter.

Moisten 3 spoonfuls of bread crumbs lightly with 2 spoonfuls of beef consommé and mix well with 3 spoonfuls of Parmesan cheese. Cover one side of each chop with this mixture by pressing it on with a knife or spatula.

Melt 4 spoonfuls of butter in a pan that can be put into the oven and is large enough to contain the chops side by side without over-lapping. Lay the chops, cheese side up, in the pan. Mix $\frac{1}{2}$ cup white wine and $\frac{1}{4}$ cup beef consommé and pour into the pan but *not* over the chops. Bring to a boil, then put the pan in a 350° F. oven without covering and cook for 2 hours, basting every 15 minutes for the first hour or so. Then sprinkle the cheese-covered surface of the chops with a little melted butter.

While this is going on, chop up some truffles and heat them— *do not boil them*—in sufficient Sauce Madère (see page 5) to serve with the chops (about $\frac{3}{4}$ cup).

Lift the chops to a hot serving platter, with great care not to break them up after the long cooking. Reduce the liquor in the pan to a few spoonfuls and mix this with the Sauce Madère. As the chops will be lightly browned on top (the cheese side), the sauce should be served around them and *not* over them.

TENDRONS DE VEAU
[Veal Tendrons]

The French word *tendron* as applied to cookery or butchery is translated in most dictionaries as "gristle." This is reminiscent of Dr. Johnson's reply to the question "Why do you say in your dictionary that the pastern is the knee of the horse?" "Ignorance, pure ignorance." Culinarily speaking, *tendrons* comprise some gristle or cartilaginous tissue but also meat, and they should be cut from the upper part of the breast of veal without any bone. Good Paris butchers prepare *tendrons* in sections about a finger's length and two or three fingers' width.

TENDRONS DE VEAU À L'ESTRAGON
[Veal Tendrons with Tarragon]

For each person to be served, take about 4 ounces of veal strips cut from the cartilage joining the ribs to the breast, without any bone. Brown in hot clarified butter (see page 10) until a golden color, but avoid burning. Dust generously with all-purpose flour, turning the pieces around, and brown the flour lightly, stirring and scraping the bottom of the pan.

Moisten with a mixture of half white wine–half water, continuing to scrape and stir and keeping the pan on medium-high heat, so that the liquid boils moderately, for 5 minutes. Transfer the contents to a cocotte and add several tarragon stems and leaves, salt, and white pepper. Bring to a boil, then cover tightly and set in a 300° F. oven for an hour or an hour and a half, according to the quantity of meat.

Add some tarragon leaves a moment before serving, and remove the stems that cooked with the veal. Skin off the excess fat. If the sauce is too liquid, remove the meat to a hot serving platter and reduce the sauce. If the sauce is too thick or broken down or lumpy, thin it with white wine mixed with hot water.

N.B. Boiled white rice, boiled potatoes, or noodles go well with this dish.

TENDRONS DE VEAU CHASSEUR
[Veal Tendrons with Mushrooms in White Wine Sauce]

In a cocotte, sauté *tendrons* in oil. Add well-washed mushrooms trimmed of their root ends and sauté them too, stirring. Then add chopped shallots, reduce the heat to medium, and dust the whole with a spoonful or so of all-purpose flour, which you should allow to brown only lightly.

Moisten gradually with a mixture of half white wine–half water, stirring and scraping to make a rich sauce. Bring to a boil, then cover and put in 350° F. oven for 1 hour, or until the meat is tender but not falling apart. Remove from the oven and skim off excess fat.

Add a few drops of lemon juice and serve.

[Veal Tendrons with Mushrooms and Tomatoes]

This harks back (or, rather, forward) to Poulet Sauté Marengo (see page 173).

Sauté as in Tendrons de Veau Chasseur (see above) and proceed the same way, but keep the mushrooms in reserve. Instead, add several tablespoons of tomato paste (or fresh cut-up tomatoes squeezed of their water), and a little garlic.

Cover and set in a 350° F. oven to boil gently for 1½ hours, then remove the meat to a shallow pan. Set this on medium high heat, throw in the mushrooms, add a few drops of lemon juice, and stir thoroughly, then withdraw from the fire quickly. Place the meat on a hot platter and pour the sauce over it through a wide-meshed strainer (just to strain out the shallots, garlic, tomato seeds and skins—put the mushrooms back with the meat).

Surround with triangular pieces of fried bread and serve.

BLANQUETTE DE VEAU
[Veal Stew with Cream and Onions]

It is essential that the sauce resulting from this preparation be creamy white and *not* yellow.

For 4 to 6 persons

Cut ¼ pound pork fat in strips and then across, making rough cubes. Put 4 spoonfuls of unsalted butter into a thick saucepan (enameled cast iron much preferred) that has its own good lid. Melt and clarify the butter (see page 10) on medium heat. Add cubes of pork fat and stir: at all costs, prevent any browning.

When the cubes of fat have softened and become reduced in size by cooking, which should take 20 to 30 minutes, add a ½-pound veal knuckle and 2 pounds of veal *tendrons*, after removing any particle of blood (which would turn dark brown in cooking). Stir well and turn the slices of veal so they become creamy white on both sides.

Dust the veal with all-purpose flour, turning over the pieces so that all of them receive some flour—about 1½ ounces in all. (Do not let the flour turn yellowish-brown: if any signs of this appear, quickly pour in some hot water, preferably boiling, and stir thoroughly.) Mix 1 cup of dry white wine with half a cup of water. Add the mixture, little by little, to the pan, stirring as you do so until you get a creamy sauce. Let boil for 20 minutes, stirring and scraping the bottom of the pan to prevent any sticking. Add 2 medium-sized onions cut in quarters, salt and white pepper to taste, and a pinch of grated nutmeg. Boil gently for 20 minutes longer, stirring as before.

If at any time the spoon with which you stir indicates sticking at the bottom—i.e., if the edge or point of the spoon comes up with brownish "goo"—shift all the contents to another, similar pan, leaving colored matter behind. Skim off any scum that rises to the surface, and add an equal quantity of white wine.

Meanwhile, you will have cooked 10 to 15 small white onions in 2 spoonfuls of clarified butter (see page 10) in a small saucepan for 20 minutes; peel these (so that they are white). In another saucepan, bring to a boil—barely—½ cup heavy cream. Add the cream and the tiny onions to the stew and serve with boiled potatoes.

N.B. If any pork fat cubes have been left whole, do *not* serve them).

ESCALOPES DE VEAU
[*Veal Collops*]

The word generally used is not "collop" but "cutlet," which is wrong, since a cutlet, properly speaking, is a chop.

Veal *escalopes* ("collops") lend themselves readily to a variety of preparations, and it is up to the cook's imagination to conjure up others besides the well-known ones given below.

Very thin collops may be cut from the rump or the "cushion" (French *noix*). The juicier and more substantial collops should be sliced from the "round" or inside portion of the "cushion" (in French, *le rond de la noix pâtissière*). They can be ¼ to ½ inch thick and as large as medium-sized steaks. They should never be flattened by beating with a meat cleaver.

ESCALOPES DE VEAU PANNÉES
[Breaded Veal Collops]

First dry the meat with paper toweling, then salt and pepper it. Pick the collops up with a fork and roll them well on both sides in egg that has been beaten with olive oil (half a spoonful of oil per egg) and then in fine bread crumbs (some prefer to precede the rolling in crumbs with a rolling in flour).

Pour enough clarified butter (see page 10) in a skillet to cover the bottom amply and heat it until it begins to turn yellow: a collop lifted on a fork and held with one end touching the butter gives the signal—if it sizzles, the temperature is right. Lay the collops side by side in the pan and, after a minute or two, move the pan back and forth without lifting it off the heat.

Pick up one end of a collop with a fork and, as soon as the underside looks golden brown, turn it over. Continue shaking the pan and inspecting the undersides of the collops. Remove the pan from the heat as soon as all are golden brown on both sides.

An amusing trick is then to throw the beaten eggs into the warm pan and make a very thin omelette, which you cut in small portions as a garnish.

Serve with noodles and any vegetable that is not watery.

ESCALOPES DE VEAU FLAMBÉES
[Flamed Veal Collops]

After drying veal collops with paper toweling, flour lightly and sauté in clarified butter (see page 10). Turn them over when one side is light brown, and, when the other side has browned equally, pour a small glass (or spoonful) of Cognac in the pan and light it— taking care not to drop the head of the match in the pan. Shake the pan, then put out the flame, if necessary, by waving a hand over it or putting a lid over the pan. Stir the sauce, season with salt and pepper, cover, and keep *warm* for two minutes.

As accompaniment, any vegetables and mashed potatoes or chest‑ nut puree will do.

Serve with the sauce, well stirred, poured over the meat.

N.B. There are two good variants: (1) add prepared mustard to thicken the sauce before serving; (2) use dry London gin instead of Cognac, and mix in the sauce some crushed juniper berries and a little thick cream (fresh or sour).

ESCALOPES DE VEAU À LA MILANAISE
[Veal Collops, as in Milan]

Proceed as for Escalopes de Veau Pannées (see above), but mix finely grated Parmesan cheese with the bread crumbs.

Serve with macaroni well dusted with Parmesan cheese and lightly topped with a ribbon of tomato sauce.

FILET DE VEAU
[Veal Tenderloin]

The tenderloin in the calf is small and is generally included in the loin. But this delicate morsel can be cut like miniature tournedos or filets mignons and sautéed in butter.

Cooking should be slower and more thorough than in the case of beef, veal being rather indigestible when underdone.

Sauce Allemande (see page 7) should be poured over them, and a purée of green beans or peas or artichoke hearts should be served on the side.

CHAPTER 13

Pork (Fresh)

RÔTI DE PORC
[*Roast Pork*]

For normal home preparations (except for large families or parties), the cut chosen for roasting should be the rack or undivided chops, boned or not. If boned, the addition of the bones to the roasting pan is advisable: they give flavor, color, and some gelatinous substance.

For 6 persons

Rub 2 pounds pork chops (undivided, boned, in one piece) with salt and pepper, sage, thyme, and powdered bay leaf. Set in a dish with 2 cups red wine for 4 or 5 hours before cooking, turning it several times to impregnate it with the marinade.

Place the pork directly on the roasting pan, with 2 spoonfuls of butter, 4 carrots (chopped) and thick slices of 2 onions under and over it. Add to the pan a few spoonfuls of cold water, possibly mixed with a little leftover dry wine.

Put a few slices of apple on top of the roast, then place the roasting pan in a 300° F. oven for an hour (30 minutes per pound). In that period, baste the roast four or five times with the pan juices, and, after the first 15 or 20 minutes of cooking, remove and discard the apple slices.

Carve the roast on the pan in order to make the most of the meat juices. Mix these with half water–half white wine, and use the mixture to deglaze the pan and make a thin sauce.

N.B. Cored apple rings cooked in butter in the oven are a good accompaniment. If the roasting pan is large enough, they can be cooked with the meat, turning them over as needed, removing the cooked ones to a warm plate, and replacing them with fresh ones.

Mashed potatoes are also excellent with roast pork.

CÔTELETTES DE PORC
[Pork Chops]

Generally speaking, pork chops may be treated like veal chops (see page 148); but grilling is also recommended for pork chops, though not advisable for veal chops.

CÔTELETTES DE PORC À LA CHARCUTIÈRE

Wipe the chops well, butter them, season them, and bread-crumb them (or, better, cover them generously with prepared French mustard, and then bread them). Put them some 5 inches under a red-hot caloroid or gas flame. When browned, turn them over and lower them some 2 inches, in order to have the heat penetrate without burning them.

Meanwhile, on gentle heat, cook chopped onions in butter until they "melt," and mix them with Sauce Espangole (see page 3) (or, if this is not available, add to the pan as much all-purpose flour as you put in of butter and stir well until the flour turns yellow brown; with half wine–half beef consommé dissolve to the consistency of heavy cream), strain, and add coarsely chopped pickles to the strained sauce.

Serve mashed potatoes in a heap, with the chops around it like a crown. Serve the sauce in a sauceboat.

A VARIANT: Instead of grilling the chops, sauté them in clarified butter (see page 10) and then simmer them in sauce made as above.

CÔTELETTES DE PORC À L'ARDÉNNAISE

Sauté the chops in clarified butter (see page 10) together with finely chopped onion on *gentle* heat, keeping the onion from burning. Meanwhile, separately, blanch bacon dice and sauté them in lard. When there is sufficient fat in the pan, add quartered potatoes to cook with the bacon, turning them as they brown.

Remove the chops from their pan when done and deglaze the pan with dry white wine; thicken this sauce with arrowroot (see page 65). Verify the seasoning, and add a few crushed juniper berries.

In the middle of a hot serving dish, make a heap of the potatoes and bacon dice. Arrange the chops as a crown around the heap and pour the sauce over the whole.

CÔTELETTES DE PORC À LA GRENELLE

Sauté the chops in clarified butter (see page 10) on gentle heat, and season with salt and pepper and sage. When they are half cooked (when you turn them over), add finely sliced onion and brown it lightly.

Separately, sauté thick slices of cored apple, with the skin on, in butter—say, 1/2 apple per chop—dusting them lightly with granulated sugar.

Remove the chops to a hot dish. Deglaze the chop pan with dry white wine, then strain the pan juices over the chops.

Serve the apple slices on the side. Boiled potatoes may also be served with this.

CÔTELETTES DE PORC À L'ALSACIENNE

Put 4 chops (backbone and ribs trimmed by the butcher) in a cocotte on which you have laid a bed of 4 ounces of bacon (chopped), 3 carrots (chopped), and 3 onions (chopped). Season with salt, pepper, a pinch of thyme, and a bay leaf. Half cover the chops with dry white wine (about ¾ cup; preferably Alsatian). Place, uncovered, on high heat and let the wine reduce to a spoonful or two. Add beef consommé—as much as you did white wine—and bring to a boil, then cover, and set in a 350° F. oven for 45 minutes.

Meanwhile, on medium heat, covered, cook sauerkraut (or—this is easier and can be quite satisfactory—take it already cooked out of a tin and bring to a boil) in 1 cup of dry white wine with half a handful of juniper berries, an onion stuck with a whole clove, and a little pork lard. Fluff up the sauerkraut with two kitchen forks.

Separately, poach 4 frankfurters.

Serve on a hot dish, the sauerkraut in the middle and on it the frankfurters, the chops forming a ring round the whole with the cooking liquor strained over them.

CHAPTER 14

Mutton and Lamb

MUTTON SUCH AS FOUND in the British Isles and at times in the United States is rare in France. *Mouton* as sold by French butchers ordinarily is what in the United States is called "lamb." *Agneau,* which is the French word for "lamb," is spring lamb, that is, about six months old and castrated. Then there is *agneau de lait* ("milk lamb"), not yet castrated and under six months old, supposedly milk fed. Sometimes very young lamb meat is labeled *agneau de Pauillac* —i.e., lamb from the great wine-growing region of Pauillac, where there are meadows swept by sea winds that give a special quality to the meat. These salt meadows are called *prés-salés*, and this term is used generally not only for *agneau* but for *mouton*.

Here *mouton* (castrated yearling lamb) will be considered first, and then *agneau*.

GIGOT DE MOUTON RÔTI
[Roast Leg of Lamb]

Paris butchers prepare their lamb legs below the stifle joint, saw off the shank joint, remove the thin bone, and open up the meat round the shank. (They also like making little patterns on the fat underside with a knife.) The portion near the shank, which has meat streaked with fine nerves and veins, is called the *souris* ("mouse"), and is greatly favored by some.

Unless the scent of garlic is anathema, put a crushed clove of it into an orifice that you can pry open next to the bone on the large, or hip, end.

Sprinkle the leg with freshly ground pepper and rosemary on both sides, lay on a trivet or short-legged rack in a roasting pan, and set in a 375° oven. *No salt.* (The addition of salt would result in bleeding the lamb: the meat would be dry at the end of the cooking period.)

For nicely underdone meat, cook 45 minutes; for well-done, 55 minutes. After the first 15 minutes of roasting, reduce heat to 350° F. *No basting and no opening of the oven door.* (For roasting on the spit before an open fire or for roasting in a proper open electric roaster, you may allow 5 minutes more, tempering the heat at mid-point in the time.)

If a delay is inevitable before carving, remove the leg from the oven at the indicated time and keep it between two hot plates: it is better to have such a splendid piece of meat cold but properly cooked than hot and overdone.

Small white beans, green beans, or a combination of both, termed in restaurants *haricots panachés*, are the usual accompaniment of a *gigot*. Potatoes in any form are also recommended.

SELLE DE MOUTON
[*Saddle of Lamb*]

This fine piece comprises the whole loin on both sides behind the prime chops and above the hind legs. (When the piece includes the two legs, it is called a *baron* or *bas-rond de mouton*.) The butcher removes the kidneys and the fat inside and trims the flank, then rolls and ties up the piece with string.

It is best roasted in a 350° F. oven at the rate of 10 minutes to the pound of raw weight.

Follow the directions for Roast Leg of Lamb (see above).

ÉPAULE DE MOUTON
[*Shoulder of Lamb*]

Many connoisseurs prefer this cut to a leg of lamb. The butcher should remove the shoulder blade from the underside or cut side, including the nerves close to it. Some butchers saw off the long (humerus) bone at the middle and remove it to make carving easier, rolling up the joint with string.

Follow the directions for Roast Leg of Lamb (see above); although the cut is smaller, it takes just about the same roasting time.

CARRÉ DE MOUTON
[*Rack of Lamb*]

This is equivalent longitudinally to half a saddle, but farther forward and should comprise 8 or 9 chops. The butcher trims the chop bones, saws through the vertebrae without cutting down between the chops, and peels off the skin, for which he substitutes a thin layer of lamb kidney fat, all tied together with string.

The piece should be laid on a short-legged rack or trivet, backbone side down, and then sprinkled with pepper and rosemary, or daubed with French prepared mustard. *No salt*. Set in a 375° or 400° F. oven for 10 minutes, and 350° for 10 or 15 minutes longer: by watching the thermostat you can manage this, if necessary by opening the door of the oven for the required time.

Carving is simple: just cut through and separate the chops.

Any vegetable or green salad goes very well with this succulent dish.

CÔTELETTES DE MOUTON
[*Lamb Chops*]

There are 5 ribs next to the loin that are called *premières* in French, "prime" in English: they are the best and fleshiest. When two are cut as one and the second rib bone is removed at the backbone (this cut is called a "*double* chop") they are incomparable. The lesser chops forward can be operated on in the same way—but can never be as good as the *premières*.

All chops should be peeled of their skin. The backbone should be trimmed close with the cleaver, the rib bones should be shortened, and the extra fat adhering to them should be cut away. Paris butchers give the chops a slap with the cleaver to flatten them slightly: a useless gesture.

Lamb chops should be wiped with paper toweling, especially to remove bits of bone left by the butcher's cleaver. *They must not be salted, but they can be peppered: in cooking them, use no other condiment.*

They should be grilled: place them on a grill about 3 inches under a red-hot caloroid or gas flame, and turn only when the fat (which should be topside to begin) *begins to burn black*. Then lower them an inch or so, and reduce the heat to medium low: this is the moment to watch them especially, for, as soon as they brown lightly on the lean side now exposed to the heat, they must be withdrawn from it. Thus you will have juicy chops.

Any vegetable, cooked or raw, can be served with them.

COLLET DE MOUTON
[Neck of Lamb]

It is a rare Paris butcher who calls this piece otherwise than *collier*, which of course means "necklace"; whereas *collet*, its proper name, is a diminutive of *cou* ("neck"). For one use for this piece, see Navarin de Mouton (below).

NAVARIN DE MOUTON
[Lamb Stew]

It may seem wrong to translate this term as "lamb stew," yet that is what it really is.

For 4 to 6 persons

Cut 2 pounds of lamb necks, spareribs, and breast (all boned) into chunks that will require no knife at table (about 2-inch cubes). Brown them in 2 spoonfuls of very hot pork lard, turning them over only when one side is well browned: this is essential because it keeps the juices *in* the meat. (It is preferable to do this in a wide, shallow frying pan rather than crowd the pieces in a deep pan, where their juices will ooze out.)

Then dust the meat with all-purpose flour, and stir vigorously to brown the flour a russet color. Turn the meat out into a heavy cocotte, then drain the frying pan of excess fat and deglaze its bottom with boiling water. Pour this into the cocotte, and add enough boiling water to cover the chunks of meat. Set on high heat and bring to a boil while stirring and scraping the bottom to prevent sticking (the flour is bound to *try* to do this). Lower and regulate the heat to keep the liquor boiling gently when the cocotte is covered, with only a tiny chink open.

Add 1 or more spoonfuls of tomato paste (according to its strength and your taste—the sauce should be reddish brown, not too red), salt to taste (remember that the liquid will reduce in cooking and the salt not), a pinch of thyme and another of rosemary, a bay leaf, and 1 crushed garlic clove (its pungency will vanish in the cooking). Cover well and let *simmer* for 1½ hours, stirring from time to time.

Add 6 turnips (peeled and cut up) and 6 medium carrots (peeled, cored, and cut up). After 10 minutes, add 12 *small* potatoes (peeled), sinking them well in the liquor. Stir and scrape the bottom. Increase the heat to gentle *boiling*, cover, and let cook for 45 minutes.

Meanwhile, peel a cupful of tiny onions and brown them in a spoonful of clarified butter (see page 10). Add them to the cocotte just before serving.

If the sauce is too greasy, skim off all the top fat. If necessary, add a few drops of vegetable caramel (Kitchen Bouquet or Gravymaster) to darken the sauce. If the sauce *separates*, add a little cold water and stir vigorously (before stirring, however, remove the meat momentarily so as to avoid its disintegration).

A VARIANT: Navarin Printanier is spring lamb stew that is made as above and includes precooked fresh peas, or green beans.)

GIGOT D'AGNEAU RÔTI
[*Roast Leg of Spring Lamb*]

Proceed as with Gigot de Mouton Rôti (see page 160) but in a 300° F. oven for the larger roasts and 275° or even 250° for the smaller ones, at the rate of 10 to 12 minutes the pound, and baste well with melted butter.

NOISETTES D'AGNEAU

These are the meaty hearts of spring lamb chops. Sautéed in butter, they may be dressed in a great variety of ways with practically any vegetable or sauce.

ÉPIGRAMMES D'AGNEAU

Braise a breast of spring lamb, and bone it. Cut small triangular pieces out of it. Dip these in beaten egg, and then roll them in bread crumbs. Sauté them in hot butter. Bread-crumb likewise an equal number of boned chops, and sauté them.

On the service dish, top these and the pieces of breast with Sauce Espagnole (see page 3) and surround with fresh Petits Pois à la Française (see page 236) or any other tender spring vegetable.

CHAPTER 15

Poultry

POULET
[Chicken]

ALTHOUGH FRENCH AUTHORS on gastronomy have separate sub-chapters for cocks and hens, that arrangement is not followed here: chickens, without regard for their sex, are satisfactory in practically all hot-dish recipes.

Farm-raised chickens that have been allowed a certain amount of liberty and not fed forcing-rations are obviously the most flavorful; and such chickens are still available in France, although penned-up, artificially developed ones are, alas, becoming more and more common there.

French chickens seem much less leggy than their American counterparts; also, they certainly smell fresher at the butcher's. A bad habit, however, is gaining favor in French butchery: drawing the birds and "dressing" them (sewing them up in an unnecessarily fancy way) quite a while before selling them. This procedure is, of course, simply another application of assembly-line, mass-production methods.

The following recipes are meant for what is called in French *un poulet de grain*, roughly equivalent to an American broiler weighing 1¼ to 2 pounds after being plucked, drawn (eviscerated), and trimmed (head and shanks cut off). Besides being plucked, drawn, and trimmed, the chicken should be perfectly singed (free of feathers or hair).

LE POULET RÔTI
[Roast Chicken]

The principal objective here is to serve a *juicy* chicken—one that does not need any gravy other than its own juice and what you deglaze from the pan by the addition of a very little water.

For 4 persons

Stuff a whole chicken (a broiler, 1¼ to 2 pounds) with an onion stuck with 2 whole cloves, half a clove garlic (crushed) (if not objectionable), a branch of celery (broken up), a bay leaf, a good pinch of thyme, and freshly ground black pepper. Close the hole through which the bird was drawn and stuffed either by sewing it with needle and thread or by thrusting thin, sharp nails or wooden toothpicks from side to side over it and tying it up with thin string. Lay fine slices of smoked bacon on the breast to cover it entirely and on the legs likewise, fastening the slices in place with wooden toothpicks.

Set the bird thus prepared on a short-legged rack or trivet and this in a roasting pan or even dish of proper size (the chicken should be rather snugly accommodated so that there will not be too much drying of the juices that drip off it). Add 2 or 3 spoonfuls of *cold* water to the pan or dish, then put it in a 350° F. oven for 50 to 55 minutes. *Never baste: that only dries the chicken.*

When you observe that the bacon is *beginning* to burn, remove the slices with a long kitchen fork. The chicken will by then be perfectly anointed with the melting bacon fat, and its skin will now begin to acquire a golden color. (If, on removing chicken from the oven and carving it, you find the joints of the legs too pink or even a little bloody, it is simple to put the pan on high heat for a minute or so, with the offending side down, and the pinkness or bloodiness will disappear.) After carving, deglaze the pan with a little hot water.

N.B. Roast potatoes (*pommes château*) and lettuce salad on the same plate are recommended.

LE POULET BRAISÉ
[Braised Chicken]

For 4 persons

Put 2 or 3 slices of bacon (chopped), 1 onion (roughly chopped), and 3 or 4 smallish carrots (roughly chopped) in an oval cocotte (enameled cast iron, preferably) with 1 spoonful of butter, a bay leaf, and a pinch of thyme. Sprinkle a whole chicken (broiler, 1¼ to 2 pounds) not tied up or otherwise "dressed" with a little salt and white pepper, and put it in the cocotte on one side. Set the cocotte on high heat, uncovered. As soon as one side (including the second joint) becomes golden, turn on the other side. Once that is lightly browned, turn on its back and brown that, too.

Now pour enough dry white wine to come up to half the second joints, and boil this wine down to a few spoonfuls.

Add concentrated beef consommé in the same quantity as the wine, and boil *this* down to half its volume. Lay a piece of aluminum foil right on the bird to cover it, and close the cocotte with its own well-fitting lid. Put it in the oven for 40 minutes at 350° F. (If, on opening it, you want the chicken to cook longer, put it all back as it was. But do not overcook: it will fall apart and lack flavor.)

There should be enough sauce in the cocotte to serve with the chicken, either strained or with the total contents.

N.B. Carrots Vichy (see page 216) and small browned onions, if the vegetables in the cocotte are not served, go very well with this dish.

LE POULET AU POT
[Chicken in the Pot—Boiled Chicken]

The standard French name is *la poule au pot* ("The-hen-in-the-pot"), and the tradition persists that King Henri IV promised this dish to all his countrymen/subjects. The availability of excellent chicken bouillon cubes makes it possible to prepare the dish more quickly and easily than in the old days.

For 4 persons

Exactly as for roasting (see page 167), stuff and close a whole chicken (broiler, 1¼ to 2 pounds) and lay several slices of smoked bacon on its breast, to cover it entirely, and on the legs likewise, fastening the slices in place with wooden toothpicks. Place the bird breast side up in a cocotte with enough cold water almost to cover it.

Set the cocotte on high heat. As the water begins to boil, skim off very thoroughly all the gray scum that comes up, and continue skimming until nothing but white froth rises to the surface. Then add 1 chicken bouillon cube cut in small pieces. (If, on tasting the broth, you find this insufficient, add more to suit you; but beware of too much salt, bearing in mind that the bacon on the chicken as well as the cube will provide salt, and that some of the broth will evaporate in cooking.) Cover, leaving a little chink to allow steam to escape, and adjust the heat for gentle boiling. Boil for 30 minutes.

Add 3 or 4 young turnips (peeled and quartered), ½ bunch of celeriac (cut in pieces), 3 or 4 carrots (peeled, cored, and cut in 3-inch sections), the white of 2 or 3 leeks, and 8 small potatoes (peeled). (If there is not enough room for the potatoes, cook them separately: the broth will be all the clearer for this.) Add the gizzard, cover again, bring to a boil, and control the heat so that the broth will continue boiling gently for another 30 minutes. Five minutes before serving, add the liver and the heart.

Serve, after carving in quarters, with the vegetables and the bacon and a little of the juice, with a small bowl of the broth on the side.

POULET GRILLÉ
[Grilled Chicken]

For 4 persons

If the chicken (broiler, 1¼ to 2 pounds) has not already been halved, cut from neck to tail with a knife and then with poultry shears, first along the back and then down the breast. Snip off the wing tips and the neck.

Daub both sides of both halves with French (Dijon) prepared mustard—no salt or other seasoning is needed—and dust generously with fine bread crumbs. Place, skin side up, on a grill, about 7 inches from a red-hot caloroid or gas flame.

As soon as blackish spots appear on the surface of the skin, turn the chicken and moderate the heat. The first side requires about 10 minutes, the second about 15.

N.B. Green salad or any vegetable goes well with it.

POULET À L'ESTRAGON
[Chicken with Tarragon]

Stuff into a whole chicken (broiler, 1¼ to 2 pounds) a small fistful of tarragon leaves. Poach the bird for 50 minutes in water with 1 chicken bouillon cube cut in small pieces—breast side up and just enough liquid to half cover the breast—then remove to a warm dish and cover it.

Reduce the liquor, watching out for possible excess of salt. (If you have too much liquor for a sauce, put the excess away.) Bind the rest of the *hot* (not boiling) liquor with beaten egg yolks (2 should do) and pour over the chicken evenly. With the points of your kitchen scissors, pick up a number of tarragon leaves and arrange them in a pattern on the breast of the chicken.

Serve with a ring of white rice (see page 45) around it.

FRICASSÉE DE POULET
[Fricassee of Chicken]

For 4 persons

Divide a whole chicken (about 2½ pounds) in two as for grilling (see above). Then run a sharp knife round the leg where it springs from the lower portion of the belly, leaving the skin with the second joint; or run the knife at the point above (toward the neck) the "oyster," and with its point pierce the joint of the backbone, which you can break with your hands, and then separate the leg quarter from the breast quarter by cutting down with the knife. Now bend the drumstick joint and cut the skin and sinews to expose its condyles, which you then cut through, separating the drumstick from the second joint. Trim off the bar ribs below the breast, the wing tips, and the neck. With the poultry shears cut off all the backbone.

Put all the chicken pieces, including trimmings, into a cocotte of appropriate size, on a layer of 3 onions (chopped) and 3 carrots (peeled, cored, and cut up) and 1 chicken-bouillon cube (cut up in small pieces). Fill with hot water up to half the breast and bring to a boil on high heat. Lower the heat to a simmer, and cover well. Cook thus for 55 minutes.

Meanwhile, poach a handful of tiny onions in 2 or 3 tablespoons of the chicken liquor and half a spoonful of butter for as long as the chicken simmers. Also, put a handful of small mushrooms (washed, root ends cut off) in *cold* water with a spoonful of butter and the juice of half a lemon, salt, and pepper; place on medium heat and boil for 10 minutes.

After the 55 minutes, remove the chicken from its liquor to a warm plate and cover it.

With a spoonful of butter and another of all-purpose flour, make, in a saucepan, a white "binder," stirring it over medium heat and preventing any coloration. After a few minutes pour some of the chicken liquor on this "binder" and stir well to make a thick paste. Gradually dissolve the paste with more of the chicken liquor from the cocotte, always stirring, until you have a creamy sauce. Boil this, removing the scum that rises to the surface and stirring and scraping the bottom: it must not stick, for it will *burn* there—i.e. turn dark brown. This skimming should take a good quarter of an hour.

Add to the sauce a few spoonfuls of the mushroom cooking liquor, if possible without the floating butter oil. Remove the sauce from the heat. Beat 3 egg yolks and add them *very* gradually to the sauce, thus binding it again. Set the pan of sauce in a larger pan with hot water, off the heat. Add 2 or 3 spoonfuls of heavy cream and mix well, then verify the seasoning.

Set the chicken pieces as nearly together as possible, breasts and legs, on a hot platter. Around the chicken place the mushrooms and the onions, both drained with a skimmer (save the liquor of both for future use), and strain the sauce over the bird.

Serve with white rice (see page 45) in little mounds all round or buttered noodles in a ring.

POULET SAUTÉ
[Sautéed Chicken]

Sautéed chicken invites the originality and fancy of any passionate cook. The principal procedures and elements are indicated below. Almost all vegetables lend themselves to these compositions, and any wine (or cream, sweet or sour) is acceptable.

After the chicken is cut up as for a fricassee (see above), it is cooked in hot clarified butter (see page 10), browned on one side before being turned over on the other side. The dark meat is put in first and, 2 or 3 minutes later, the white meat. Then the pieces are put in a sauce prepared with the residue at the bottom of the pan—deglazed with wine or bouillon, etc. (Or, if the pieces are to be kept from coloring, they are gently cooked in clarified butter and then put in a cream sauce.) Once they are in the sauce, this should *never boil*: otherwise you have a stew.

POULET SAUTÉ ARCHIDUC
[Sautéed Chicken with Onion Sauce]

This is best when fresh spring onions, mild and juicy, are available.

Peel and cut 8 spring onions in fine wheels. Throw these into *warm* clarified butter (see page 10) and cook on medium-*low* heat, stirring to make sure not a speck of brown appears—if one does, remove it instantly. Once they are well softened (so-called *melted*), remove with a skimmer to a warm plate and cover.

Add more clarified butter if the pan looks dry.

When the butter is hot but *not* yellowing, put in the dark meat of 1 chicken (broiler, 1¼ to 2 pounds, cut up as on page 171) and (after 2 or 3 minutes) the white meat, moving the pan over the heat without lifting it. Every few minutes, turn the pieces over: cook them thoroughly, but *do not let them brown*. After about 15 minutes remove the pan from the heat. Remove the chicken to a warm plate, using two forks but without piercing the pieces. Cover the plate.

Return the onions to the pan. Pour in a small glass of good Cognac and boil it down on high heat, but without browning the onions.

Prepare separately Sauce Béchamel (see page 8) sufficient for the chicken, and add it to the pan with the onions. Stir well on medium heat and then strain, squeezing the onions with a spoon to get all possible juice. Add 3 spoonfuls of Madeira wine, or very dry Spanish sherry (Fino), and heat, but do not boil. If this sauce is too liquid, thicken it with snippets of butter.

Cover the pieces of chicken with the sauce.

N.B. A purée of celeriac and potatoes is recommended with this.

POULET SAUTÉ MARENGO
[Sautéed Chicken with Tomatoes, Olives, and Herbs]

Tradition has it that after the Battle of Marengo in Italy, Napoleon Bonaparte was served this dish, which had been made with whatever the army cook could lay his hands on: chicken, olive oil, garlic, tomatoes, olives, wine, herbs, eggs and bread.

For 4 persons

Cut up a broiling chicken weighing about 2 pounds into the usual pieces. Heat 3 spoonfuls of olive oil, and in it sauté the pieces of chicken, browning them on all sides (put the dark meat in first and, after 2 or 3 minutes, the white). Remove the chicken from the pan to keep warm while you fry in it 3 or 4 eggs (see page 33), which you reserve with the chicken. And if you can get 4 live crayfish, sauté *them* and set them aside.

In the same pan, make a sauce with some sliced onions, 1 clove of crushed garlic, 20 pitted green olives, a handful of fresh basil leaves (or a spoonful of dried), 3 ripe tomatoes (peeled, seeded and squeezed of their water), and ½ cup dry white wine, all seasoned with salt and pepper.

Pour the sauce over the chicken and serve with the reserved eggs and crayfish.

POULET SAUTÉ CHASSEUR
[Sautéed Chicken with Mushroom, Herb, and White Wine-Sauce]

This is a more French and less elaborate version of Poulet Sauté Marengo.

For 4 persons

Heat 2 spoonfuls each of butter and olive oil together, then, sauté a chicken (broiler, about 2 pounds, cut up as on page 171), browning the pieces on all sides (put the dark meat in first and, after 2 or 3 minutes, the white). Remove the chicken to warm plate and cover.

In the same pan, sauté a handful of sliced mushrooms. As these cook, sprinkle with all-purpose flour (this will later serve to bind the sauce). Pour into the pan a small glass of Cognac, and light it. Add 2 spoonfuls of tomato paste, 4 shallots (finely chopped), thyme, a bay leaf, and a few stalks of parsley stems. Stir all this over medium high heat to boil, preventing it from sticking at the bottom by adding squirts of dry white wine (up to ½ cup). When you have a sauce, with the mushroom slices incorporated, add 2 tablespoons chopped tarragon leaves. Taste for seasoning.

Pour the sauce over the pieces of chicken, nicely arranged on a hot serving platter.

POULET SAUTÉ PARMENTIER
[Sautéed Chicken with Potatoes and White Wine Sauce]

This name is derived from that of the man who is supposed to have first brought the potato from the New World to France. Dishes in which the potato is a prime ingredient often bear his name.

In 4 spoonfuls of clarified butter (see page 10) sauté a chicken (broiler, about 1¼ to 2 pounds, cut up as on page 171) browning the pieces on all sides (put the dark meat in first and, after 2 or 3 minutes, the white). Meanwhile, in another pan sauté in clarified butter ¾ pound of potatoes (peeled and nicely cut in 1-inch cubes). Chicken and potatoes should cook separately but simultaneously, and be turned as they brown. Season both with salt and pepper, then remove both when browned and join them on a warm platter, which you cover.

Deglaze the chicken pan with ½ cup each dry white wine and chicken broth, or sufficient to make a little sauce. Pour this over the pieces of chicken, arranged with white meat together and dark meat flanking it, surrounded with the potatoes. Sprinkle a little chopped parsley over all.

Any root or green vegetable may accompany this dish.

CANARD
[Duck]

The domestic breeds best known to Paris butchers are the Barbary duck, the Nantes duck, the Rouen duck, and the Peking duck (not to be confused with the lacquered duck of the Peking cuisine). They are recommended in inverse order to this list. Since the Rouen duck should be prepared only in a special way (smothered, in order to keep its blood), the Peking duck (*canard de Pekin*), which is quite unusual at Paris butchers', and the Nantes duck (*canard Nantes*) are those meant in the following recipes.

In the United States, the China duck is generally the best pro-curable.

CANARD RÔTI
[Roast Duck]

Invariably choose a young bird and a female (*duck*) rather than a male (*drake*).

For 2 or 3 persons

Proceed in its preparation for the oven exactly as for Le Poulet Rôti (see page 167), but omit the bacon slices, ducks having almost always sufficient fat to prevent the meat from drying in the oven. However, it is a good precaution to melt some of the interior fat and to swab the bird with it. If you salt it, do it inside the duck before introducing the onion, celery, etc.

After stuffing and closing a young duck (female if possible), set it on a low trivet or rack as for the chicken. Put it in a 400° F. oven for 15 minutes, then reduce the heat to 350° for another 30 or 35 minutes—depending on how red you want the meat on the breasts. It should not, in any case, be brown.

Deglaze the cooking dish or pan with ½ cup red Burgundy (or any similar) wine and ½ cup water to make a sauce.

N.B. Any green salad, especially watercress, and sautéed apple rings, chestnut purée, and creamed sorrel are recommended to go with roast duck.

CANARD AUX NAVETS
[Duck with Turnips]

This must be prepared in the spring or early summer, when turnips are tender and sound.

For 2 or 3 persons

Brown a young duck (female, if possible) in ½ cup clarified butter (see page 10), first with breast down and then all around. Decant the butter into another pan, and in it cook 12 white turnips, cut and shaped like small plums, slowly on medium-low heat.

Meanwhile, remove the duck to a warm plate. With 1 wineglass of dry white wine, deglaze the pan in which the duck cooked. Add to this 3 or more spoonfuls of Sauce Espagnole (see page 3), and mix well. Place the duck in a cocotte, breast side up, and pour the sauce over it.

Dust the turnips with a pinch of sugar and, once they are nicely brown, add them to the duck. Put a sheet of aluminum foil right over the bird, and cover the cocotte with a properly fitting lid. Set for 40 minutes in a 300° F. oven.

Serve with the turnips and the sauce poured over the duck.

A VARIANT: The same instructions are applicable for Canard aux Olives, duck with olives, except that olives (pitted) are added to the duck in the oven only 15 minutes before serving, and a squirt of Marsala wine is added to the sauce and well mixed just before serving. (Port wine can be substituted.)

CANARD À L'ORANGE
[Duck with Orange]

For 2 or 3 persons

Brown a duck in ½ cup clarified butter (see page 10) or 2 spoonfuls of lard, then put it into a cocotte into which it fits snugly. Peel an orange (if possible, not artificially colored). Reserving the peel, squeeze the juice of the orange on the duck through a strainer. Season the duck with salt and pepper, then cover the cocotte and set it on low heat barely to simmer for 30 minutes.

Meanwhile, scrape very carefully every bit of white off the *inside* of the reserved peel so as to leave its orange color, as well as little pores showing: this is important, as the white underside is bitter. Slice the peel into slivers and put them into boiling water for 5 minutes. Remove them with a skimmer and reserve them.

Add to the duck in the cocotte ½ cup of Sauce Espagnole (see page 8), and mix this well with the liquid in the cocotte, rolling the duck in it all. Bring to a boil, add the orange zest slivers, and cover. Set in a 325° F. oven for 30 minutes.

Five minutes before serving, sauté *lightly* in clarified butter the peeled segments of 2 more oranges, carefully stripped of all the small white strings clinging to them.

Verify the seasoning of the sauce. Skim off extra fat.

Serve the duck with the sauce poured over it and the orange segments all around it. (If the orange you squeezed on the duck at first was *very* juicy, you may have to thicken the sauce finally with arrowroot, as on page 65).

CANARD AUX CERISES
[Duck with Cherries]

For 2 or 3 persons

Brown a young duck (female, if possible), on all sides in hot clarified butter (see page 10) in an open pan. Season with salt and pepper, then put the duck in a cocotte with a close-fitting lid on low heat while you make a sauce composed of 20 preserved (if possible wild) cherries (pitted), port wine (a small wineglass), the peel of 1 orange (grated) and the juice from the pan the duck was browned in, mixed with 3 or 4 spoonfuls of Sauce Espagnole (see page 3); and if the duck in the cocotte has oozed out more juice while waiting, mix it in, too.

Set the duck on a hot platter, and pour over it the sauce with the cherries.

DINDE OU DINDON
[Turkey Hen or Turkey Cock]

Dinde means turkey *hen*; a turkey *cock* is called *dindon*. In France huge turkeys such as are fancied in the United States are not sought after. The requisite for a prized turkey in France is *tender age*: not more than twelve months.

DINDE OU DINDON FARCI
[Stuffed Turkey Hen or Turkey Cock]

For 6 to 8 persons

This is for a turkey (preferably hen) weighing about 9 pounds.

If using fresh chestnuts, make an incision on the shell of each (for a total of 2 handfuls) with a small, sharp knife. Put them in an oven-proof pan with a few spoonfuls of water, enough for a good film on its surface, and set them in a 200° F. oven. Leave the oven door open; after some 5 to 10 minutes the chestnuts should be ready to shell. Take them out, a few at a time, and with the heel of the knife remove shell and inner skin. Put the shelled and skinned chestnuts in a saucepan with chicken bouillon (made with 1 cube) to cover. Bring to a boil, reduce the heat, cover, and boil gently for 30 minutes. Drain and let cool.

Meanwhile, put through the meat grinder 1 pound each of fresh lean pork and smoked bacon, with 1 small onion (finely chopped) and a spoonful of spices: ground thyme, pepper, a bay leaf, and 2 cloves. Add a pinch of garlic powder (or half a clove of garlic, minced).

Chop up the chestnuts coarsely (those you cooked, or tinned ones), and combine these thoroughly with the ground meat. Add a small glass of Cognac and mix well again, then stuff the turkey with the mixture, and close it up like a chicken to be roasted (see page 167). Cover all the turkey with 8 or 9 thin slices of bacon, fastening these with wooden toothpicks.

Set on a low rack in a roasting pan with a few spoonfuls of water. Cook in a 350° F. oven at the rate of 18 minutes to the pound, raw weight. *Do not baste.*

OIE
[Goose]

In France the goose is not appreciated as in England and in the United States for its meat, although the great authors proclaim its excellence. However, in the southern portion of France called the Languedoc (which means the "goose-Language") one of the great dishes of French cuisine has been perfected: *le confit d'oie*, which may be translated as "goose preserve." The recipe given below is somewhat simplified, but reliable. Of course, one of the great achievements of French gastronomy is foie gras, erroneously called in English "pâté de foie gras," which is by definition a "fat liver pie,"—i.e., with a crust; but, generally, this term means a *terrine de foie gras*, which is ground fat goose liver. The best foie gras is of course the freshly prepared liver (see page 181) and second best the tinned section of one.

CONFIT D'OIE
[Goose Preserve]

Cut up a fat goose like a chicken for sautéing, taking great care not to damage the liver, which you should put away for other uses. Rub the pieces all over with coarse salt mixed with a teaspoon of sodium nitrate and powered thyme, bay leaf, and cloves. Put the pieces in a stone crock and cover them with more of this mixture. Place a piece of cardboard over the crock to keep the dust off and set the crock for 24 hours in a cool place.

Now take all the fat of the goose and melt it on low heat: there should be enough to cover the pieces of goose, which you should remove from the salt and carefully wipe clean. Put the pieces into a cocotte with a close-fitting lid, and cover them with the melted fat.

Set the cocotte on medium-low heat to cook, covered, for 1½ to 2 hours. (The meat should be cooked when a wooden toothpick penetrates it easily.) Then put the pieces again in the crock, which you will have washed thoroughly, and cover them with the hot, liquid fat. Set in a cool place, covered as before, and, when the fat has solidified completely and the crock is cool to the touch, add a little melted pork lard (it should not be very hot) to the surface of the goose fat, which by then might show little cracks. (Lard hardens better on cooling and so protects the meat.)

When this is cold and hard, cover the crock with a piece of cellophane or similar odorless chemical sheet and secure around the crock with an elastic band. Put it away in a cool place—not the refrigerator, of course—and it will keep perfectly for some months, if you take care every time you remove a piece from the preserve to cover the remainder with the fat that isolates it from the air. These pieces are warmed up in some of the goose fat with cooked vegetables, fresh or dried, and well repay the original job of preparing the *confit d'oie*.

FOIE GRAS À LA GELÉE DE PORTO
[Fresh Foie Gras in Port Wine Jelly]

In the autumn it is possible in Paris to obtain splendid fat goose livers and large black truffles, fresh. Of course, they are very expensive. The job of preparing the foie gras is not arduous. What takes time is picking away the nerves from the lobes, especially between them. Then the truffle must be brushed (although often sold as such it often is not) with a stiff or wire brush to remove the sand.

Then you must have a sufficient quantity of *clear* homemade jelly made from consommé and calves' feet (though you can buy this as well, or use the excellent concentrated beef consommé available in tins in which you dissolve one or two sheets of leaf gelatin on medium heat). And, finally, a heavy flameproof pottery cocotte of the right dimensions to accommodate the liver, 10 inches or so in length, and about 4 inches in width (inside measurements), is indispensable.

With this equipment and components you first cut the truffles in pencil-thick one-inch bits and then introduce them into the liver with a larding needle—not by piercing it right through but just enough to leave the truffle imbedded a fraction of an inch beneath the surface of the liver. (Handle the liver as little as possible after picking away the nerves.) Pour into the cocotte some of the jelly-consommé-port mixture; lay the liver sprinkled with Cognac and stuck with the truffles on this, distributing whatever truffle parings there are over it, and fill the cocotte with the rest of the liquid, which should amply cover the whole liver. Clap on the well-fitting lid and set in the oven to cook at 300° F. for 35 minutes. Watch it and temper the oven if there is any tendency to boil. (If the cocotte is not very thick it is best to set it in a larger pan with boiling water up to $3/4$ its height for 45 minutes. Some cooks insist on the merits of sautéing the whole truffle in butter for a few minutes and then putting it in a small cocotte with half Madeira–half consommé, covered, for 10 minutes in the oven.)

Once the time has elapsed, withdraw the cocotte from the oven and let it cool naturally, covered, in a corner of the room. As soon as the jelly has set the foie gras is ready to serve. To remove it from the cocotte, place a very clean napkin on the surface of the jelly to form a cushion and on it an inverted flat dish of the right dimensions; then turn the cocotte over, holding the napkin and the dish tight to it, and wrap a hot towel around the cocotte: in a few minutes the jelly on the inner surface of the cocotte will melt and release the whole contents. Watch it. (If you have a very thin, small knife with which to loosen the jelly around the sides, so much the better, before turning the cocotte upside down.)

N.B. It is advisable to put the foie gras covered with jelly in the refrigerator vegetable/fruit compartment.

PIGEONNEAU
[Pigeon]

It is difficult to find good pigeon squabs in Paris.

PIGEONNEAUX À LA CRAPAUDINE
[Squabs à la Crapaudine]

Cut the pigeon squabs down the back through the bone and open them up like a book, bending them back to keep them open. Brush them generously with melted butter, season with salt and pepper, and dust lightly with very fine bread crumbs. Set them on a grill, about 6 inches below a red-hot caloroid or gas flame, for 15 minutes with the skin side up and 10 minutes turned over. Serve with green salad.

PIGEONNEAUX EN COMPOTE
[Braised Squabs]

For this it is preferable to have a rather shallow kind of Dutch oven of relatively wide diameter. In it heat 4 spoonfuls of clarified butter (see page 10) and sauté on medium heat a handful of bacon cubes (about ½ pound) until they are golden. Remove them to a warm plate with a skimmer, and in the same pan throw in a handful of peeled tiny onions (about 20). Move the pan back and forth without raising it from the heat so that the onions will brown without losing any part of their unending skin. Remove the onions, add them to the bacon, and repeat the operation with a handful of cleaned mushrooms.

Put 4 squabs, breast side down, on this fat and turn them when the breasts are golden (all this on moderate heat). Remove the birds to join the foregoing on the plate, and add as much all-purpose flour to the pan as there is fat (about 3 spoonfuls): if the fat has been consumed add clarified butter and wait until it is hot before adding the flour. Stir the flour thoroughly to make a binding, then add ½ cup white wine and 1 cup chicken broth (made with 1½ chicken bouillon cubes) and scrape and mix it all to the consistency of a fairly thick sauce.

Add the squabs and other contents of the plate all around them, and spoon the sauce over the birds several times. Cover with aluminum foil and then the lid, tight. Set in a 300° F. oven, after bringing to a boil, and simmer for 40 minutes. Serve in the dish, wrapped in a fresh napkin.

PINTADE
[Guinea Fowl]

PINTADE RÔTIE
[Roast Guinea Fowl]

A young guinea hen should be stuffed and roasted in the oven exactly like a chicken (see page 167), but not more than 15 minutes per pound, raw weight, drawn.

PINTADE À LA CRÈME
[Guinea Fowl Braised in Sour Cream]

Brown a young guinea hen lightly in clarified butter (see page 10), then season with salt and white pepper and put in a cocotte, with the butter in which it was browned and a roughly chopped onion. Cover tightly and set in 350° F. oven for 30 minutes. During this time, turn the bird every 10 minutes so it will be cooked on all sides.

In a saucepan, bring to a boil 1 cup of cream seasoned with salt and white pepper. Add the juice of half a lemon to the cream and pour it on the bird. Cover the cocotte again and cook for another 15 minutes. If the sauce is too thin, bind it with arrowroot (see page 65).

CHAPTER 16

Gibier a Plume
(Game Birds)

ON THE CONTINENT of Europe no bird is safe from the gun and the kitchen, except possibly canaries. The lark, the thrush, the blackbird (remember the four and twenty blackbirds baked in a pie?) are all candidates for the reverence of the gastronome, not so much for their music. However, let us be mindful of the holier-than-thou principle by looking back on the wholesale slaughter of game in the United States a few years ago in the name of the birthright of every free citizen and assume a modest and discreet attitude of mind.

N.B. As this is a French cookery book, no attempt is made to advise the reader on the preparation of native American birds, such as the wild turkey, or American migrant birds, such as wild geese. However, in view of some American recipes which begin with some prescriptions to *wash* the birds or *wipe them clean with a damp cloth*, it may be admissible to recommend the good French method of singeing the birds after plucking and proceeding as for Le Poulet Rôti (see page 167), timing the roasting at 15 to 18 minutes the pound, raw weight.

The exquisite way of cooking small game birds is with *very* hot oil dripped on the bird as it turns on the spit. This is done with a funnel (entonnoir) fitted with a trap, which you release by pressing with the thumb. This used to be a specialty of the Hôtel Saint-Louis at fabulous Aigues Mortes.

Now let us consider the game birds available in the United States also known to French cooks, in French alphabetical order.

BÉCASSE ET BÉCASSINE
[*Woodcock and Snipe*]

The hard-bitten game fancier insists on woodcock being roasted without being drawn—except for the crop—and, furthermore, on having a special delicacy called the *rôtie*, which is nothing else than the intestines of the bird lightly sautéed, seasoned, and spread on a piece of toasted bread. But the moderate gastronome may agree that this delicious bird should not be eaten too freshly killed nor too well done: it must be hung (with its feathers, of course, like all game birds, because the flavor is greatly impaired by plucking long before cooking) for a few days; and it should be roasted not more than 18 minutes in a 450° F. oven—or, better, on the spit for 20 minutes, about 4 inches below a red-hot caloroid or by a bright fire on the hearth. And it should *not* be drawn: its intestines being very small and "innocent." Of course, it should, preparatory to roasting, be wrapped in a very thin sheet of bacon and its long beak should be thrust through its second joints and body.

An old recipe calls for stuffing the woodcocks with oysters poached in their juice and then moistened with cream and fish fumet (see page 57), then roasting them as above and serving them with toasted slices of bread spread with the lightly sautéed intestines seasoned with anchovies, nutmeg, and pepper.

For snipe the cooking process should be the same, but shortened to 10 or 12 minutes.

CAILLE
[Quail]

The wild bird shot down is incomparably better than the usual quail fed in captivity sold by Paris butchers. The native American quail is of course a very superior bird, like the one shot in Europe and North Africa.

CAILLES RÔTIES
[Roast Quail]

Plucked just before cooking, quail are singed over an alcohol flame (*never* wood alcohol) rapidly and wrapped up first in a grapevine leaf and then in a thin sheet of pork fat or bacon, and roasted on the spit 3 inches below a red-hot caloroid for 10 minutes. They are served on fried toast.

CAILLE EN CAISSES
["Boxed Quail"]

This is quite complicated.

Bone each bird by opening it up along the back, then stuff it with its liver and foie gras and sautéed bacon ground up, the whole moistened with Cognac and seasoned with pepper, nutmeg, shallots (finely minced), a pinch of thyme, and salt, bound with egg yolk. Wrap up the birds in a piece of oiled paper and put them, well pressed together, in an oven dish; spoon some melted butter over them, cover the dish, and bake in a 350° F. oven for 15 minutes.

Remove them to a hot serving platter, strip off the paper, and set them in individual, thin cardboard boxes that have been oiled and dried in the oven for a few minutes. Deglaze the pan with some Madeira wine and pour the juice over the birds. If insufficient, this juice can be laced with a little Sauce Madère (see page 5).

FAISAN
[Pheasant]

Again, the wild bird is incomparably better than the farm-raised product. It should hang during cold weather for a week; freshly killed it lacks flavor. If the weather turns damp the hanging period may be cut down by half. For simple roasting follow the recipe for Le Poulet Rôti (see page 167). The oven should be at 400° F. and the time 30 minutes. If it is roasted on the spit, 35 minutes and 6 inches below a red-hot caloroid.

FAISAN EN CHARTREUSE

This is a presentation piece and therefore complicated in its final touches. Birds past their tender years may be utilized.

First, surface-lard (see page 123) the breasts of a pheasant and brush the whole bird with melted butter (about 2 spoonfuls). Put it in a 400° F. oven for 7 minutes, then set it in a cocotte in which you will have put a layer of cooked cabbage (10 minutes of boiling in salted water) squeezed of its water, an onion stuck with 2 whole cloves, and 4 ounces of fresh pork fat cut in fine strips 1 inch long. Season the bird with salt and white pepper and a good pinch of thyme, then put around it sections of peeled and cored carrots, 4 fat pork sausages, and more cabbage as before. Deglaze the dish or pan in which the pheasant was roasted with consommé (about 2 or 3 cups) and pour the liquid into the cocotte. Cover and bring to a boil. Put in a 350° F. oven for 2 hours; but after 20 minutes examine the contents and withdraw the sausages if they begin to disintegrate; keep them warm.

Meanwhile cook in butter and water with salt and pepper 10 small, tender turnips (peeled), 5 carrots (peeled and cored), and ½ pound each of green beans and peas—all separately, of course. Cut the turnips and carrots in pieces 1½ inch in length and ½ inch in width.

Line the bottom of a buttered charlotte mold with the tailored pieces of carrot and turnip, alternately, to form a pattern to your fancy. On this put a layer of finely ground veal (1 pound) seasoned with salt and white pepper, mixed with 6 well-beaten eggs and 4 spoonfuls of thick Sauce Béchamel (see page 8)—the whole well worked into a very fine puree. Cut up the pheasant in quarters (2 breasts and 2 legs) and dress these on the purée, surround with cabbage squeezed of its water, and all around on the sides of the mold cut carrots and turnips as before, slanting them slightly for the effect. Pack more veal puree round the pieces of pheasant and more cabbage squeezed as before, and put now a ring of peas on the edge of this, touching the mold. Again more purée and more cabbage, and another band of turnips and carrots and peas, until the mold is almost full. Finally, add a slice of raw ham cut in small triangles. Cover with aluminum foil, set in a larger pan filled with boiling water up to three-fourths the height of the mold, and bake in a 350° F. oven for 45 minutes.

Let the mold, once removed from the pan, remain to consolidate for 5 minutes before unmolding on a platter. Decorate with the cooked green beans on top surrounded with thin sectional slices of the sausages, and around the base arrange a pattern of the cooked vegetables and sausage slices. Warm for a few minutes in a very mild oven with the door open and serve a Sauce Madère (see page 5) in a sauceboat.

N.B. Any colorful salami cut in crescent shapes may be substituted for the sausages.

PALOMBE
[Wild Pigeon and Dove]

Follow the recipes for partridge (see below).

PERDREAUX, PERDRIX
[Partridge—young and mature]

There is a mocking saying in France: "*A la Saint-Rémi, perdreaux sont perdrix.*" As this saint's day is the first of October, it means that after that all partridges are mature. And, of course, only the young birds lend themselves to roasting. You can tell the difference by examining the long feathers: if they are pointed at the ends it is a young bird, but if they are rounded it is an old one.

PERDREAU RÔTI
[Roast Young Partridge]

This delicate bird must be plucked—especially—just before it is cooked, so that the natural scent at the root of its feathers will not dry out and fade. Besides, it must be wrapped up in a living leaf like a grapevine leaf, buttered on its top side, which should then be applied to the bird, with a thin sheet of fresh pork fat over it, both fastened around the bird with a wet string tied crisscross over all. Some gas-tronomes prescribe a pinch of coarse salt inside the bird: this might make it bleed, so it seems preferable to withhold all seasoning until it is cooked.

Spit your partridge and set it some 4 inches below a red-hot caloroid or on a low grill, in a dish, in a 400° F. oven, and roast it for 15 minutes. Remove its wrappings and expose to the same heat, by either method, for 3 minutes.

If roasted in the oven, the bird should be served with the pan juice obtained from deglazing it with boiling water. Season with salt and pepper and a few drops of lemon juice.

PERDRIX AUX LENTILLES
[Mature Partridge with Lentils]

Lard the breasts of 2 mature partridges through with 2 slices of fresh pork fat which you have cut into thin strips. Lay the birds on a bed of coarsely chopped carrots and onions (2 of each) and bits of pork fat and a spoonful or two of melted butter. Add a bay leaf, a pinch of thyme, salt, some whole peppercorns, then cover with aluminum foil and a well-fitting lid and set on medium heat to "sweat" for 20 minutes. Uncover and pour in half a wineglass of dry white wine. Increase the heat to reduce this to a spoonful or so and then moisten with enough consommé to come up two-thirds on the bodies of the birds. Cover tight again and set in a 300° F. oven to simmer for 1 hour.

Serve surrounded by cooked lentils (see page 252) moistened with the cooking liquor of the birds.

CHAPTER 17

Four-Legged
or Furry Game

As WITH FEATHERED GAME, no attempt is made here to consider the native American wild animals unknown in France.

CHEVREUIL
[Venison]

The English word, derived from the Latin *venari* meaning to hunt, is now used to designate deer meat. In French the word *venaison* means any kind of game meat.

CHEVREUIL RÔTI
[Roast Haunch of Venison]

After carefully skinning and wiping off any bits of fur and trimming off the hock of a leg of venison, lard it on the surface with 3 ounces of fresh pork fat, cut in slivers and dipped in onion salt, white pepper, and powdered rosemary. Put the venison haunch in a deep dish, one that holds it snugly, with 4 carrots (peeled and sliced) and 4 onions (sliced), a sprig of fresh thyme (or ¼ teaspoon dried thyme), a bay leaf, half a clove of garlic (crushed), salt, and freshly ground peppercorns—under the haunch and on top—and pour over it gently 2 cups of strong white wine (Sauternes) mixed with 1 cup of white vinegar and 4 spoonfuls of good, fruity olive oil. Keep it thus, covered with a piece of aluminum foil, in a cool place for 24 hours, turning it over several times.

Before cooking, lift the leg to a low rack and wipe off all the vege-tables on it, taking care to mop up all moisture on the bits of lardoons on the surface: moisture prevents proper roasting. Proceed to roast it like a leg of lamb, either on a spit (50 minutes) or on a low rack in a 450° F. oven for 20 minutes, reduced to 350° for 25 minutes longer. Deglaze the pan with some of the marinade and add this to 1 cup of Sauce Poivrade (see page 5), served apart.

N.B. Chestnut purée, celeriac and potato puree, and braised celery go well with this.

TOURNEDOS DE CHEVREUIL
[*Venison Tournedos*]

As the deer has too little tenderloin, the tournedos are really boned chops and, of course, the prime ones. Proceed as for Tournedos à la Louis (see page 130).

N.B. Louis was a French headwaiter at the old Copley-Plaza Hotel in Boston, Massachusetts, and the inventor of this dish, which he cooked over a spirits lamp in the finest of French traditions. *Eheu fugaces!*

LAPIN
[Rabbit]

This means, of course, wild rabbit, which in France is called *le lapin de garenne*. Perhaps the best way to prepare wild rabbit is given by Alexandre Dumas: "Cut the rabbits in quarters, reserving the liver. Lard them with spiced lardoons, on the surface, of pork fat and of ham. Garnish the bottom of a casserole with pork fat and slices of veal, seasoned with salt, pepper, herbs, fine spices, onions, scallions, parsley, carrots, and parsnips. Arrange the pieces of rabbit in the casserole, season them on both sides, and cook in the oven with heat above and below." Then he directs the reader to make a mush of the same vegetables as above plus the livers of the rabbit, plus truffles and mushrooms, pieces of bread, and veal juice—all strained and poured over the pieces of rabbit, which are then warmed in this mush.

GIBELOTTE DE LAPIN À L'ANCIENNE MODE

Again, this is Alexandre Dumas's recipe: "Cut up a rabbit in pieces and a medium eel in sections, make a binding (butter and flour) and heat your rabbit and sections of eel in it when it is nicely light brown; lightly sauté in this some mushrooms and little onions; when everything is lightly cooked moisten with $\frac{1}{3}$ white wine and $\frac{2}{3}$ broth; season with salt and pepper, parsley, scallions, and thyme; lift the sections of eel and the onions, to cook the rest on high heat; when the liquor is reduced to $\frac{1}{3}$, put back the eel and the onions, finish on low heat, skim off the fat, and serve."

LIÈVRE
[Hare]

Again, wild hare is understood. It should be young—i.e. of the year—which you tell by the tenderness of the ears and by the weight, which should be not more than 6 pounds (raw and not dressed).

CIVET DE LIÈVRE
[Hare Stew]

This is the best known of French hare dishes. It requires the blood of the animal; so, if you see that it has been shot around the ribs, the likelihood is that it has bled and therefore is not acceptable. If it shows signs of having been shot in the head and hindquarters, take it and skin it and bleed it over a bowl, adding a teaspoon of good wine vinegar to prevent it from coagulating. Keep the liver and throw away the rest of the offal. Wash the liver well and dry it with paper toweling. If you are not finicky, cut off the head, gouge out the eyes, and chop off the teeth, but keep the head for the stew just to add flavor but not to be served.

Now cut the hindquarters from the body and divide them into six pieces, two from the upper leg and one from the lower leg, on each side. Cut the forelegs in two pieces each, and the neck in two also. Make two or three sections through the ribs, and four or five through the loin (which is the best piece). Put all these pieces in a marinade of Cognac (a good wineglassful), 3 spoonfuls of fine olive oil, salt, 1 onion (finely sliced), a bay leaf, a pinch of thyme, several stalks of parsley, and freshly ground black pepper.

Throw into boiling water a good handful (about ½ pound) of lean bacon cut in rough dice and lift them out with a skimmer after 2 minutes; drain them, and when *dry* sauté them in hot butter until golden. Join 2 onions (roughly chopped) to the bacon. Make a bind-ing in the fat with 2 or 3 spoonfuls of all-purpose flour, and when it is beginning to turn yellow add the pieces of hare, scraping off the marinade from the surface *only*. Turn them as they cook, and stir and scrape the pan on medium heat.

Transfer the whole to a cocotte with a well-fitting lid and set it on high heat. Pour enough red Burgundy wine in (about 1½ cups) to just cover the meat and add half a clove of garlic (crushed). Stir and scrape the bottom until boiling begins; then clap on the lid and put the cocotte in a 300° F. oven for 1 hour. Inspect it from time to time to make sure the sauce is simmering only, and regulate the heat accordingly.

Meanwhile brown some 20 tiny onions in 2 spoonfuls clarified butter (see page 10) and sauté 2 handfuls of well-cleaned mushrooms likewise; season the latter with salt and pepper and a few drops of lemon juice. Slice the liver after sautéing it in the same butter, and season it with salt and pepper; take some of the sauce from the cocotte in the oven and mix it gradually with the blood you reserved. When the 1 hour of cooking is up, remove the pieces of hare (minus the head) to a hot serving platter, surround them with the bacon dice, the little onions, and the mushrooms, and strain the sauce mixed well with the diluted blood, heated just under boiling point, over the whole dish. Cover the platter and set it on a plate warmer, or similar warm spot, while you prepare some triangles of fried toast.

LE RÂBLE DE LIÈVRE
[Saddle of Hare]

Strictly speaking, this is the entire back from neck to tail, but is generally understood as just the loin, sometimes including the hind-quarters. This is the piece for roasting: it should be marinated as above, wiped dry, seasoned, and not only surface larded (see page 123) but carefully gone over to remove numerous nerves just under the surface of the flesh, as well as the thin membrane that covers it. Roast, well basted with melted butter, on a low rack in a 350° F. oven for 25 minutes, and serve with the drippings deglazed with a little white wine, or a Sauce Poivrade (see page 5).

MARCASSIN
[*Young Wild Boar*]

Marinating the really young wild "boar" (in fact, the young female is preferable) is not at all necessary. For cooking advice follow that for venison (see page 192), but prolong the cooking one-fourth longer, since you are dealing with a member of the pig tribe.

CHAPTER 18

Pâtés, Croquettes, Godiveau, Rissoles

PÂTÉS

A PÂTÉ IS A PIE—i.e., either a two-crust pie or just a top-crust pie. What is commonly called "pâté de foie gras" is not a pâté (it has no crust) but a terrine. Terrines are served cold and will be found under The Cold Buffet (pages 256ff). Pâtés can also be served cold; but it would seem that cold salt pastry with meat could be improved upon by serving it hot, freshly prepared. In France, however, hot pâtés are fairly unusual, especially so in Paris; so much so that to see on a menu—and even in famous cookery books—the term *pâté en croûte* ("pie with a crust") is not unusual. Of course the English word *pie* is not the translation of the French *pâté*, because in the English-speaking world a pie has two crusts, or something closely resembling them, or just a top crust, whereas in France no sweet pie, practically speaking, is called a "pâté," or only rarely, and then it has just the under crust (more usually called a *timbale*).

LES PÂTES À PÂTÉS DE VIANDES
[Pastes for Meat Pies]

Three kinds of paste can be used for top crusts: *feuilletée* (trans-lated as "puff paste"), *demi-feuilletée* (containing half the proportion of butter), and *pâte à foncer* (as given below). The last mentioned is best for lining pie dishes and the two other for top crusts, especially the first. For directions see page 273.

LE POULET AUX MORILLES EN CROÛTE
[Chicken Pie with Morels]

Morels are native to North America as well as Europe, but they are rarely obtainable in the United States, especially in the markets. They are perhaps the most highly flavored of all mushrooms (wild). In Paris they are sold mainly in small cellophane bags, dried: even so, once soaked in lukewarm water for an hour or so, they are deli-cious. The dish is simple enough: it is Poulet Sauté (see page 172), flamed in Cognac and then warmed in a Sauce Madère (see page 5) mixed with tomato paste; the whole is put into an ovenproof porcelain or pottery dish, covered over with Pâte Feuilletée (see page 273), and baked in a 375° F. oven for 40 minutes.

PÂTÉ DE VEAU À LA PARISIENNE
[Veal Pie à la Parisienne]

Line an ovenproof pottery dish with the following pie paste (*pâte à foncer*).

On a marble slab put a mound of 8 ounces of all-purpose flour. Make a hollow in the center and put into it 1 cup of cold water with 1 teaspoon of salt and ¼ pound of softened butter cut into small pats. Work the flour from the inside of the hollow toward the edges with your fingers, as quickly as possible, to mix the butter, flour, and water without breaking down the outer wall of the mound until there is no liquid to spill over. With your fingers, again, work the paste quickly into a sort of ball, wrap it up in a clean napkin or cheesecloth, and put it away for at least 2 hours in a cool place (or the fruit compartment of the refrigerator, where it can not freeze). The longer the paste remains thus the better.

Roll the paste out to make a lining for your pie dish and a top crust. Line your pie dish, and on it put a fine puree (called in French a *farce*, strange as it may sound to English speakers) consisting of 4 ounces of fresh white bread (without the crust) worked with a wooden spoon over high heat with about 1/4 cup of boiling water, a pinch of salt, and a spoonful of butter until it no longer sticks to the pan; 1 pound of lean veal cut in small pieces and then pounded in a mortar with a pestle into a paste, seasoned with onion salt, white pepper, and a pinch of nutmeg; 2 eggs (well beaten); and 4 spoonfuls of very thick béchamel sauce (simply made with a little butter and an equal amount of flour, stirred for a minute or two and moistened with 4 spoonfuls of milk).

Mash all this together, and put one-half of it on the bottom crust of the pie, reserving the other half to spread over all the meat layers, which consist of 1 pound of very thin slices of veal from the *noix* or "cushion," marinated for 1 hour in 1/2 cup white wine, a small glass of Cognac, onion salt, a pinch of thyme, and white pepper, and then lightly sautéed in 2 spoonfuls of butter. Alternate the meat layers with sautéed, chopped mushrooms sprinkled with a few drops of lemon juice.

Pour over the whole 1/4 cup of melted butter and cover with the top crust, sticking the paste to the sides of the pie dish with a little cold water. Brush with beaten egg. Make a 1/2-inch hole in the middle of the pie and surround this hole with a ring of paste. Bake in a 375° oven for 50 minutes.

CROQUETTES

For making croquettes, a wire frying basket and a saucepan in which it fits easily are recommended.

CROQUETTES DE VEAU ET JAMBON
[Veal and Ham Croquettes]

Sauté ½ pound of veal and ½ pound of ham (or whatever other proportion of the meats you prefer) in 2 spoonfuls of butter, and season with onion salt, pepper, parsley leaves, thyme, and onion juice (cut an onion and scrape with a small knife onto a plate). Grind half the meat and cut the other half in fine dice.

If you are using Sauce Espagnole, thicken ½ cup of it with arrow-root (see page 65), and reserve another ½ cup over warm water. If you are using thick Sauce Béchamel (see page 8) or Sauce Mornay (see page 9) it should not require thickening. Mix the ground and diced meats with the ½ cup of thick sauce to make a fairly solid mass. Spread this over a lightly oiled (or buttered) piece of glazed paper so that you have a rectangular slab of an even thick-ness of about 2 inches. Brush this with melted butter and let cool entirely, covered with aluminum foil. Some 20 minutes before serv-ing, cut the slab into equal sections and roll each into a wine-cork shape about 3 inches long by 2 inches wide. Dust lightly with all-purpose flour.

Beat 3 (or, if small, 4) whole eggs with a teaspoon of olive oil. Roll the croquettes first in the eggs and then in very fine bread crumbs, and slide into a frying basket. Plunge them into a quart of very hot, smoking oil.

As soon as they turn golden or light brown, lift the basket and, after letting it drip over the pan, lay it on a plate. If the croquettes are still greasy, lift them carefully with a fork slid under each one and place them on a piece of brown wrapping paper.

Serve as soon as possible with the other half of the sauce in a boat, and accompanied by any vegetable that is not watery.

CROQUETTES DE POISSON
[Fish Croquettes]

Proceed as above, but add minced sautéed mushrooms (one-third the quantity of the fish), and mix 2 eggs (well beaten) with the ground fish.

The seasoning should be salt, white pepper, dill powder or flakes, and onion juice; and the sauce a thick Sauce Béchamel (see page 8).

Fried parsley (see page 53) is a recommended garnish.

N.B. Potato croquettes made with mashed potato, breaded and fried the same way, but rolled in small balls (like golf balls) can be served at the same time.

GODIVEAU POUR QUENELLES DE VIANDE
[Godiveau for Meat Quenelles]

It is regrettable that there is no translation for either French term, unless we use the word "dumpling."

First, with 1 ounce of all-purpose flour thrown into $\frac{1}{2}$ cup of boiling milk and 1 spoonful of butter, make a batter that by vigorous beating and stirring no longer clings to the pan. Add a pinch of salt and beat it again.

Cut 4 ounces of raw, lean veal into dice and pare off all nerves, etc., so that you can pound the meat in a mortar with a pestle into a fine, smooth paste. Season with salt, white pepper, and nutmeg, and add not quite twice the amount of raw suet (the fat off a veal kidney), also chopped fine and stripped of all membranes, and mash them together with the first batter preparation. When it is reduced to a fine homogeneous paste, add 2 beaten eggs, one by one, while mashing. Gather this fine puree together, wrap it up in a piece of buttered paper and put away in a *cool* place, preferably overnight.

This puree can be poached, when shaped into small balls or elongated sections the shape of a wine-bottle cork no longer than $1\frac{1}{2}$ inches long, in boiling water; or it can be pressed in pellets out of a pastry bag onto a buttered and floured cookie sheet and baked in a 250° F. oven for 10 minutes.

These morsels are an excellent addition when added to sweet-breads, brains, etc., and warmed in a sauce to fill a *vol-au-vent*.

N.B. Alexandre Dumas quotes the "Maréchal de Richelieu's cook" to the effect that *chipped ice* should be ground into this composition to give it the proper velvety consistence *during the summer months when it is hot*; other authors prescribe this peculiar addition at all times. It would seem that what is required is an addition of very cold water and storage until use in a cold place.

RISSOLES
[*Pasties*]

These are small discs of *pâte à foncer* (see page 275) or ordinary pie paste filled in the center with ground cooked meat of any kind, or of fish, or of vegetables, then folded over to enclose the filling, pinched along the semicircular edge firmly, lightly dusted with all-purpose flour, and fried in hot pork fat or oil until golden.

CHAPTER 19

Cured Beef
and Pork

LE BOEUF SALÉ
[Corned Beef or Salt Beef]

CURED BEEF IS NOT a usual dish in France; at least, not as usual as in English-speaking countries. American corned beef is as good as if not better than any French competitor, so the only novelty that can be presented under this heading for the American reader of culinary experience is the French manner of cooking it.

After washing off the salt under the tap for a minute or so, it is treated just like the raw cuts that go into a *pot-au-feu* and served accordingly, surrounded by the vegetables it boiled with (of course, omitting salt in the seasoning).

LANGUE DE BOEUF SALÉE et FUMÉE
[Smoked Beef Tongue]

In Paris few pork butchers (*charcutiers*) sell smoked tongues: one has to order them in advance. They are generally an Alsatian specialty. Like corned beef, American smoked tongues are better than their French rivals, generally speaking. The method of cooking is the same as for ham (see below).

JAMBON
[Ham]

Paris *charcutiers*, or pork butchers, generally sell two kinds of ham, *jambon de Paris*, which is boned and molded and rather bland in flavor, and *jambon de York*, which is cured with, and carved off, the bone—lightly smoked and more flavorful. The superior establish- ments also sell the sliced raw hams of Bayonne (French), of Parma (Italian), and rarely the Spanish pressed hams, which are consumed as hors d'oeuvres, frequently with melon or figs. Whole hams for cooking are sold as Prague hams, and like all hams need soaking (preferably overnight) and boiling—beginning with cold and of course unsalted water—20 minutes to the pound, without any sea- soning. The famous New York restaurateur Rector tells in his memoirs that he bet a pretentious customer that a ham boiled in Champagne was no better than one boiled in ink: he won his bet but had a devil of a time getting enough ink for the operation; this was, however, nearly one hundred years ago, and then, perhaps, ink was not as "civilized" as today.

However, the point is that ham with its skin on does not absorb the flavor of its cooking liquid—nor, presumably, its tint. Boiled ham is generally served in Paris with Sauce Madère (see page 5) and spinach.

SAUCISSES
[Sausages]

The more ambitious Paris *charcutiers* have on display a consid- erable variety of sausages, French and foreign. The real Frankfurt sausages, made of beef and pork, and smoked, are generally one of the components of Choucroute Garnie (see page 207), but are also served with mashed potatoes: they should be cooked for 10 minutes in boiling water. French pork sausages are put in boiling water for an instant and then pricked with any fine instrument to prevent the casing from bursting when grilled or sautéed, which in either case takes only 6 to 7 minutes. The favorite French recipe for these sausages is:

Sauté them in butter, after the boiling-water ducking and pricking, and remove them to a hot plate; deglaze the pan with white wine; thicken this liquor with a binding of flour and butter, mixed with meat glaze or Sauce Espagnole (see page 3) or thicken the white wine liquor with egg yolks. Mashed potatoes, mashed chestnuts, or almost any vegetable will do for accompaniment.

BOUDINS BLANCS ET NOIRS
[Pork or Chicken Quenelles and Blood Puddings]

The white *boudins* are really quenelles made of fresh pork and chicken, or chicken only. The finest contain fresh foie gras and truffles as well. They should be pricked with a pin and then wrapped up in buttered paper and grilled, at a distance of 5 to 6 inches, under a medium-hot caloroid or gas flame for 15 minutes: this is really a warming up, as the *boudins* are already cooked. The black *boudins* are blood puddings made from fresh pork blood, onions, pork fat, cream, and seasoning: they are grilled the same way as the white *boudins* but without wrapping *and*, moreover, lightly scored all around like a fish before roasting. The white *boudins* are served with a Sauce Madère (see page 5) or Sauce Périgueux (see page 6) as a first dish. The blood puddings are generally accompanied by applesauce and mashed potatoes.

LA CHOUCROUTE GARNIE
[Sauerkraut with Cured Pork]

Here we jump to the other end of France, Alsace. Unless you have a very sure source of homemade sauerkraut, it is best to rely on the tinned article put up in Alsace in 1¼-pound tins. It must not contain any meats, and it is preferable if prepared with Alsatian wine.

For 2 persons: Take a piece of smoked bacon weighing ½ pound, cut it in 2 or 4 pieces across and heat these in a heavy cocotte on medium heat, stirring, until you have a film of fat at the bottom. Shred a 1¼-pound tin of sauerkraut and put the shreds into the cocotte in a 2-inch layer, and spread over this about 1 spoonful of juniper berries lightly crushed in a mortar and in the middle 1 onion stuck with a whole clove. Make a second 2-inch layer of sauerkraut, put in in shreds, and on it lay here and there 4 pieces of pork spareribs (pickled in salt for 12 hours, known in France as *petit salé*). Cover with a third layer of sauerkraut, then moisten with enough Alsatian wine so that you can see it between the shreds of sauerkraut.

Cover and bring to a boil on high heat, then let it boil gently for 1 hour, regulating the heat accordingly. Add then 4 Frankfurt sausages pricked with a fine-tined fork, and a few minutes later 2 small slices of smoked, cooked ham. Cover again and cook for 20 minutes longer.

Serve with boiled potatoes and sharp mustard.

CHAPTER 20

Vegetables

THERE IS IN FRANCE a general contemptuous attitude toward English cookery. Nevertheless, as one studies in detail the French art and science of culinary excellence, one becomes quite familiar with the term *à l'anglaise* ("English fashion") as applied to many preparations. This is especially so with regard to vegetables. Not that they are cooked in England today in an exemplary manner! But the tradition surely is there: vegetables *à l'anglaise* are boiled for a certain prescribed time in salted water and then served with fresh butter on the dish.

Undercooked vegetables can be more or less indigestible—depending on the vegetable—but overcooked ones are bound to be unappetizing and probably have little nutritious value.

ARTICHAUTS
[*Artichokes*]

Artichokes should be bought with their stems on, because, by grasping the stem with the right hand and holding down the head with the left on the edge of a table, one can break off the stem by bearing down on it and thus tear off a good portion of the spiny fibers from the bottom of the heart, which otherwise are very hard to pick off.

The tougher leaves at the bottom should be torn off (or cut off) at their base. Also, the top leaves should be sawn off at a line with the tender leaves rising from the choke (this can also be done by cutting with a large, sharp knife).

ARTICHAUTS BOUILLIS
[Boiled Artichokes]

The artichoke prepared as above should be put into boiling salted water and boiled steadily for 40 minutes.

Against many opinions to the contrary, it is recommended that the artichoke be trimmed around the base or bottom of the heart *after cooking, not before*, because the fibers left thus can be more easily picked off without much waste; also, the choke can be taken off much more easily after cooking, by using a pointed teaspoon.

Boiled artichokes can be served warm (*hot* would burn your fingers) or cold—if warm, with Sauce Hollandaise (see page 9); if cold, with Vinaigrette (see page 11), Sauce Gribiche (page 11), or even Sauce Mayonnaise (see page 12).

ARTICHAUTS FARCIS
[Stuffed Artichokes]

For 4 artichokes

Make a fine hash by putting ¾ pound lean fresh pork twice through the fine plate of the meat grinder. Season it with onion salt, freshly ground pepper, and a pinch of powdered sage. Mix thoroughly.

Prepare the artichokes for boiling (see above), but boil them in salted water for *only 15 minutes*. Pare off the bottom fibers, if any, and remove the choke, with a spoon, and the thin leaves around it.

Make a binding by cooking 4 spoonfuls of melted butter and 4 spoonfuls of all-purpose flour until it turns yellow—5 to 10 minutes. Add about ½ cup of chicken bouillon or broth, and on medium-low heat stir the mixture into a thick cream or paste. Mix this with the hash and with 3 eggs (well beaten).

Stuff the hollow center of each artichoke with this mixture, pressing it down but leaving a low domelike effect on top. Lay on top of each a thin slice of bacon, which you then tie with crossed string.

In a heavy cocotte with a good lid, melt 4 or 5 spoonfuls of butter on medium heat. Set the artichokes side by side in the cocotte to brown their bottoms lightly. (This should take about 12 minutes, during which you should shake the cocotte occasionally to prevent the butter from burning.) With two large kitchen forks or similar implements, remove the artichokes to a warm plate, then add to the butter in the cocotte 3 or 4 spoonfuls of flour to make a yellow-brown binding, stirring carefully. Add beef consommé (2 cups concentrated consommé mixed with 2 cups water) gradually on medium heat, stirring constantly to avoid lumping; then bring to a boil. Immediately put the artichokes in this mixture, side by side: the liquid should come up to more than one-third their height. Cover and put in a medium-moderate oven (325° F.) to boil very gently for 50 minutes, removing the lid three or four times to baste the artichokes with the cooking liquor.

Remove the strings before serving, and brown the bacon slices lightly under gas flame or caloroid. Set the artichokes on a hot platter and strain the cooking liquor over them, after skimming off the surface fat.

Decorate the bacon on top of each artichoke with a pinch of finely chopped parsley.

FONDS D'ARTICHAUTS
[Artichoke Hearts]

Prepare boiled artichokes as instructed above. Let cool, then remove all the leaves. Pare the bottoms carefully to give them a smooth
appearance, then cut them in quarters. Sauté lightly in butter.

N.B. When used as garnishing *à la Clamart*, do not quarter them
but fill the hollow upper side with cooked peas.

ASPERGES
[Asparagus]

White asparagus is the classical variety in France, even though
the green ones have become fashionable in Paris restaurants catering
to foreign, especially American, customers. The green are referred
to by nineteenth-century authors as *pointes d'asperges* ("asparagus
tips"), the inference being that they could serve only as garnishing
and not as a course in a meal. The best white asparagus comes from
Argenteuil, nine miles from Paris.

ASPERGES BOUILLIES
[Boiled Asparagus]

The white asparagus must be carefully peeled and cut at the desired
length to fit the cooker (either vertical or horizontal). The green
variety does not need peeling: it should be lightly scraped, and it is
easily broken off at the point where the tender portion ends.

If a deep casserole or other deep utensil is chosen as cooker (vertical
method), the asparagus must point upward and be tied up in a bunch
or bunches.

If an asparagus boiler of the horizontal method, with a sleeve or
movable shelf, is used, tying the spears in bunches is not recommended, because those in the center will not get cooked uniformly
with those on the outer edge of the bunches. With this method you

can move the spears as they cook, so that those at the bottom of the boiler will be shifted to the top, thus ensuring uniformity of cooking.

In either way of cooking, the asparagus should, after careful wash' ing, be submerged in salted boiling water, kept covered until boiling resumes, and then allowed to cook vigorously, uncovered: for white asparagus, about 15 minutes; for green, 10 or 12 minutes. A prick with a fork indicates whether they are just soft enough to eat. Over' cooking spoils their flavor.

As soon as they are cooked, they should be drained over the boiler for a few seconds and then arranged on a grill over a dish to dry completely. Cold asparagus are served with Vinaigrette (page 11).

Lukewarm asparagus may be served right away, wrapped in a napkin, with Sauce Hollandaise (see page 9) or drawn (melted) butter in a sauceboat. As you eat them with your fingers, they are never served piping hot.

HARICOTS VERTS
[Green Beans—commonly called "String Beans"]

The name "string beans" is purposely avoided here, as really fine green beans have no strings.

Sometimes in the United States one hears of "Frenching" green beans, which seems to mean a manner of cutting them lengthwise or diagonally. This is not normal French practice.

The beans are nipped at each end to remove only a tiny tip. If longer than 3½ inches, they may be broken or cut in two, across. They are thrown into a large bowl with cold water, which is renewed if necessary to ensure their cleanliness.

HARICOTS VERTS BOUILLIS
[Boiled Green Beans]

Plunge the green beans into a large saucepan with plenty of boiling salted water (a good pinch of bicarbonate of soda helps their green' ness and their digestibility, and is *not* perceptible to the taste when they are served). Do not cover the saucepan once the beans are in. Watch for boiling to resume, then allow 10 minutes of steady boiling on high heat. Remove the pan immediately from the heat and drain it of all the water.

If possible, serve the beans immediately with a pat of butter on each helping—this is known in French culinary language as *beurre à l'anglaise* ("butter in the English manner"). You will find beans thus cooked full of their own flavor and not mushy, as when cooked longer.

N.B. As for sautéing green beans, it is definitely *not* recommended.

BETTERAVES
[*Beetroots—Beets*]

In Paris it is difficult to find raw beets. They are almost without exception sold cooked, unpeeled, and are consumed, after peeling, in combination with other vegetables or greens in a salad. This man-ner—strange to an English-speaking person—of dealing with this delicious vegetable, may be due to the fact that unknowing people peel beets before cooking them, which of course "bleeds" them.

They must be left with not only their skins but the fatter portion of their roots and an inch or so of their tops, and plunged thus into salted boiling water to boil for 30 to 40 minutes. Then they can be peeled easily with the back of a knife, and the root and top cut off.

The best French recipe simply directs that they be served hot, sliced or cut in cubes, with pats of butter *à l'anglaise*, leaving to each person the addition of pepper at table. Other French recipes for cooking beets are unnecessarily complicated and do not improve the natural flavor.

CHOU BROCOLI
[*Broccoli*]

This is unusual in Paris greengrocers' or open markets.
Cook it in boiling salted water for 10 to 15 minutes *without cover-*

ing the saucepan (this is important in cooking the entire cabbage family, as thus the pervading aroma is somewhat minimized).

Serve with Sauce Béchamel (see page 8), drawn butter, pats of butter *à l'anglaise*, Sauce Mornay (see page 9), or Sauce Mousseline-Moutarde (see page 10).

CHOUX DE BRUXELLES
[*Brussels Sprouts*]

Cook like broccoli (see above), but for all of 20 minutes.
Serve like broccoli or, after complete drying after cooking, covered with Sauce Mornay (see page 9) and browned in the oven.

CHOU
[*Cabbage*]

CHOU BOUILLI
[*Boiled Cabbage*]

There is a certain aversion in France to plain boiled cabbage, which when cooked in boiling salted water for 30 minutes, well drained, and served with pats of butter can hardly be improved upon as an accompaniment to roast beef or mutton—a case of the lily that needs no gilding.

French authors prescribe cutting up the cabbage before boiling, but this is not recommended unless the specimen is so large that it will not fit in any saucepan available. One of the reasons offered for the French procedure is the likelihood of finding worms and other live creatures among the leaves—which is most unlikely if you wash the cabbage well under the cold water tap and remove all leaves that have brown or other discolored marks.

The cabbage (white or green) should then be pared at the stem, cutting deep into it to facilitate cooking, and put into boiling salted water to boil steadily, uncovered, for 30 minutes.

It should be well drained but kept in the same saucepan until about to be served, when it should again be drained, squeezed of all water —without mashing—and served with a pat of fresh butter on each helping.

CHOU FARCI
[Stuffed Cabbage]

Put 2 spoonfuls seedless raisins in warm water and let soak for 30 minutes. Meanwhile, boil a head of cabbage whole, as above, *but for only 15 minutes*. Boil 2 ounces of smoked bacon for 2 minutes. Put it through the grinder, together with ½ pound cooked pork or beef or with 4 ounces of each. Add to this mixture the seedless raisins and also a few tablespoons of Sauce Espagnole (see page 3).

Open the leaves of the boiled cabbage very delicately and introduce some of the mixture into each layer. Re-form the cabbage, and tie it together with several turns of string, crisscross and over and under.

Pour a little melted butter on top and set in a 350° F. oven to *warm* for 15 minutes.

Serve with white boiled rice (see page 45).

N.B. If desired, rice may be mixed with the stuffing, in which case it is not served on the side, of course.

CAROTTES
[Carrots]

Although their natural season is late spring to early autumn, young and tender ones are obtainable in Paris practically the whole year round. Like most vegetables found on this market, they are of very good quality. The early (May-June) carrots are really sweet, and the short ones shaped like a spinning top are of merit in fancy stuffing operations.

Very tender young carrots should *not* be peeled but may be scraped with a wire brush or, according to an old French practice, with very coarse salt in a piece of canvas. All other carrots should be delicately peeled (a swiveled peeler is recommended).

Most carrots of any size should be cut in four, lengthwise, and cored—i.e., the green or paler core should be removed with a quick stroke of a knife: this core is tasteless. This does not apply to the very young and small carrots, which would be sadly reduced by such an operation; nor to the *grelot* or spinning-top variety, whose yellow-green center can be scooped out with the point of a small knife.

CAROTTES VICHY
[Carrots Cooked in Vichy Water]

The water of the Vichy region is soft, hence the merit of carrots cooked there (it is surprising that only this vegetable should have claimed the label). In order to compensate for the hardness of the water elsewhere, add a pinch of bicarbonate of soda to the water or even a Vichy Célestins tablet. Otherwise their cooking is quite ordinary.

Peel and core the carrots, and cut them either in sections across or strips lengthwise (or have them whole if very tender and small).

Put them in a pan, and *just* cover with cold water. Add a spoonful of butter for every cup of water, ½ teaspoon salt, a good pinch of granulated sugar, and a few white peppercorns.

Set on high heat and bring to a boil, then temper the heat to let boil gently for 30 minutes, covered. Remove the lid and let the liquor boil down to a syrupy consistency.

Serve with finely chopped parsley sprinkled over.

CAROTTES À LA CRÈME
[Carrots with Cream]

Cook as above for Carottes Vichy. Before serving, add a small amount of a carefully stirred mixture of Sauce Béchamel (see page 8) and heavy cream in equal amounts.

CAROTTES BRUNOISE and CAROTTES JULIENNE

The first designates carrots very finely diced; the second, carrots sliced in strips. (*Brunoise* and *julienne* are terms that can be applied to other vegetables, too.)

CHOUFLEUR
[*Cauliflower*]

French authors generally prescribe that the delicate clusters or *bouquets* should be separated with a knife before cooking—even that the stems of these be finely peeled. This is not recommended.

The cauliflower should be very white and compact, with no dark marks indicating the invasion of vermin. The stem should be cut as short as possible, and the center of it should be gouged out with the point of a knife. All leaves should be removed. The cold water tap should be run quite strong on the base, upside down, to free it from any marauding creatures.

CHOUFLEUR BOUILLI
[*Boiled Cauliflower*]

An ample saucepan with sufficient boiling salted water (with a pinch of bicarbonate) should be ready for it: put the cauliflower in carefully, stem side down, and do not cover. Keep the saucepan on sufficient heat to maintain boiling for 20 to 25 minutes. When done, drain the saucepan by putting its lid on but leaving a chink open through which to pour.

Serve as soon as possible, with a pat of butter on each helping. If the cauliflower is served whole, pour some melted butter over it.

CHOUFLEUR GRATINÉ
[*Cauliflower with Cheese Sauce*]

Cook as above, *but for only 15 minutes*. Drain well, and set in a round oven dish well rubbed with butter. Pour over the cauliflower a little Sauce Mornay (see page 9) and on its surface lay small pats of fresh butter.

Place some 5 inches under a medium-hot caloroid or gas flame until brown on top.

CÉLERI-RAVE
[Celery Root—Celeriac, Root Celery, Knob Celery]

No matter how it is to be prepared, celeriac must be peeled carefully to remove the dark exterior discolored by contact with air. Then it should be cut in pieces ½ inch thick and 2 to 3 inches long, and these put in cold water to prevent browning.

CÉLERI-RAVE À L'ETOUFFÉE
[Stewed Celeriac]

Put in a cocotte a handful or two of pieces prepared as above. Add a spoonful of butter, enough cold water to cover the pieces, onion salt and peppercorns to taste, a bay leaf, and a few drops of lemon juice. Cover and bring to boil, then reduce the heat to medium, to just keep boiling steadily for 45 minutes.

Take off the lid and boil on high heat until only 1 or 2 spoonfuls of liquid remain. Serve with this liquid over the pieces.

PURÉE DE CÉLERI-RAVE ET POMMES DE TERRES
[Puree of Celeriac and Potatoes]

After stewing the celeriac as above, test the pieces to see if they can be mashed; if they cannot, add enough boiling water to prevent burning and boil for 15 to 20 minutes longer, covered.

Mash them with a kitchen fork, and add half their quantity of mashed potatoes. Beat with a mechanical beater, or put through the grinder. Add butter if too dry for your taste, and ground white pepper and a pinch of nutmeg. Mix thoroughly and serve.

This puree goes very well with game.

CÉLERI
[Celery]

In old English cookery books, celery plants are called "heads," but in French they are called *pieds* (feet).

Choose, if possible, plants with their roots on, because they can be pared off and the heart trimmed into a point: this heart is very flavorful.

Cut off the leafy portion, which can be used for soup. Trim off all discolored portions. Run the cold water tap on the celery, parting the overlapping stalks and washing off all sand, earth, and live creatures that hide in them: this must be done carefully to avoid breaking off the stalks. Then run a small knife over the outer layers of the stalks to scrape off the tougher filaments.

Having made sure that there are no black or brown spots on the surface, plunge the celery into boiling water (no salt) and boil it for 10 minutes. Remove it to a large bowl, into which you turn the cold water tap to cool completely.

This process does not so much blanch the celery as it cleans it of what you have been unable to detect.

CÉLERI AU JUS
[Celery in Its Own Juice]

Tie the completely cooled celery (blanched as above) with fine kitchen or butcher's string once around. Lay it in a cocotte on a piece of bacon rind, fat side down, with 1 teaspoon of butter and enough chicken bouillon or broth (may be made with bouillon cubes) or a mixture of consommé and water (half and half) just to cover the celery. If the bouillon (broth) or consommé is not seasoned, add salt, pepper, and 2 or 3 stalks of parsley.

Butter a piece of waxed paper of appropriate size and put it *into* the cocotte to touch the celery. Bring to a boil on high heat, covered, and set in a 350° F. oven for 1½ hours.

Inspect the contents after 20 minutes to make sure the boiling is not too violent: it should be boiling, however, and not just simmering. Regulate the oven heat accordingly.

To serve, reduce the liquor in an open saucepan on high heat until you have just enough for a sauce, tasting it now and then to make sure it is not becoming too salt. Bind the sauce with ½ teaspoon of arrow-root powder dissolved in a teaspoon of cold water: add this to the sauce as it boils, but remove the sauce from the heat the moment it starts boiling again. (If it boils again with the arrowroot, it is likely to lump, which ruins the sauce.)

Remove the celery to a hot serving dish, remove the string, and pour the sauce over the celery.

N.B. If you have beef marrow on hand, slice it ¼ inch thick and put it in a small quantity of boiling water, then set on low heat and keep the water simmering for 5 minutes: the addition of the marrow gives the celery a special succulence.

MARRONS
[Chestnuts]

These are generally included with the vegetable tribe by most French authors, although of course they should be classed among the nuts. However, when prepared as follows, they are used as a vegetable to accompany meats.

PURÉE DE MARRONS
[Chestnut Puree]

With a sharp, pointed knife, make a little incision on each brown shell. Put nuts thus treated on a roasting pan in one layer, and pour into the pan enough water to form a good film on the bottom—(this is to prevent the chestnuts from scorching). Put them in 300° F. oven for 5 minutes.

Turn off the oven and take out a few chestnuts at a time with a spoon. Shell and skin them with a small knife while they are hot. If you break the nut meats during this process, it does not matter, be-cause they are going to be mashed.

Put the meats in a cocotte with 2 spoonfuls of butter per pound of peeled chestnuts, a good pinch of granulated sugar, and enough chicken bouillon (may be made with cubes) or a mixture of con-centrated consommé and water (half and half) just to cover the chestnuts. Set on medium-high heat, cover, and simmer for 1 hour, or until the chestnuts can be mashed.

If the chestnuts do not absorb all the liquid while being mashed, it is simple to stir them over medium heat and obtain this result. If they still have too dry a quality, add butter to make them unctuous. A little heavy cream, too, is not a bad addition.

CHICORÉE
[Chicory]

CHICORÉE À LA CRÈME
[Chicory in Cream]

Remove all discolored and withered bits from one or two frizzled chicory heads, as well as the tough stems. Wash the heads carefully under the cold water tap—they often contain inhabitants as well as mud—then boil them for 15 minutes in salted water with a pinch of bicarbonate of soda. Drain them, and cool them completely immedi-ately thereafter. Then squeeze all the water out of them.

Chop them up and sauté them in hot butter, sprinkling a little onion salt, white pepper, and a pinch of grated nutmeg over them, at the same time stirring them vigorously to get rid of most of the water.

Add *boiling* heavy cream, stir well again, and serve. (If the cream is not thick enough, add 1 or 2 spoonfuls of Sauce Béchamel, page 8).

CONCOMBRES
[Cucumbers]

There are two schools in the preparation of cucumbers for cooking: the majority opt for peeling, the minority for not peeling. *Not* is recommended.

Wash the cucumbers, which should be bright shiny green and not of great size, scraping if necessary any tarnished spots. Dry them with paper toweling.

CONCOMBRES À L'ETOUFFÉES
[Stewed Cucumbers]

Cut 1 or 2 medium or small cucumbers across into sections of 1½ inches. Put these in a cocotte with enough butter to make a good base (about a spoonful, according to the size of the cucumbers). Add a little salt and white peppercorns, then cover with a tight-fitting lid and set on high heat.

Inspect after a couple of minutes and regulate the heat to keep actively cooking but prevent burning, turning the pieces from time to time. The water in the cucumbers is sufficient to cook them, if the lid is lifted only momentarily, in 15 minutes. (A slight browning of the skins is not harmful; however, if you are going to add cream as a finishing touch, this is not desirable.)

Bind the sauce by dissolving ½ teaspoon of arrowroot in 1 teaspoon cold water and adding to the boiling liquid. Stir well, but do not let boil again, and remove quickly from the heat before it lumps.

CONCOMBRES FARCIS
[Stuffed Cucumbers]

Cut 1 or 2 large cucumbers into 2½-inch sections, and scoop out of these sections most of the seed *center*, going not deeper than three-quarters their length.

Set the sections side by side in a well-buttered cocotte. Pour around them—not into them—enough boiling water to come up to half their height. Set on high heat, then regulate to keep the water simmering for 15 minutes. Sprinkle a little salt over the whole.

Meanwhile, make a fine hash of 1 slice of ham and 3 or 4 chicken livers, seasoned with onion salt, white pepper, and basil, and mix it with one-quarter its volume (about 1/4 cup) of thick Sauce Béchamel (see page 8). Stuff the hollowed-out sections of the cucumbers with this mixture, topping each with a very small pat of butter.

Set the sections side by side in a buttered ovenproof dish and heat in a 350° F. oven for 10 or 15 minutes.

This can be served as garnishing for a meat dish, like any other vegetable.

AUBERGINE
[Eggplant]

Its skin should be bluish purple, smooth, even, and shiny. It should have no dents or soft spots.

AUBERGINE FRITE
[Fried Eggplant]

Cut off the stem and the very end. Slice in 1/4-inch wheels, and line these along the edges of soup plates or shallow bowls, side by side without stacking. Sprinkle them with fine salt and leave them for 30 minutes to allow their water to ooze out.

Scrape the salt off with a knife and dry the slices with paper toweling, then fry them in hot oil, renewing the oil as needed, eggplant being a thirsty customer.

Season them after frying, taking care not to oversalt, because some of the original salt may have remained in the pulp.

AUBERGINE FARCIE
[Stuffed Eggplant]

Cut a medium-large eggplant in half along its long axis.

With a small, sharp knife held near the point, cut through the pulp without wounding the skin—an operation requiring patience and dexterity. Repeat these cuts, making a checkered pattern, then put the cut halves thus scored, pulp side down, on hot oil or clarified butter (see page 10) to cook for about 30 minutes, depending on the thickness of the eggplant, and adding butter or oil as needed.

Meanwhile, slice a large onion, and saute in clarified butter, cooking until well softened; sauté 2 slices of bacon lightly in clarified butter. Chop up the onion and bacon and set aside.

When you see that the eggplant pulp is fairly brown, take out the eggplant and scoop out the pulp with a sharp-pointed spoon, without damaging the skin. Mince the pulp well and season it lightly with salt. Then mix it with the finely chopped onion and bacon and with 3 or 4 spoonfuls of thick Sauce Béchamel (see page 8). Stuff the eggplant skin (both halves) with this mixture. Spread on top a good layer of bread crumbs, and pour melted butter over that.

Set the stuffed halves in a buttered ovenproof dish, and place in 350° F. oven for 25 to 30 minutes. (If not browned on the surface by then, open the door of the oven and set the dish briefly under a hot caloroid or gas flame.)

ENDIVE

This is a variety of chicory that the grower usually blanches by covering with earth.

Choose creamy white, tight-leafed endives. Remove all discolored leaves and nip off the tip if brown.

Wash well.

ENDIVES BRAISÉES
[Braised Endives]

Lay endives in a thickly buttered cocotte, side by side, tightly packed but not stacked, head to tail, with 3 or 4 spoonfuls of cold water, a light sprinkling of fine salt and white pepper, and the juice of half a lemon. (The water may be replaced by a mixture of consommé and water (50/50), but in that case no salt should be added here.)

Cover, set on high heat, and bring to a boil. Place a thickly buttered piece of waxed paper or aluminum foil right on the endives. Cover the cocotte with a well-fitting lid and set in a 250° F. oven for 1 hour to 1 hour 15 minutes.

Remove the endives to a hot plate. Thicken the liquor in the cocotte by adding to it, while boiling, $\frac{1}{2}$ teaspoon of arrowroot dissolved in 1 teaspoon of cold water. Stir and remove quickly from heat without letting boil again. Verify the seasoning.

Pour over the endives and serve.

ENDIVES MORNAY
[Endives with Sauce Mornay]

Cook the endives as above, but drain off the cooking liquor. Set the endives side by side on an ovenproof dish, cover them with Sauce Mornay (see page 9) and a few pats of butter, and brown in the oven.

ENDIVES À LA MOËLLE
[Endives with Beef Marrow]

Cut beef marrow in $\frac{1}{4}$-inch sections and drop them into boiling consommé; quickly lower the heat to simmer for 5 minutes. Spread these bits of marrow over endives that have been cooked and drained as above, and pour Sauce Espagnole (see page 3) over the whole.

FENOUIL
[*Fennel*]

This is, of course, the cultivated variety with a bulbous base.

Pare off the root end; cut off the branch stems at the height of the bulb. Scrape the surface of the bulb with a vegetable peeler or a knife, after tearing off any damaged or discolored layers. Cut in two from top to root end.

FENOUIL BRAISÉ
[*Braised Fennel*]

Put the fennel into a cocotte with a spoonful of butter, a bay leaf, a sprinkling of onion salt and white pepper, and a few drops of lemon juice. Add enough cold water to come up to the vegetable, cover with a proper-fitting lid, and set on high heat to bring to a boil. Then turn down the heat to simmer for 30 minutes.

Remove the fennel with a skimmer; reduce the cooking liquor on high heat to a spoonful or so, which you pour on the vegetable when served on a hot dish.

TOPINAMBOURS
[*Jerusalem Artichokes*]

There are two disadvantages to this delicious vegetable: they are hard to peel because of their extremely irregular surface, and they are likely to produce flatulence.

To make peeling easier, cut them in portions that permit the action of the knife without too much elaborate carving. After peeling, wipe well but do not wash.

TOPINAMBOURS AU BEURRE
[Jerusalem Artichokes Stewed in Butter]

Put them in a cocotte with enough clarified butter (see page 10) to cover its bottom generously. Sprinkle with a little salt, white pep‑ per, and grated nutmeg, then cover and set on medium heat. Inspect after a few minutes to regulate the heat accordingly. Move the pieces of vegetable about in the cocotte.

Cook for 15 or 20 minutes more, then try them with a fork. If not easily pierced, continue cooking a few minutes only: too prolonged cooking may toughen them.

Serve them with their butter, or with that butter mixed with a little Sauce Béchamel (see page 8), to which you may, if you prefer, have added some heavy cream.

POIREAUX
[Leeks]

These are called in France *les asperges du pauvre* ("the asparagus of the poor") because when stewed and cooled they can be eaten, like asparagus, with one's fingers and vinaigrette or oil. Their strong odor while cooking *is* a drawback.

POIREAUX BRAISÉS
[Braised Leeks]

Cut off the green portion and the roots, and wash the white remain‑ der under the cold water tap, parting the leaves to make sure there is no sand or earth hidden there.

Put the leeks in a heavy cocotte with 2 or 3 spoonfuls of butter and enough chicken bouillon to come halfway up the leeks. Cover and set on high heat to bring to a boil; then reduce the heat to boil very gently for 35 minutes.

Remove to a hot plate with a skimmer. Boil down the liquor, *if necessary*, to make a sauce with which to serve them. A little Sauce Béchamel (see page 8) or Sauce Espagnole (see page 3) mixed with it is an improvement.

FLAMICHE AUX POIREAUX
[Leek Pie or Tart]

Cut ½ pound leeks, very finely, across—using only the white part —and sauté in 4 spoonfuls of butter on medium heat for 15 minutes, *without browning at all.* Add the same quantity (not weight) of flour that you used of butter, sprinkling it over the leeks. After a few minutes, add warm milk, sufficient to make a thick béchamel (about 1¾ cups). Season with very little salt, white pepper, and grated nut' meg. Cover and set aside in a warm spot.

Cut up 3 ounces of smoked bacon in small dice (proportion of bacon to leeks should be about 1 to 3). Throw the dice into cold water to cover; bring this water to a boil, and boil for 5 minutes. Drain the bacon well, and add it to the leeks in their sauce. Mix well to dis' tribute the bacon.

Turn the mixture, which should be quite thick, into a baked pie shell. Set in a 350° F. oven for 10 minutes, just to warm (if the shell has already baked a deep brown, which is an error, shorten to 5 minutes).

LAITUE
[Lettuce]

(For lettuce as salad, see page 253.)

In summer, when lettuce abounds, it can be an excellent cooked vegetable.

LAITUE BRAISÉE
[Braised Lettuce]

Choose the tougher kind with very green leaves and a good stem. Cut this off without going so far as to dismember the entire head. Wash the whole head under the cold water tap and make sure there are no intruders.

Tie 3 heads of lettuce together with kitchen or butcher's string, 3 or 4 times around: the object being to cook the stem part more than the leaftips. Plunge the heads, stem end down, into a saucepan with lightly salted water boiling furiously. Count 7 minutes after it boils again, then lift the heads to a large bowl filled with cold water. Turn the cold water tap on to this water—not hitting the lettuce—until no warmth is left in the heads.

Remove the strings and separate the heads. Drain them, squeeze them between your hands to get the water out, and then fold them into rectangular shapes.

Cover the bottom of a cocotte with bacon rind (fat side down), 1/2 cup chopped onions, 1/2 cup cored, chopped carrots, and 1/3 cup chopped bacon. Put the lettuce in the cocotte, cover, and set on medium heat for 10 or 15 minutes.

Add a mixture of beef consommé and water (50/50) just to cover the lettuce (about 1 cup in all). Add 1 or 2 spoonfuls of melted butter, pouring it slowly all over. Place a sheet of buttered waxed paper on the lettuce, and cover the cocotte with its lid. Set in a 325° F. oven to simmer for 1 hour, then if, on inspection, the lettuce seems undercooked, cover again and prolong the cooking for 30 minutes.

Lift the packets of lettuce to a large colander, and press them lightly to squeeze out the excess juice. Arrange them nicely on a hot serving dish, and cover.

Reduce the cooking liquor to the amount desired to pour over them as a sauce; bind this with a little fresh butter (about 3 spoonfuls), and, when thick, spoon over the packets of lettuce.

CHAMPIGNONS
[Mushrooms]

The white, round-headed mushroom cultivated in France in underground establishments is the principal variety that interests the cook for the multiplicity of its uses in garnishing meats and fish: it is called in France *champignon de couche*. It is, of course, cultivated in all civilized countries.

CHAMPIGNONS DE COUCHE (or DE PARIS) POUR GARNITURES
[Mushrooms for Garnishings]

The standard method requires peeling by rotating the head against the knife held in the right hand; but many experienced cooks protest that this is sheer waste and insist that all you need do after washing the mushrooms and snipping off the root end is to rub them with a lemon cut in half—and not to put them in water.

When, let us say, you have what both your hands can hold of mushrooms and you have trimmed and washed them and rubbed them with lemon, put them in a smallish saucepan with a wineglass full of cold water, 2 spoonfuls of butter, a good pinch of salt, 3 or 4 peppercorns, and the juice of half a lemon. Set it on high heat, and, as soon as it boils, moderate the heat but have it continue boiling, *covered*, for 8 minutes.

Withdraw the pan from the heat and let the mushrooms cool in their liquor, which can be put away for sauces, especially Sauce Poulette (see page 7). The mushrooms can be used whole or sliced for garnishing meat dishes.

CHAMPIGNONS DE COUCHE SAUTÉS
[Sautéed Mushrooms]

After paring and washing, dry the mushrooms with paper toweling and slice them downward through the stem.

Throw them into hot clarified butter (see page 10), season with salt and white pepper, turn with a spatula, and withdraw from the heat after 10 minutes. Sprinkle with chopped parsley and chives and give them another turn of a minute over the heat.

Serve on buttered toast or on top of a grilled steak.

TARTELETTES DE CHAMPIGNONS
[Mushroom Tartlets]

These can be made with any edible mushroom.

Fill baked, empty, pie-pastry tartlets with sautéed mushrooms well mixed with Sauce Béchamel (see page 8), Sauce Espagnole (see page 3), or (better) Sauce Poulette (see page 7). Heat them in a 300° F. oven for 10 minutes.

They can accompany a veal or chicken dish.

MORILLES
[Morels]

Considered by many as the most flavorful of mushrooms, and here much recommended, these are obtainable in Paris mainly in the dried form. However, after soaking in lukewarm water for an hour they swell and then can be cooked like fresh ones very satisfactorily. The water they are soaked in has some flavor but is generally full of sand and had better be thrown away. The *morels*, as they are rightly called in English, can be sautéed in butter like Champignons de Couche, but they are best in a chicken pie (see page 199).

CÈPES

This wild mushroom found in the woods (*Boletus edulis*) is greatly prized in France. As it is the only nonpoisonous of the "boleti," it is not recommended that any but the highly specialized experts pick them for the table. Preserved and sold in tins, when these are of recent packing, they can be prepared as follows.

CÈPES À LA BORDELAISE
[*Wild Mushrooms Bordeaux Style*]

Wipe the mushrooms dry. Slice them not too fine and sauté them in hot olive oil. Season them with salt and white pepper, and when they begin to brown throw in some chopped shallots and twice as much of white bread crumbs. Squeeze the juice of half a lemon on them; add enough Sauce Espagnole (see page 3), according to the quantity of *cèpes*, to garnish them, and a springling of finely chopped parsley.

CÈPES À LA CRÈME
[*Cèpes in Cream Sauce*]

Chop an onion and "melt" it in clarified butter (see page 10) without coloring. Meanwhile, wipe dry the *cèpes* and sauté them in clarified butter as well, but without browning them. Combine the two and dust them with enough all-purpose flour to make a binding, after cooking and stirring, with heavy cream. The sauce should boil with the mushrooms and the onion for 2 or 3 minutes, while you stir constantly: its color should be as white as possible.

N.B. Quantities depend on how many *cèpes* you are dealing with.

GIROLLES, PIEDS DE MOUTON, TROMPETTES DE LA MORT
[Chanterelles, "Sheep's Feet," "Trumpets of Death"]

The first are the best of this selection: they are orange-yellow and should be firm and large; otherwise they are not recommended. They require very careful washing and cleaning before sautéing in clarified butter (see page 10), and they must not be overcooked or nothing much will be left of them; but they are one of the most flavorful. The other two are not very attractive, but the last named, although black, repulsive in name and appearance, does have a truffle flavor. Sautéing is the method recommended, preferably in hot oil and sprinkled at serving with finely chopped chives and parsley. All these mushrooms, of course, should be seasoned with salt and white pepper.

OIGNONS
[Onions]

To mitigate the unpleasant effect of onion peeling on the tear ducts, conduct this operation near the sink, where you should run the cold water tap: silly as it may sound, this affords some relief to all except the most sensitive. To peel very little onions, plunge them into boiling water for 1 minute and lift them immediately with a skimmer: the peel will come off fairly easily.

PETITS OIGNONS GLACÉS
[Small Glazed Onions]

These should be the size of a boy's marble.

FOR LIGHT SAUCES: If they are to accompany dishes with white or very light-colored sauces, prepare as follows:

Peel them as indicated just above, and put them in cold chicken bouillon just to cover, with butter (4 spoonfuls per cup of bouillon). Bring to a boil, and then reduce the heat to keep boiling very gently —if the onions are very fresh, just barely simmer—for 35 minutes to 1 hour, uncovered.

They are ready when the liquor has all but disappeared by evapora-tion. They must not be brown.

FOR BROWN SAUCES: If the onions are intended to go with brown sauces, prepare as follows:

Put them in a saucepan with clarified butter (see page 10). Season with salt, white pepper, and a little confectioners' sugar (for the caramel), then sauté for about 20 minutes, moving the onions about with a spoon (be very careful not to tear the white outer layer).

OIGNONS FARCIS
[Stuffed Onions]

The onions for this dish should be medium sized and rather pointed (not flat), because they must be cut at two-thirds their height to hollow them out for the stuffing.

Cut them across thus at the stem end, which should be fatter, and just pare them at the other end, cutting a cross-shaped incision on that surface so they will sit up squarely and absorb the cooking juices.

Put them in a saucepan—standing side by side and close together, holding each other upright—and pour boiling water on them. Set the pan on high heat, add salt (1 spoonful for a dozen onions), and bring to a boil, then reduce the heat to keep the water simmering, un-covered, for 30 minutes. Lift the onions carefully with a skimmer, and put in another saucepan with cold water—and let cold water run into the pan until the onions are cold.

Scoop out the inner layers of the onions, leaving enough outer shell or wall to hold them upright when stuffed. Mince very finely what you have scooped out and mix it with finely ground meat of any kind, well seasoned with salt and pepper and aromatic herbs (thyme, bay leaf in powder form, powdered sage if the meat is pork). Fill the cavity you made in each onion with this mixture, and sprinkle on top of each a little confectioners' sugar.

Arrange the stuffed onions on a well-buttered ovenproof dish, and set in a 300° F. oven for 10 minutes.

Serve with a little Sauce Espagnole (see page 3) poured on top of each stuffed onion.

N.B. The stuffing can be as varied as you wish: cooked rice with chopped tomatoes well squeezed of their water and lightly sautéed, or with sweet peppers, or finely minced, sautéed mushrooms, etc.

PURÉE D'OIGNONS SOUBISE
[Onion Puree]

The onions should preferably be white and not yellow inside—and never red, as the puree should be as white as possible when finished.

Peel the onions and cut into thin slices. Throw these into plenty of boiling water and boil for 8 minutes, then drain them in a strainer. Put them in a cocotte with butter (4 spoonfuls of butter to 1 pound of onions) and "melt" them—i.e., soften them—on medium to low heat, stirring often, without letting them color at all, for about 5 minutes. Add ⅔ cup of chicken bouillon and set, covered, in a 300° F. oven for 40 minutes.

Lift out the onions with a skimmer (reserve the broth for other preparations) and mix with an equal amount of thick Sauce Béchamel (see page 8). Strain this mixture through a fairly fine mesh into a wide, thick skillet and set on high heat to dry out the puree, stirring and scraping constantly for just a few minutes, without letting any browning occur.

Remove from the heat and add as much warm, heavy cream as you can without making the puree liquid (it must not be soupy, but rather like very soft mashed potatoes).

SALSIFIS
[Oyster Plant]

Either peel with a swiveled peeler very delicately, or scrape off the skin. Cut off and discard tops and roots, and immediately throw the retained portions into a bowl of water with several spoonfuls of strong vinegar to keep them from turning dark.

Take out two or three pieces at a time and cut them in strips about 2 inches long and ¼ to ½ inch thick. Throw these into a pan of lightly salted boiling water. In the boiling water, dissolve some all-purpose flour (1 spoonful for 2 quarts of water). Cover the saucepan, regulate the heat to keep the water boiling, and cook for 1½ to 2 hours: when you find the vegetable tender to the tooth, it is done.

It can then be sautéed in butter and seasoned with onion salt and white pepper; or it can be served in a hot Sauce Béchamel (see page 8) or Sauce Mornay (see page 9), or even a Sauce Mousseline-Moutarde (see page 10). It can also be served cold with Vinaigrette (see page 11) or with a green salad.

PETITS POIS
[Green Peas]

These should, of course, be very young and fresh. If the shells are spotted, the peas, as a rule, are tough. If in the lot you buy there are some that are large when shelled, reserve these for a soup or a puree, and cook only the little ones.

PETITS POIS À LA FRANÇAISE
[Green Peas Braised with Lettuce]

For 6 persons

Pare and wash a head of green lettuce, then cut it in two, length-wise. Peel 8 or 10 small onions (they need not be diminutive), then put them, along with the lettuce, 4 cups of freshly shelled small green peas, 6 spoonfuls of butter, and ½ cup cold water, into a heavy enameled cast-iron cocotte with a well-fitting lid (preferably hollowed in the middle).

Add a good pinch of salt, another of sugar, and a few stalks of parsley, then cover tightly and set on high heat. As soon as steam leaks out, reduce the heat to medium. Then, if you have a lid with a hollow center, put a few pieces of ice on it: the steam will cease to come out but will condense on the underside of the lid and rain down on the peas. (If you do not have a lid with a hollow center, place a soup plate right side up in its stead: it does very well.) As soon as the ice turns into hot water on the lid, remove it with a spoon (or, better, with a giant dropper) and replace it with fresh ice, and so on until 35 minutes have elapsed.

Uncover the cocotte. The peas should be done and there should be a very small amount of liquid. Remove peas, lettuce, and onions to a warm saucepan and cover. (If, because of the moisture from the lettuce, there appears to be too much liquid, reduce it by boiling.) Bind the cooking liquor with fresh butter lightly creamed with a little all-purpose flour, and put the peas back into it.

Serve the lettuce and the onions in equal portions, with the peas around them.

N.B. Peas thus cooked and left over can be used on artichoke hearts as a meat dish accompaniment: the tag *à la Clamart* is then tacked on.

PETITS POIS À LA FLAMANDE
[*Green Peas and Carrots*]

When you do not have many peas, this recipe may be useful.

Take small young carrots—about one-third the amount of your shelled peas. Scrape or peel the carrots delicately, and stew them in butter with very little water, salt, and sugar until almost done.

Meanwhile, cook the peas in the same way and with the same seasoning and to the same degree as the carrots, then combine the peas and carrots, and finish by cooking them, covered, for 30 minutes.

Bind the sauce with a little fresh butter.

PIMENTS DOUX ou POIVRONS
[*Sweet Peppers*]

To peel, put the peppers in the oven, on a low grill on a pie plate, at 350° F.—in a few minutes the skin is ready to come off. Or you can plunge them in boiling water for 1 minute and get the same result. *They must be peeled while hot.*

If they are to be stuffed, cut the stem end across, after the peppers have cooled, and dig out the seeds without piercing the flesh. Stuff them with finely ground, cooked meat and onion, spiced with pepper, garlic, and herbs, all mixed up with boiled rice and Sauce Espagnole (see page 3) that has been cut with tomato paste by one-fourth its volume. (This is *not* "La Grande Cuisine"!)

POMMES DE TERRE
[Potatoes]

POMMES DE TERRE BOUILLIES
[Boiled Potatoes]

Even the simple process of boiling potatoes must be done carefully.

No potato should be bigger than what you can hold in the palm of your hand. Peel them and, as each is peeled, put it immediately into cold water. Drop the peeled potatoes into salted water (1 spoon-ful per 2 quarts) that is boiling furiously and boil them for 25 minutes (less if *new*) and not more, and drain immediately.

POMMES DE TERRE CHÂTEAUBRIAND
[Sautéed Potatoes]

Choose potatoes of the same size, about that of a large egg, and peel them carefully so that they present a smooth surface. As you peel them, put them in cold water.

Bring a saucepan of salted water (1/2 tablespoon of rock salt per quart) to a furious boil. Throw the potatoes in, cover, and regulate the heat to keep boiling for 15 minutes. Drain them and *dry* them.

Put enough clarified butter (see page 10) in a skillet to cover its bottom amply, and place on medium heat. When the butter is beginning to turn yellow, throw the dried potatoes in and brown them on all sides, shaking the pan and also turning the potatoes over with a wooden spoon. Lift them with a skimmer onto a piece of brown wrapping paper to remove any fat on their surface.

Serve on a hot dish. A little fine table salt may be sprinkled over them.

POMMES DE TERRE SOUFFLÉES
[Souffléed Potatoes]

Cut the potatoes with a sharp knife into regular blocks and then into slices ⅛ inch thick, with parallel sides.

Fill two large saucepans with cooking oil up to 2 inches of their brim. Heat one to 225° F. and the other to 425° F. Put the potato slices (they must be dry) into the *less hot* oil, putting them in one by one so that they will not stick together. As soon as the slices rise to the surface, remove them with a skimmer and put them into the *hotter* oil. Let them swell, and then remove them with a skimmer (keep the skimmer in the hot oil so that it remains hot).

Put the blown-up potatoes on a piece of brown paper to drain, and then sprinkle them with a little fine salt. Cover them on a hot plate until they are served.

N.B. Restaurants have great advantages: large basins of hot oil and *constant practice!*

GRATIN DAUPHINOIS
[Scalloped Potatoes with Cream]

Slice peeled potatoes very fine, and throw the slices into a bowl of cold water.

Butter an ovenproof china pie plate. Arrange the potato slices around the bottom, each slightly riding on its neighbor and in concentric circles. Sprinkle this layer lightly with onion salt and white pepper, and repeat the same operation, layer upon layer, until the dish is full. Distribute small pats of butter on top, and then pour in as much heavy cream as the dish will hold.

Put in a 350° F. oven for 40 minutes, or until the surface is nicely browned.

N.B. It is not recommended that you add grated cheese or beaten egg, as some great authorities prescribe; but you may, of course, try that if you wish.

POMMES DE TERRE DUCHESSE
[Mashed Potatoes for Garnishings]

Potatoes prepared this way are especially good and attractive for rings around a meat or fish dish in the center of an ovenproof platter.

Choose large Idaho or similar potatoes. Wash well and dry without peeling, then roll in cooking oil, put in a roasting pan in a 400° F. oven, and bake for 50 to 60 minutes.

Cut each potato open and scoop out the pulp. Mash it thoroughly, using any power tool you have handy, so that there will be absolutely no lumps (putting through a colander or strainer is advised). Sprinkle with fine salt and white pepper to taste. Mix thoroughly with butter (4 spoonfuls per 2 pounds of potatoes) and then with beaten egg yolks (5 per 2 pounds).

The ring around the oven dish can be squeezed out of a pastry bag or distributed with a spoon and in patterns of your fancy. The surface should be lightly sprinkled with melted butter and the dish put in 350° F. oven until the ring is nicely browned. It is best to add the meat or fish in the center after this, just before serving.

POMMES DE TERRE À LA LYONNAISE
[Lyonnaise Potatoes]

Boil your potatoes as indicated on page 238. Meanwhile, sauté about one-quarter as much onion (finely sliced) in clarified butter (see page 10) until golden. Cut the potatoes in 1/4-inch slices and mix them with the onions. Sauté them together.

Before serving, sprinkle the surface with finely chopped parsley and white pepper.

QUENELLES DE POMMES DE TERRE
[*Potato Quenelles*]

Prepare potatoes à la *Duchesse* (see above) and mix them very thoroughly with one-third their volume of Pâte à Choux (see page 275). Shape them like little croquettes with a spoon and drop them into boiling salted water. Lift them with a skimmer to a warm buttered dish as they come up. Arrange them side by side, sprinkle them with finely grated Parmesan cheese and a little melted butter, and set them in a 350° oven just to brown.

Serve lightly sprinkled with butter melted with finely chopped parsley.

LES FRITES
[*"French Fries"*]

In Paris bistros the words *pommes de terre* are understood when a client orders *des frites* with his steak—in fact, *les frites* come automatically with it. The peeled potatoes are trimmed into blocks, sliced about $\frac{1}{4}$ inch thick and $2\frac{1}{8}$ inches long, and thrown into a basin full of very hot oil. When well browned, they are removed to dry, sprinkled with salt, and served.

OSEILLE
[*Sorrel*]

This is best when it is tender and the acid tang is less pronounced. Fold the leaves and tear off the nervature, then wash carefully.

PURÉE D'OSEILLE
[*Puree of Sorrel*]

Put the sorrel in a thick (to help prevent burning) saucepan or cocotte with $\frac{1}{2}$ glass of water and 4 spoonfuls of butter for 2 pounds of sorrel. Set on high heat for 10 minutes, then reduce the heat to medium while you turn over the leaves to cook them evenly.

In 15 or 20 minutes they will have turned a grayish olive green. Stir them vigorously over high heat to reduce the juice to a creamy consistency, then remove from the heat. Add (for each pound of sorrel) 1 whole egg (well beaten) and 2 spoonfuls of fresh butter, and stir thoroughly. Verify the seasoning, and sprinkle a pinch of granulated sugar and another of white pepper over all. Stir again and serve.

N.B. This puree cooks down so that 4 pounds of fresh leaves serve no more than 8 people.

It is excellent in combination with fish, and is used in finishing the cooking of filets and John Dory, brill, and sole.

ÉPINARDS
[Spinach]

Nip off the stems and discard all damaged leaves. Wash in plenty of water two or three times, and make sure there is no mud or grit on the leaves.

ÉPINARDS EN BRANCHES
[Boiled Spinach]

Cook in a small amount of boiling water with salt and bicarbonate of soda—1 teaspoon of the first and a good pinch of the second. (The water need be not more than 1/2 glassful for 1 1/2 pounds of leaves.) Stir and turn the leaves over to cook evenly. In 10 minutes they should be done. Do *not* overcook them.

Drain them and squeeze the water out of them gently, just so that they will not make a puddle on the plate, and serve with pats of butter on top and a sprinkling of white pepper.

ÉPINARDS À LA CRÈME
[Creamed Spinach]

Cook as above.

Chop very fine and force through a strainer, then dry on high heat, while you stir vigorously, with 4 spoonfuls of butter per pound of leaves. Mix well with heavy cream, a pinch of nutmeg, and a pinch of granulated sugar: the finished product should be not too creamy.

Heat before serving.

N.B. To doll the dish up, fry triangles of white bread (2 inches at the base) in butter and stick them, point down, on the mound of spinach on the dish. Also, chop up finely a hard-boiled egg and sprinkle it over the mound.

CRÊPES ET SUBRICS D'ÉPINARDS
[Spinach Crêpes and Subrics for Garnish]

After drying cooked spinach as in the recipe just above, mix with an equal amount of the mixture for Crêpes Mar'Jeanne (see page 41). Season the mixture fairly highly, then either sauté like an ordinary pancake or fry it by spoonfuls in clarified butter (½ inch deep in the pan) (see page 10).

In the latter case, the mixture should be solid enough to hold its shape; it is pushed off the spoon with the index finger into the hot butter, turned over after a minute, and removed with a skimmer when golden brown.

N.B. The spoonfuls, termed *subrics*, are served as garnishes for meats.

SOUFFLÉ D'ÉPINARDS
[Spinach Soufflé]

Dry the spinach after cooking, as in the recipe above for Épinards à la Crème. Add 3 spoonfuls of it and 1 spoonful of finely minced cooked ham to the heavy béchamel base of a soufflé (see page 38). After thorough mixing, add 4 beaten eggs, separated as in basic soufflé recipe, and bake 25 minutes.

The addition of 1 or 2 spoonfuls of grated Gruyère cheese is acceptable.

PATATES or PATATES DOUCES
[*Sweet Potatoes*]

The first Spaniards who brought back sweet potatoes from the Caribbean islands called them, in imitation of the name the natives gave them, *batatas*. This was later confused with *patatas*, the name given by Spaniards to the potatoes that were and are known by the Andean natives as *papas*. Sweet potatoes are known in tropical South America as *camotes*.

All good American cookery books have excellent recipes for cooking sweet potatoes. Perhaps the best way is to wash them un-peeled, dry them thoroughly, brush them with melted bacon fat and bake them in a 375° F. oven for 1 hour. Remove them and cut them down the middle, salt and pepper them lightly, and mash them in their skins with plenty of butter.

BLETTES or BETTES
[*Swiss Chard*]

The variety grown in France that one sees most in the markets has fine large leaves and wide central nervatures. The latter are carefully —painstakingly—peeled—i.e., the stringy layers are removed and only the tender hearts are left to cook in *very* slightly salted boiling water for 45 minutes. Drained, they are spread on a dish with a few spoonfuls of Sauce Béchamel (see page 8) or Mornay (see page 9), layer upon alternating layer of sauce. The leaves may be cooked like a rough kind of spinach or added to vegetable soups.

TOMATES
[*Tomatoes*]

Tomatoes should be peeled by plunging them into boiling water 15 seconds on one side and 15 seconds the other: the skin comes off easily while hot. They should be sliced and the seeds should be carefully removed and discarded. Better still: they should be quartered, seeded, and gently squeezed to remove the water, which is tasteless. The real tomato juice is in the pulp.

TOMATES FARCIES
[*Stuffed Tomatoes*]

Do not peel the tomatoes. Either cut them in half or cut off enough of the tops to allow stuffing.

Scoop out the center pulp (be very careful not to pierce the skins), then squeeze gently upside down to get rid of the water, and dig out the seeds. Set on a lightly oiled roasting pan (or on a cookie sheet on a roasting pan) and put in 350° F. oven for 5 minutes.

Take out, and stuff with ground, cooked meat of any kind mixed with boiled rice and chopped sautéed mushrooms and onions, seasoned with salt, pepper, and basil (the herb that marries best with tomatoes); or stuff with scrambled eggs, mixed or not with minced ham; or stuff with any cooked vegetable, mixed or not with Sauce Mornay (see page 9); or stuff with bread crumbs, cheese . . . and so *ad infinitum*.

The stuffing should be topped with a little butter, and the tomatoes then baked for 10 minutes at 350° F.

TOMATOES SAUTÉES
[*Sautéed Tomatoes*]

Peel the tomatoes, cut them in half, seed them, squeeze them gently of their water, and set them upside down on a grill or flat sieve to drain for a few minutes.

Chop up a handful or two of fresh basil leaves (if not available, have on hand dried basil) and heat clarified butter (see page 10) or, better, fruity olive oil, and slide the tomatoes, cut side up, into it. Move the pan back and forth for 10 minutes, then remove the tomatoes to a hot serving platter. Season them with salt, pepper, a small pinch of granulated sugar, and plenty of basil.

Dust the hot butter or oil with white bread crumbs and pour it over the tomatoes.

VARIANTS ARE: *Tomates à la lyonnaise* and *Tomates à la proven-çale*, the first requiring sautéed onions; and the second, chopped-up garlic.

TRUFFES
[*Truffles*]

Although there are "white" truffles (their color is not pure white but rather creamy gray) in southeastern France, these are character-istic rather of northwestern Italy. So, here only the black truffles are considered. Today they are all but prohibitively expensive in Paris. Truffles are found in England as well, but not in the abundance of France; and there is no reason, apparently, why they should not be produced in the United States—hence the following recipe for the preparation of the fresh raw underground fungus.

As the truffle grows underground, it is covered with earth, which when largely clay is difficult to remove. Therefore, put it in lukewarm water and work off the earth between your fingers, changing the water as needed. When you can no longer remove the clay that sticks to the minute clefts on the surface, rub it gently with a hard vegetable brush free of any odor. When no particle of earth clings any longer to the truffle, put it into a saucepan with chopped onions, chopped carrots (peeled and cored), sautéed lightly in clarified butter (see page 10). Moisten with Madeira, Champagne, or a great white Burgundy or Bordeaux (in this order of preference), and season with salt, white pepper, and a small bay leaf. Cover tightly, interposing a piece of buttered paper under the lid. Cook on low heat for 15 to 20 minutes, maintaining a steady but moderate boiling.

Remove the truffle, without any trace of the other components, to a warm plate or saucer and cover. Strain the contents of the saucepan through fine mesh and mix with a little Sauce Madère (see page 5); pour this over the truffle the moment of serving.

N.B. In order to impart the truffle flavor to meats, it is necessary to introduce the truffle, whole or in pieces, *deeply* into the meats. The slice of truffle under the skin of a bird is almost nothing but show.

TRUFFES BLANCHES
[Fresh White Truffles]

If you have the good fortune to come by this great delicacy, which is at its best in the Piedmont in early September, slice it very fine, combine it with equally finely sliced white mushrooms, and dress the two with fine olive oil and lemon juice, a little salt, and white pepper. Eat them thus, raw, as an hors d'oeuvre.

NAVETS
[White Turnips]

Turnips are an excellent addition to most stews.

In the spring they are sold in Paris with their fresh green leaves —which are delicious boiled in salted water, after being stripped of their central nervatures, for 30 minutes, served with fresh butter, or in vegetable soups.

Root and stem centers should be cut off. Also, unless the turnips are very young and tender, care must be taken to strip the rather thick peel off.

NAVETS GLACÉS
[Glazed Turnips]

Put turnips into salted water with a few white peppercorns and 1 spoonful of butter (for a handful of turnips), bring to a boil, cover, and cook at a steady boil for 45 minutes.

Remove the lid and reduce the juice until the turnips are "glazed."

Alternatively, they can be mashed into a purée, with some butter being added as the purée is being dried out over high heat.

COURGETTES
[Zucchini]

These need not be peeled, but they must be carefully washed and, if necessary, scraped wherever damaged. The two ends should be snipped off.

COURGETTES SAUTÉES
[Sautéed Zucchini]

Cut the zucchini across into 1½-inch sections.

Cook these, without water, in butter (preferably clarified, see page 10), or olive oil, with salt, white pepper, a bay leaf, and a very small bit of garlic, covered and on low medium heat, for 40 minutes. Turn them over a few times.

COURGETTES FARCIES
[Stuffed Zucchini]

After washing well and drying cut zucchini lengthwise in half. With the point of a small knife, all over the cut surface, make little chequered incisions in the flesh without piercing the skin, then, in a pan big enough to hold the zucchini easily, pour enough olive oil to cover the surface amply. Place on moderate heat and put the zucchini in the hot oil, cut side down. If the flesh begins to brown in 10 minutes, moderate the heat so that it will be cooked in 25 minutes.

Lift the zucchini out with a skimmer and let cool enough for the next step: scraping off the flesh without spoiling the skin.

Mash the flesh with a little tomato puree and bread crumbs. Season with onion salt and white pepper (plus, if you wish, garlic powder in moderation; also, if you like, you may add finely grated cheese), then stuff the skins with the mixture and place them, stuffed side up, on an ovenproof dish. Brown them in the oven.

Sprinkle a little chopped parsley on them, and serve.

CHAPTER 21

Dried Beans, Lentils, and Peas

HARICOTS ROUGES ET BLANCS
[Red and White Beans]

For 6 persons

Never soak beans overnight: this causes the beginning of fer-mentation, spoiling the flavor and your digestion.

Soak 1½ cups dried beans for 2 hours in lukewarm water—just a little warmer than your hand—with a good pinch of bicarbonate of soda, and change this water after 1 hour. Then put them in a thick cocotte to ensure gradual heating, with a rasher of smoked bacon, an onion stuck with a small whole clove, a bay leaf, a few thyme leaves, 1 teaspoon of salt, and a few white peppercorns. Fill with *cold* water to cover by more than ½ inch. Turn on the heat very gently, so that boiling will not start before 30 minutes or so, and skim when the water begins to boil. If after 30 minutes there is no sign of boiling, increase the heat gradually. Boil steadily, covered, for 1½ to 2 hours, depending on the freshness of the beans. From time to time scrape the bottom of the cocotte with a spoon to make sure nothing has "caught" there.

N.B. If your water is hard, add a good pinch of bicarbonate to it in the cooking.

LE CASSOULET
*[Beans Baked with Sausage, Duck, and Goose Preserves,
"as prepared in Castelnaudary"]*

This dish from the Languedoc, in southern France, must have garlic; so, those who do not care for its redolence had better not try it. Secondly, its mainstay is beans, dry white beans. Thirdly, as you will see at a glance, it is a dish for strong digestions.

For 8 persons

Take 3 cups of dry white beans of the current year and soak them for 2 hours in lukewarm water (with a pinch of bicarbonate of soda, as an extra to the recipe). In a thick, enameled iron cocotte with a nicely fitting lid put 6 ounces of fresh pork fat rind with 2 cups of cold water and bring it to a boil gradually; simmer it for 5 minutes, then remove the rind, throw away the water, and rinse the cocotte well. Put back the rind, fat side down, and add 1 peeled onion stuck with 2 whole cloves, 1 spoonful of pork lard or goose fat, and the beans after they have duly soaked. Season with ½ teaspoon of salt, cover with cold water, and bring to a boil very gradually. Skim off the gray froth that comes up, replacing with hot water what you remove, and cover, leaving a chink for steam to escape and regulating the heat to prevent boiling over.

After 1 or 1½ hours of boiling, add 4 ounces of large garlic sausage and 1 garlic clove (cut in tiny pieces), 1 sprig of fresh thyme (or ¼ teaspoon dried), and a bay leaf.

Meanwhile, heat some pork lard in a frying pan and brown a duck on all sides; then cut it up in quarters, plus the bony back (also used for its juice). Bury these pieces in the beans, taking care not to mash the latter. Cover and continue cooking on medium heat. After 1 hour of gentle boiling, the beans should be soft but whole; then add a piece of Confit d'Oie (see page 180) and cook for 1 hour, covered, in a 350° F. oven. (If then you find the sauce too thin you may thicken it by dissolving some white bread [without crust] with a small quantity of the liquor.)

LENTILLES
[*Lentils*]

First spread the lentils out on a piece of white paper to detect bits of stones, gravel, etc. Soak and cook like Haricots Rouges et Blancs, above.

POIS CASSÉS
[*Split Peas*]

As these have no skin, they need less water to start with: it can easily be replenished, boiling, as needed. Otherwise, soak them and cook them like lentils.

CHAPTER 22

Salads

SALADES VERTES
[Green Salads]

IN FRANCE tender and very green lettuce is preferred to the green-white-yellow iceberg lettuce of the United States. Besides the six or seven varieties of lettuce obtainable in Paris according to the season, there are escarole, chicory, dandelion, and lamb lettuce (*mâche*), some of which, though, are not really green. All these are dressed with Vinaigrette (see page 11).

Nowadays, under American influence, green salads are often served with cheese in private houses; but this is not a French custom. Simon-pure green salads are not customarily served as hors d'oeuvres as in Italy—a most recommendable habit—although Salade Niçoise (as given below) is.

As for the addition of mustard to *sauce vinaigrette*, all that need be said is that it is not according to Hoyle: besides vinegar and oil, salt, and pepper, the sole ingredients permitted are herbs, such as tarragon, chives, chervil, and parsley. Garlic powder or garlic salt may be added, or the bowl may be rubbed with garlic (which is removed).

The proportions of oil and vinegar are not rigidly canonical. It is amusing to recall that four men are needed to make a good *vinaigrette*: a miser with the vinegar, a spendthrift with the oil, a sage with the salt, and a madman with the pepper.

Finally, lettuce leaves are *not* cut with a knife, but are invariably pulled apart to be put in the salad bowl.

N.B. Lamb lettuce requires great care in washing, as it contains a great deal of sand hidden in the leaf stems, especially the smallest and tenderest, which should be taken apart and thoroughly washed, or you risk breaking a tooth.

SALADES DE LÉGUMES CUITS
[Salads of Cooked Vegetables]

Cooked beets, potatoes, celeriac, and green beans lend themselves to mixing with Vinaigrette (see page 11).

A good practice is to add the Vinaigrette to cooked potatoes while they are hot and just after you slice them: thus they absorb the flavor of the dressing much more than when they are cold.

For the cooking of beets, oven roasting is generally preferred to boiling, as any wound on the surface of the beet makes it bleed in the water: they need 1 hour or more, according to size, in a 325° F. oven, and should be peeled only after cooling.

Rubbing the salad bowl with garlic is recommended for cooked vegetable salad though not for delicate lettuce salad.

SALADE DE TOMATE, CONCOMBRE, CÉLERI
[Salad of Tomato, Cucumber, Celery]

Tomatoes should be peeled after immersion of 30 seconds in boiling water, while hot, then finely sliced with a very sharp knife (even better, with a razor) and cleaned of their seeds (which are indigestible).

Fresh basil leaves should be chopped up roughly and added to the Vinaigrette (see page 11).

Only young cucumbers with practically no seeds should be used in salad. In most instances they should be sliced fine and dusted with salt to lose their water for 1 hour on a soup plate, then wiped care' fully. (Some varieties of cucumbers, however, do not need this treatment.)

Celery should be carefully scraped of its strings and cut lengthwise in thin strips, then put into water with pieces of ice for an hour or so before serving.

SALADE NIÇOISE
[Combination Salad with Anchovies and Tuna,
Tomatoes and Olives]

Even in Nice there is considerable irregularity in this combination. Almost always tinned anchovies and tuna, olives and tomatoes enter into it, often supported by sweet red peppers (peeled and seeded), green beans, lettuce, and hard-boiled eggs, all well moistened with a Vinaigrette generously seasoned with garlic and herbs.

CHAPTER 23

The Cold Buffet

LA GALANTINE DE VOLAILLE
[*Galantine of Chicken*]

FOR THIS A PULLET of mature age is recommended, because the first requisite is a good, strong skin. It is possible if you are very dexterous to remove the skin whole, after drawing the pullet, by forcing your fingers with delicate persistence between the skin and the flesh of the bird, and save for a few minor cuts, such as at the wings, to pull the skin off as you would take a glove off inside out. However, for the impatient cook the usual method is to cut the skin straight down the back of the bird and then proceed to pull it free from the flesh.

The elements necessary are: cooked ham (5 to 6 ounces), fresh pork fat back (5 to 6 ounces), fresh lean pork (¾ pound to 1 pound), peeled pistachio nuts (a handful), a red cured tongue (5 to 6 ounces), the breasts of the pullet, half a wine glassful of Cognac and another of Madeira wine, and 2 or 3 truffles in slices: all the solids to be diced in 1½-inch pieces as neatly as possible, excepting the pistachio nuts and the truffles, and to be marinated in the Cognac and Madeira until you have prepared the following hash.

Cut up and then put through the fine plate of the meat grinder 1 pound of lean fresh pork, ¾ pound of fatter fresh pork, the meat of the pullet left after cutting away the breasts (but not the skins and gristly parts, which go to make the broth in which the galantine is cooked), the trimmings of the other meats, salt, pepper, and parsley.

Now the art is to combine the diced elements, plus the peeled pistachios and the sliced truffles, and the hash—which you have to do with your hands—so that when the galantine is cooked, cooled, and sliced it will present a pretty, mottled effect. To stuff the skin, then, if you have removed it whole, tie one end with several turns of string and stuff the mixture of hash and dice, etc., toward this end carefully but making it as compact as possible, until you reach the other end, which tie as well: you then have a fat sort of sausage of 3 to 4 inches in diameter. If you have cut the skin, distribute the composite stuffing as evenly as possible over the underside (or inside) of the skin, which you then wrap over it with an overlap and tie at both ends. Wrap this fat sausage up in turn—*and this applies to the first method of the uncut skin as well*—in a double fold of per' fectly clean cheesecloth that has been lightly buttered all over; tie it carefully, not too tightly but just to keep the package secure.

Deposit the galantine in a heavy enameled cast-iron cocotte of the proper dimensions to fit it fairly snugly, first laying down a layer of 4 or 5 pieces of bacon rind (fat side down), 3 each onions and carrots (chopped), a bay leaf and 1 sprig of fresh thyme (or ¼ teaspoon dried). Over the galantine and around it add the trimmings and bones of the pullet. Cover and let "sweat" over low heat for 15 minutes, then add enough dry white wine (about a bottle) to come up to half the girth of the galantine, and fill up with chicken broth (bouillon cubes are fine) to cover it by about 1 inch over. Increase the heat to bring the liquid to a boil and boil very gently, tightly covered, for 1 hour. Turn the galantine over completely with two spoons, not to damage the wrappings, and continue the gentle boiling for 1½ hours longer, tightly covered. Then remove the galantine to a plate to cool.

Strain the cooking liquor and let it cool, then measure it and add 1 ounce of unflavored powdered gelatin to 2½ cups of the liquor—

in that proportion. Rinse out the cocotte, put the gelatin and cooking liquor mixture in it on medium heat; stir constantly until it begins to boil, and then withdraw it from the heat. Remove the cheesecloth and strings from the galantine and lay it carefully in the cocotte with the *lukewarm* liquid, rolling it around it once or twice, for 30 minutes. Lift the galantine to a dish where it can cool completely (overnight or in the refrigerator), and strain the liquid into a wide, shallow pan to cool and solidify.

Before serving, set the galantine on a platter decorated with lettuce leaves, on them little piles of the solidified jelly cut up in small cubes.

N.B. Red cured tongue, called *langue écarlate* ("scarlet tongue") in French, is recommended because of its decorative color, but if not obtainable in the United States it can be substituted by red corned beef.

LE CHAUD-FROID DE VOLAILLE
[Cold Chicken in Cream Jelly]

Take a 3½-pound pullet, prepare and cook it just like Le Poulet au Pot (see page 169). Remove it to a plate (reserving the cooking liquor) and skin it entirely once it is cold. Cut away the legs and separate the drumsticks from the second joints. Cut away the wings and sever the tips off; they are not used in this preparation. Now carve the breasts out, each side, in one piece, taking as much meat as you can from the wishbone. Thus you will have 8 pieces, which you should trim to present no ragged edges. Set aside and cover.

Make a binding of 1 spoonful of butter and 1 spoonful of all-purpose flour, and dilute it with the strained cooking liquor before it browns: this must be done very gradually, and the result should be a whitish, creamy sauce. To this you add half a wineglassful of mushroom cooking liquor (see page 230). Set it on high heat, placing the saucepan so that it will boil at one place, thus facilitating skimming, which you perform for 20 minutes, adding as much dry white wine as you remove of broth—i.e., about ½ cup. Strain through fine mesh and keep warm, covered, stirring from time to time to prevent it forming a skin.

Meanwhile, beat lightly 3 egg yolks and mix them with ¾ cup of heavy cream. Reheat the sauce and add it, spoonful by spoonful, to the egg and cream mixture, without allowing to boil for a second; set aside and cover.

Now dissolve 1 ounce of unflavored powdered gelatin in a pint of half water–half white wine, bring it to a boil while stirring, and quickly remove it from the heat. Verify salt and pepper seasoning, cover, and let cool.

When the creamy sauce is cool, dip the pieces of cold chicken in it, gathering a good coating, and lay them nicely arranged on a cold platter with a thin slice of truffle on each piece. When the jelly begins to set, dip a brush in it—or even a spoon—and brush with it (or delicately pour over) the pieces of chicken to form a film over them. The platter may be put in the refrigerator for an hour or so to insure the setting of the jelly, but should be removed a good half-hour before serving to wear off the blighting cold. The dish should be decorated with lettuce leaves, etc.

ASPICS

These are jellies that contain meats and/or vegetables.

Dissolve unflavored powdered gelatin in half water–half dry white wine, bring to the boil while stirring, remove from the heat, and *let cool—but do not let set.*

Pour enough of it to make a ½-inch layer at the bottom of a platter, distribute there your cold cooked meats and/or vegetables in an attractive pattern, and pour the rest of the dissolved gelatin over it all.

Let set *without refrigeration*, thereby preventing the surface from hardening excessively. Then, if you must wait some time before serving, put in the refrigerator.

EGGS

OEUFS EN GELÉE
[Eggs in Jelly]

Coddled eggs and poached eggs are used for this preparation, the latter being preferable because they are easier to handle and make a better presentation.

Dissolve 1 ounce of unflavored powdered gelatine in 2 cups of half white wine–half water. Set on medium heat and gradually bring to a boil, while stirring. Withdraw from the heat and let it cool, but not set.

Meanwhile, poach your eggs (see page 30): for this quantity of jelly, up to 12, depending on the size of the molds.

Oil the inside of the molds with any edible oil. (Butter is not advisable, as it hardens too much in the refrigerator and makes unmolding difficult.) Pour a little cool jelly into each mold, just enough to form a film when cold and set. Put the molds in a cool place until the jelly sets *semihard*. (If the film of jelly at the bottom of the mold is allowed to become set or hard, the rest of the jelly will not stick to it when added later—and when you unmold your eggs they will fall apart. So, the trick is to have the film at the bottom still soft enough to coalesce with the rest of the jelly and to have the latter cool but liquid.)

If necessary, trim the eggs neatly with a knife or cookie cutter (there should be room all around the egg, when in the mold, for the jelly).

Place on the film of jelly at the bottom of each mold two crossed leaves of tarragon, or parsley, and a snippet of tomato to decorate it, and then put a poached egg in, pretty side down. Fill each mold with liquid jelly almost to the brim and top with a thin slice of ham. Then put the molds in the least cold portion of the refrigerator. To unmold, set the molds on a hot towel and have your platter or plates ready to receive the eggs turned right side up.

OEUFS À LA REINE
[*Eggs with Chaud-Froid Sauce*]

Poached eggs covered with *chaud-froid* sauce (see Chaud-Froid de Volaille, page 258) topped with a thin slice of truffle, painted over with jelly, exactly like the chicken, and sitting on a piece of ordinary white bread cut to the dimensions of the egg and generously buttered with foie gras puree or any well-seasoned chicken puree.

N.B. This dish could be a good afterthought of Chaud-Froid de Volaille.

OEUFS À LA NIÇOISE
[*Poached Eggs on Tomato, Garnished à la Niçoise*]

Poached eggs are placed on slices of tomato, decorated with Sauce Mayonnaise (see page 12) and surrounded by the elements of Salade Niçoise (see page 255) cut in minute pieces.

OEUFS DURS FARCIS
[*Stuffed Hard-Boiled Eggs*]

Warm the eggs in tepid water to prevent their bursting when boiled. A wire basket is recommended for convenience in lowering and then lifting them. Plunge them into boiling water. (If you put them in cold water and then bring them to the boil, you risk having them lopsided—i.e., the yolk not in the center of the white—which spoils the presentation. They must *boil* for 10 minutes. Do not overcook them: that spoils the flavor and the color of whites and yolks.

Put the eggs in cold water as soon as the 10 minutes of boiling are up, and then shell them and cut each one lengthwise in two. Take out the yolks and strain them through medium mesh (better than mashing, which makes them doughy), then mix with any fine puree—meat, vegetable, or fish. Refill the whites with the mixture.

Cold vegetables, such as asparagus tips, and a cold sauce, such as Sauce Gribiche (see page 12) or Sauce Mayonnaise (see page 12) should complete the offering.

FISH

POACHED SMALL FISH, SAUCE GRIBICHE

Poach any small fishes in a vinegar court-bouillon (see page 51) for 20 to 25 minutes. Let them cool, then serve them surrounded by parsley and lightly moistened with Sauce Gribiche (see page 12), which you also serve apart in a sauceboat. Place quartered lemons on the platter or plate.

RIVER OR BROOK TROUT IN JELLY

Poach river or brook trout in dry white wine with sliced onions, salt, and pepper for 20 minutes. Lift them to a grill over a dish to drain and cool.

Cool and strain the poaching liquid, then cut it with half the amount of water. In this liquid dissolve 1 spoonful of unflavored powdered gelatine and bring gradually to a boil. Remove from the heat, verify the seasoning, add a light sprinkling of dill weed, and let cool until lukewarm.

Line the fish side by side in a dish where they fit fairly snugly, and pour the liquid jelly over them to cover. Put in the refrigerator for 1 hour to set the jelly.

Decorate the edge of the dish with lemon quarters and serve.

SAUMON, BAR, OU CABILLAUD, SAUCE VERTE
[Salmon, Bass, or Fresh Cod With Green Mayonnaise]

For the sauce, see page 13. For poaching the fish, see page 50. As soon as the fish is cool enough to handle, remove the skin on the top side very carefully, avoiding damage to the flesh. The fish is to be presented with its head.

Wash some 20 tarragon leaves of about the same size, dip them in the court-bouillon of the fish, and lay them on top in a chevron pattern. With a cookie cutter, make little dots of peeled tomato and distribute them on this pattern.

Put 3 or 4 spoonfuls of the green mayonnaise in a pastry bag and decorate the fish with a snaky design. Present the rest of the sauce in a sauceboat.

BOEUF À LA MODE EN GELÉE
[Jellied Braised Beef]

Prepare Boeuf à la Mode as instructed on page 135.

At the end of the cooking, you will have a gelatinous broth.

If you wish to clarify it, decant it into another saucepan and, once it is cool, add 2 or 3 egg whites (lightly beaten), with their crushed shells. Bring to a boil gradually, stirring most of the time with a wire whisk, and boil very gently or (better) simmer for some 20 minutes, uncovered. A spoon passed along the surface to draw aside the light froth should now show the liquid below entirely clear. Pour the liquid into a conical ("Chinese") strainer lined with a double thickness of absolutely clean cheesecloth wrung out in tepid water, and let the liquor run through without any pressure.

Slice the beef neatly. Stack the slices, overlapping each other, in a dish deep enough to hold it and the liquid jelly, which you pour over the whole. The vegetables of the *boeuf à la mode* that have not disintegrated are ranged around the beef, but if none are presentable, cooked peas and minced carrots, alternating in small mounds, make a good decoration.

N.B. Keeping overnight in a not-too-cold part of the refrigerator improves this dish.

TERRINES

Terrines are often and erroneously called *pâtés* (in strictly correct usage, a *pâté* is a terrine with a crust of pastry). Terrines are preparations mainly of finely ground meat (beef, veal, pork, poultry, game, and even fish and shellfish).

FISH TERRINES

Mix a fine puree of any full-flavored fish with an equal quantity of a salt custard composition—e.g., 3 whole eggs, lightly beaten with salt and white pepper and a teaspoon of onion juice, and then mixed intimately with ¾ cup of cream—so that the two are completely amalgamated. Put the mixture into an earthenware or heavy enameled cast-iron cocotte of just the right capacity (allowing for a little swelling). Set this (covered with its lid) in a pan with boiling water up to two-thirds the height of the cocotte, and bake for 30 minues in 350° F. oven.

MEAT TERRINES

Grind the meat fine, after removing all gristle and nerves, then moisten with a little Cognac and a little port wine. Season quite highly with onion salt, ground pepper, nutmeg, and ground bay leaf and pack tight in a small earthenware or heavy enameled cast-iron cocotte lined carefully, bottom and sides, with thin slices of raw bacon.

Set the cocotte (covered with its own lid) in a pan with boiling water up to two thirds its height, and bake in a 350° F. oven for 1 hour, then take from the pan and put in a cool place.

Cut thick cardboard into a shape that will cover the terrine inside the cocotte. Put this cover in place and on it set weights totaling about 2 pounds to act as a press overnight. (As the fat or the bacon will overflow, put the terrine on a dish or plate to catch it). Remove the weights the morning after preparation.

Especially good are terrines made of poultry livers, denerved and ground. Also excellent is a terrine of calf's liver (*terrine de foie de veau*) for which a special recipe is given on page 119.

N.B. Terrines improve with keeping in a not-too-cold refrigerator 4 or 5 days.

(The word *terrine* also means an earthenware cocotte.)

CHAPTER 24

Dishes from Leftovers

A SENSIBLE COOK should throw away only the uneatable. With reasonable refrigeration, cooked fish can last perfectly well for 2 days in a receptacle with a lid; cooked meats, 4 days. Cooked vegetables outlast raw ones, and so do cooked fruits. (Bread, of course, lasts a week if tightly wrapped in a cellophane bag; if it seems a little "off" on taking out, wet it lightly under the cold water tap and heat in 350° F. oven for 5 minutes; it will revive.)

BEEF

Beef cooked in any way makes excellent patties when ground up and well mixed with 1 whole beaten egg for each patty the size of the hollow of your hand. It should be rather highly seasoned with onion salt and pepper, and fried in butter. Of course, a little sauce will help.

ROAST BEEF or BEEFSTEAK

Especially when cooked underdone, this can be sliced very thin, put into boiling Sauce Espagnole (see page 3), and served on very thinly sliced, buttered bread.

Or you may cut it into small dice with cold boiled potatoes. Dust beef and potatoes with a little flour and heat with butter. Then moisten with half wine–half water—just enough to make a creamy sauce that you can darken with a little tomato paste and a few drops of vegetable caramel (Kitchen Bouquet or Gravymaster). Season to taste.

Or you may put it through the coarse plate of a grinder with bits of cooked bacon or ham. Mix with cooked tomatoes. Cover with béchamel sauce (the simple variety: 1 spoonful butter, melted and blended with 1 spoonful flour, stirred together on medium heat to make a brown binding, moistened gradually with milk, hot or cold, and seasoned with onion salt, pepper, and thyme). Give it all a fine dusting of grated cheese, and on it place pats of butter. Then bake in a 350° F. oven for 15 minutes.

BOILED OR STEWED BEEF

This can be ground fine, seasoned highly, and used for stuffing peppers or tomatoes (top them with a simple béchamel sauce, as described above, and brown in the oven).

Or, if left over with carrots and onions, it can be simply warmed over and served on bread lightly moistened with sherry and then fried in butter.

VEAL

When only one day old, roast veal—especially when larded—can be sliced fine, heated in (not boiled together with) Sauce Espagnole (see page 3) and served with buttered noodles on the side.

Cooked veal ground up with a small amount of raw or cooked bacon makes an excellent terrine (see page 265).

Ground cooked veal may be mixed with chicken and/or turkey (see page 265).

MUTTON AND LAMB

A cook with imagination—how can a cook lack it?—can make a variety of rice dishes on a base of cooked mutton or lamb. For instance:

Soak a handful of raisins in warm water for 30 minutes. Meanwhile, chop the meat roughly and put it in a cocotte with some butter and a chopped onion or shallot. Set on high heat and, as soon as the butter sizzles, dust the meat with all-purpose flour. Stir and let the flour brown lightly. Moisten with a little broth or water, stir, then remove from the heat and cover. Drain the raisins and add them to the meat. Add a pinch of garlic powder and another of rosemary powder. Bring to a boil, stir, and serve on warmed-over boiled rice.

N. B. Mutton and lamb do not marry well with wine.

PORK

Cooked pork is especially good for stuffing cabbage (see page 215).

CHICKEN AND TURKEY

CHICKEN OR TURKEY HASH

Chicken and turkey make the best hash. They can also be mixed with ground veal, if the latter is whitish. Season with onion salt, white pepper, and a pinch of nutmeg, and moisten generously with a thick Sauce Béchamel (see page 8) or Sauce Mornay (see page 9).

Lay on a bed of leftover green beans, peas, spinach, or almost any vegetable, in a well-buttered overnproof dish. Cover with more of the same sauce, sprinkle with a little grated cheese, and dot with butter. Bake for 15 minutes in a 350° F. oven. Turn off the oven, and turn on the grill overhead to brown the surface lightly.

A *variation:* Spread the seasoned mixture of meat and sauce on the buttered dish; cover with boiled and drained noodles; add a thick covering a Sauce Béchamel (see page 8) or Sauce Mornay (see page 9), grated cheese, and dots of butter; bake for 15 minutes in a 350° F. oven; brown under overhead heat.

CHICKEN OR TURKEY CROQUETTES

Croquettes (see page 200) can be made with ground chicken or turkey that has not been overcooked, just as well as with their raw equivalent.

CHICKEN OR TURKEY VOL-AU-VENTS OR BOUCHÉES
[Patty Shells]

Vol-au-vents and their junior relations, *bouchées,* can be bought ready made. Both are delicious when filled with chopped chicken or turkey—mixed with veal, if you wish—and a Sauce Béchamel (see page 8)—enriched with cream and a teaspoon of Cognac, Scotch whisky, or good corn whiskey (bourbon). If you have mushrooms handy, they will, after being sautéed in butter, add greatly to the preparation.

CRÊPES WITH CHICKEN OR TURKEY

Pancakes (crêpes) are excellent rolled around preparations such as in the hash or *vol-au-vent* recipes above and finished with a spoonful of sauce. To make the dish a surprise: combine the chopped or ground meat *inside* the crêpe with Sauce Béchamel (see page 8), but finish the crépe *outside* with a spoonful of Sauce Espagnole (see page 3) or even Sauce Tomate (see page 7).

CHICKEN AND/OR TURKEY SOUFFLÉ

Make a really fine puree of chicken and/or turkey.

Mix this with the thick béchamel base of a soufflé (see page 38). Season with chopped fresh chives, then bake as a soufflé.

DUCK, GUINEA HEN, PHEASANT, AND GAME BIRDS

The most appropriate way of dealing with such leftovers is con-verting them into *salmis*. For this you separate all the meat left on the bones (keeping the skins, if you like them) and you heat them in enough Sauce Madère (see page 5) with a few pitted olives, washed of their salt, and a few pieces of peeled and seeded tomato, and serve on pieces of fried toast or on boiled rice or cracked wheat. The car-casses may be cut up and boiled gently in a little wine, white or red, then strained and the juice reduced by boiling to add to the sauce.

N.B. This is nothing but a rough-and-ready *salmi*. The real thing requires freshly roasted game birds, so that their carcasses can be pressed to obtain their juices, which improve the sauce.)

FISH

Leftover fillets or similar presentable portions of fish can be heated in very hot Sauce Béchamel (see page 8) or Sauce Mousseline or Mousseline-Moutarde (see page 10) with excellent results; the ad-dition of capers to the sauce is welcome.

Cooked fish reduced to a puree makes excellent molded dishes when mixed and warmed with a little thick béchamel and then allowed to cool. Top with a decoration of Sauce Mayonnaise (see page 12). (If cooked, shelled, cleaned shrimps are available, stick them all around on the unmolded fish like a crown.)

Firm-fleshed fishes like cod can be sliced and heated on an oven-proof dish and then covered with a *sauce mousseline-moutarde* heated to the boiling point and enriched at the last minute with freshly opened oysters and their water.

A fish soufflé can be made with the purée of cooked fish, plus some of the fish chopped up, incorporated with a thick béchamel soufflé base into which, if available, you have stirred a little of the cold fish-cooking liquor (see Soufflés, page 38).

Strong-flavored fish such as mackerel can be marinated in vinegar with sliced onions and a little garlic and dill for 2 or 3 hours and served as an hors d'oeuvre.

Or strong-flavored fish such as mackerel can be pureed and mixed thoroughly with mashed potatoes (one-third the amount of fish) and beaten egg yolks, shaped into croquettes, rolled in beaten egg yolks and then in bread crumbs, and either fried in hot oil or simply sautéed in clarified butter.

Leftover fish mashed into a fine puree can be combined with diced shellfish (may also be left over), a little tomato puree, and a béchamel laced with sherry or Madeira—and perhaps a little Cognac—and seasoned with paprika or powdered Spanish sweet red peppers. This thinned down a bit will make a good bisque, topped with a dollop of thick cream.

VEGETABLES

Almost any vegetable reduced to a puree and stirred in a pan over high heat (without burning) to eliminate most of its water will make, if properly seasoned with herbs and onion juice, good material for a soufflé (see page 38).

Shirred eggs can be greatly improved with puréed vegetables, preferably highly seasoned.

If the leftover vegetable is not the kind that can best be puréed, it can be reheated and served with a meat; or it can be added to a simple soup, such as a *velouté* (see page 24).

Few hors d'oeuvres can be more appetizing than leftover green beans with Vinaigrette (see page 11).

Leftover salad puréed with its dressing makes an excellent dressing for future salads.

RICE, MACARONI, AND OTHER FARINACEOUS LEFTOVERS

These can be used to great advantage in soups, and also in combination with meats in stuffing vegetables, etc. Bread, of course, should always be kept: dried in a cool oven it can be crushed into bread crumbs, always a kitchen resource, or used in thickening soups or making puddings.

CHAPTER 25

Pastry

Good cooks are not necessarily good pastry cooks. There is supposed to be a certain *cold* quality in the fingers of the pastry cook that ensures the proper handling of pastry to make it successful. At any rate, for the most delicate kinds of pastry it is certainly necessary to work on a *cold* marble slab, with very *cold* water, and to work the flour mixture with the fingers, avoiding all manipulations with the warm palms of the hands.

PÂTE FEUILLETÉE

This is unsatisfactorily translated as "puff paste" or "French puff paste," a term preferably applied to *pâte à choux*, which really puffs up in baking. The French word *feuille* means "leaf," as of a plant, and also "sheet," as of paper. The English word should be, for this kind of pastry, "foliated" or "laminated." Anyway, it is the most delicate and difficult pastry preparation to achieve perfection in.

The prescriptions are simple enough: sifted all-purpose flour (1 pound), ice-cold water (barely 1 cup), salt (a coffee spoonful). Make a mound of the flour in the middle of your marble slab, and with one finger make a crater or hollow center. Into this pour most of the ice-cold water mixed with the salt; gather up the flour inside the crater with your fingers without breaking the mound, adding the rest of the water as needed to make a soft dough, still without breaking the mound, until the last manipulation, when water and flour are completely amalgamated—all this done as quickly as possible to avoid any unnecessary handling. Roll up the dough into a rough ball, wrap it up in a clean cloth, and put it away for 30 minutes in the least cold portion of the refrigerator.

Meanwhile, manipulate 1 pound of unsalted butter to make it of the same consistence as the dough; and having taken out this dough and laid it on the marble, dusted with flour, and having rolled it out with your rolling pin into a rectangular shape about 3/4 inch thick, and having laid the butter in a similar shape but smaller dimensions right on the center of the dough, fold the dough over the butter from all four sides, without pressure, so that the dough flaps overlap on each other and the butter is totally covered.

Now—gently, so as not to squeeze the butter out—fold in three the dough enclosing the butter, then wrap it up in the cloth and put it away as you did before, this time for 15 minutes. Scrape off any bits left on the marble, dust it with flour anew, and put your dough on the middle of it. With great care roll out the dough enclosing the butter into a long rectangle and fold this in three again, and put it away wrapped in its cloth for 10 minutes more. Repeat this operation four times more, changing the position of the dough each time so that the folds will be at right angles to the rolling pin. If you have succeeded in keeping the butter inside the dough, you will have an excellent *pâte feuilletée*—by whatever name—and all you have to do is to roll it out (by no means while it is very cold) to the desired thickness and surface size.

As a top crust, brushed with beaten egg, it needs baking in a 375° F. oven for 35 to 40 minutes. About the same conditions are required for a *vol-au-vent*; cut the dough (with a fluted-edged, round pastry cutter) in two layers, which should be placed one on top of the other, the joint moistened lightly with cold water. Make sure that the fluting of both layers coincide, and cut a circular incision of hardly any depth within 1/8 inch inside the top edge: this disc is lifted after baking, and the soft pastry can be hollowed out to fill the *vol-au-vent* with its garnishing of meat, fish, sauce, etc.

Small patties can also be cut for appetizers and topped with grated cheese mixed with beaten egg yolk. On the other hand, this paste is not recommended for the bottom crust of pies, as it is difficult to bake it empty, because it puffs up (justifying the appellation?); and if baked garnished, it is soggy.

PÂTE À FONCER or BRISÉE
[*Plain Pie Paste*]

Like *demi-feuilletée* (which requires the same handling as the first paste), the *pâte à foncer* needs only one-half as much butter as flour and is quickly mixed; and requires no more ado than daintiness and speed. It is best put away for a number of hours, even overnight.

(N.B. Some authorities insist on rolling out the paste as soon as well amalgamated and then tearing it with the heel of the hand into bits which finally are rolled out and re-amalgamated into a ball.)

PÂTE À CHOUX
[*Puff Paste—that puffs up, not in layers*]

Put 4 ounces of butter, 1 cup of cold water, and a good teaspoon of salt (and if intended for sweet pastries, 1 teaspoon of granulated sugar) in a medium-sized saucepan, and have at hand 4 ounces of all-purpose flour, which you have sifted onto a sheet of white paper. Set the pan on medium heat to melt the butter, and then on high heat to bring the liquid to a boil. Throw in the flour—all of it. Now work the mixture with a tough wooden spoon, off the heat, rapidly and furiously, and once the mixture is complete set the pan again on medium heat, again to work the mixture in order to *dry* it—i.e., to evaporate the water while keeping the butter in the dough: this you can tell when the dough no longer sticks to the sides and bottom of the pan, nor to the spoon (of course, the water makes the dough stick and it has to be evaporated).

Now add 1 whole egg and beat it into the dough, off the heat, and when the mixture is perfect add another egg and mix thoroughly, and so on until you have mixed 4 eggs. The dough should now be semi-solid: solid enough to hold its shape more or less, and runny enough to form a thick ribbon when some of it is raised with a spoon.

When small balls of this dough are dropped in boiling water, they soon rise to the surface and are made into Gnocchi à la Parisienne (see page 47). Dropped in small pellets on a cookie sheet, and baked in a 350° F. oven for 15 minutes, they puff up to twice their size. Dropped in successive little pellets around a flat pie plate, they stick together as they puff up and make a nice ring: and, if you have a small cube of Gruyère cheese for each pellet and place it atop, this ring makes a pleasant first dish or family supper dish called *gougère*. Éclairs are made of this puff paste: once baked they are slit and stuffed with chocolate or coffee or vanilla cream and glazed (see page 278). *Profiteroles* and *choux à la crème*, which are small and big brothers, are also made of this paste.

N.B. For cake and sweet pastry mixes, see Desserts, pages 277–296.

CHAPTER 26

Desserts

COMPARED WITH AMERICAN GASTRONOMY, that of France is very restricted under this heading. The top Paris restaurants do not offer a great choice of sweets.

GÂTEAUX
[Cakes]

Unlike American cakes, which are almost always made with baking powder, the majority of French cakes are not made with any kind of leavening: their lightness depends on the beaten eggs.

LE GÉNOISE

This is the basis for layer cakes. Baked in a round cake pan $1\frac{1}{2}$ inches deep and $4\frac{3}{4}$ inches in diameter, the proportions of the ingredients are 4 ounces of sifted all-purpose flour, the same amount of granulated sugar, half that amount of unsalted butter, 4 whole eggs,

1 teaspoon of vanilla extract, 1 spoonful of a good liqueur (such as Curaçao, kirsch, Maraschino, or Cognac). To facilitate the blending and swelling of the ingredients, warm to body temperature the bowl in which you are going to beat the eggs, and throw in the eggs and the sugar. Start beating (presumably with an electric beater) fairly slowly, then as they blend, increase the speed, sprinkling the vanilla on the mixture.

Meanwhile you will have melted the butter in a double boiler with hot—not boiling—water, not too warm to put your fingers in it, and sifted the flour onto a sheet of white paper.

When the beater, on being stopped and raised, shows a continuous band of light yellow mixture down to the surface, called "the ribbon," it is time to add the flour. This you do by letting it drop very gradually from the sheet of paper while the beater whirls around. Then add the liquefied butter, without stopping the beating.

Meanwhile, and quickly, butter the cake pan, bottom and sides, then dust it with flour and turn it upside down to shed the excess. Pour the mixture into it, shake the pan lightly, and set it in a 325° F. oven for 35 minutes. Test the cake by pressing lightly on its surface the handle of a long fork: it should leave no depression. (For a two-layer cake you double the proportions and bake two simultaneously.) Cool on a cake rack.

Now, to glaze or frost the cake, turn it upside down and *make sure it is completely cold*. Take some apricot jam, dissolve it slightly with a few drops of warm water, and strain it onto a plate: it should be like glue. Brush the surface of the cake with it: it is thus prepared for the glaze known as *fondant*, which is the best.

GLAÇAGE
[Glaze]

Put 2 pounds of white granulated sugar into an enameled cast-iron cocotte with 2 cups of cold water and set on low heat to melt the sugar. Once this is completed, set the cocotte on high heat, and as the liquid boils remove the scum that rises. A granular deposit will begin to coat the sides of the cocotte: this you must wipe off with a bit of cheesecloth or other clean rag wrapped around a spoon, because with the heat it tends to caramelize and lend bitterness to the glaze. (Likewise, it is prudent to surround the cocotte with metal foil to receive the tiny droplets of syrup that spatter invisibly and which, on hardening on the surface of the stove, are difficult to remove.)

When the liquid boils with little bubbles, the syrup begins to take on consistency. If you stick the point of a wooden spatula in it and join the drop you pick up to the point of a dry one, you will notice the density of the syrup; so, when the drop forms a little gluey ribbon between the two spatulas, the syrup is ready for glazing and the cocotte must be removed from the heat. If you have any doubts about the consistency of the syrup and you can stand the heat, pick up a drop or so of it with a spoon and try it between your forefinger and thumb: it should be as sticky as glue. Cook it more, if necessary, until this stage is reached, but without exaggerating.

Turn the syrup on to your marble pastry slab (which should be spotless and dry), and with a large wooden spatula knead the syrup back and forth and evenly all over until it turns white and semisolid. At this point take what you need to glaze your cake and put away the rest in a dry container with a screw top. (Kept in a reasonably cool place it lasts for weeks.)

Now, add to the glaze—as it now must be called—in a small pan your liqueur, by drops, warm it slightly, and pour it gently on top of the cake (upside down and brushed with the apricot preparation). Distribute the glaze evenly all over the surface and smooth it over with the wooden spatula. As it dries, the glaze will acquire a fine sheen.

GLAÇAGE AU CHOCOLAT
[Chocolate Glaze]

Grate a 4-ounce tablet of bitter chocolate, melt it in a little hot water, and stir it to make a smooth paste. Add to it an equal amount of glaze (as above) and warm it to pour over the cake. The consis-tence must be that of very thick cream.

GLAÇAGE AU MOKA
[Coffee Glaze]

Make very strong coffee and add enough to the glaze (see above) to flavor it but not to liquefy it.

GLAÇAGE AUX FRUITS
[Fruit-pulp Glaze]

Bright colored berries reduced to a puree can be blended with the glaze (see above). For layer cakes, the fresh fruit, sugared or not, can be mixed with the glaze and smoothed over with the spatula: by fruits are meant strawberries, raspberries, and blueberries—obviously not apples and bananas, etc.

LE SAVARIN

This is the real name of the mix that makes the well-known *baba-au-rhum*. (The *baba* has currants and raisins soaked in half rum–half water.) It is baked in a ring, or, if you prefer, in a cake mold in that shape, hollow in the middle. So, for such a mold, about 10 inches in outer diameter, buttered and dusted with flour, make a good dough of 8 ounces of all-purpose flour (which you put in a proper-sized bowl) and ⅓ of a yeast cake dissolved in 4 spoonfuls of warm milk, plus a pinch of salt, mixing it delicately together with your fingers. You should have a rather liquid dough, which should be put in a wooden bowl to leaven to the point where cracks appear.

Beat 4 whole eggs lightly and add them to the dough: mix well with your *fingers*, then add gradually some 3 teaspoons of granulated sugar, plus a pinch of salt, and mix it all very thoroughly for about 6 minutes until you have a rather runny dough but with enough body to be handled. Break off a lump of dough and lay it on the mold, which you have buttered in advance and lined with ⅔ cup finely chopped almonds, and continue thus to fill the mold to one-third its depth, sticking the lumps together with your fingers to obtain an even surface.

Cover the mold with several towels, and set it in a warm place free from draughts. A peek at the surface after 30 minutes should show that the dough has risen considerably, perhaps to the brim of the mold: in that case put it in a 325° F. oven, taking the precaution to put a rolled sheet of white paper around the hollow center of the mold, in lieu of a chimney, because the dough may rise too much in that area and make the cake lopsided.

After 5 minutes the heat of the oven should be reduced if the cake tends to harden on top and brown. To counter this, you can lay over the top a sheet of aluminum foil or of white paper slightly dampened. Five minutes later you should remove the rolled piece of paper from the center of the mold. And, about 30 minutes later, the *savarin* should be well baked. Unmold it on a grill on a dish.

Now quickly mix boiling water and sugar in a small quantity (½ cup of water to 3 spoonfuls of sugar), just to moisten the cake, and a small glassful of the liqueur of your choice: pour it all over the cake while still warm, but gradually so that it will be absorbed. If you find that the cake is thirsty, give it more drink; but do not make it soggy.

BISCUITS À LA CUILLER
[Lady Fingers]

A gifted person can make lady fingers on sheets of white paper, much preferable than in tin molds; but, it is advisable to opt for the latter the first time. Also, a pastry bag will be found a comfort instead of a spoon—the shaping of these little "cakes" derives their name from this ancient implement—i.e., "spoon cakes (or biscuits)."

The dough is made of sugar and eggs principally, with flour as an adjunct: 4 ounces of fine granulated sugar and 4 eggs, and 3 ounces of flour, plus vanilla extract. The flour must be absolutely dry, and if in doubt you must spread it out on clean white paper to dry in a very mild oven for a few minutes.

First, set aside 1 spoonful of sugar and throw the rest into a mixing bowl with 1 egg *yolk*, reserving the white in a cup. Mix the two ingredients very thoroughly, and as soon as the color appears creamy add another yolk, reserving the white as before. Repeat this opera-tion until all the yolks are consumed, then add the vanilla. Again mix thoroughly and then beat with the electric whip until the mixture forms a thick ribbon on being lifted with a spoon.

Beat the egg whites stiff and cut and fold them into the egg yolk mixture, and at the same time add the flour very gradually—as it were, dusting it over from the edge of a spoon—until it is all in-corporated. Butter the molds and flour them, and with a pastry bag lay a ribbon of the mixture on each depression. Now dust the lady fingers with granulated sugar. Before putting them in the oven, count 30 seconds after shaking off the excess sugar, then bake for 25 minutes in a 300° F. oven. (The half-minute wait before baking ensures the slight moistening of the sugar dusted on top of the lady fingers to prevent its caramelization; but a longer wait might cause them to flatten out.)

CRÈMES
[Custards]

These can be quite simple preparations or very elaborate ones, but they always require great care.

CRÈMES EN PETITS POTS
[Custards in Little Pots]

Obviously, the first requisite is small ovenproof china or pottery pots or cups of about the same capacity as an afterdinner coffee cup (a demitasse in the United States) or a little over.

For 12 little pots

Bring a generous quart of milk to a boil, immediately add ½ pound granulated sugar, and remove from the heat. Make sure the sugar is well dissolved.

IF MAKING VANILLA (OR COFFEE) CUSTARD: Add 1 teaspoon vanilla extract (or very strong coffee essence to your taste, but not more than a small quantity of liquid). Beat 7 egg yolks and 3 whole eggs together without raising a froth, then, to the beaten eggs, add the *tepid* milk and sugar mixture.

IF MAKING CHOCOLATE CUSTARD: Proceed as above for vanilla custard, then dissolve about 6 ounces of grated bitter chocolate in a little hot water and add to the vanilla custard mixture. Heat the custard mixture again to make it homogeneous, then strain it through cheesecloth to eliminate all froth, which would make unsightly bubbles in cooking.

Arrange the little cups in a large pan with boiling water up to two-thirds of their height. With a ladle, fill them *not quite* to the brim. Cover them with a sheet of aluminum foil and bake them in 350° F. oven. The water in the pan should be *almost* but not quite boiling.

After about 20 minutes, inspect the surface of the cups: if, on shaking them or tipping them slightly, the custard seems still liquid, keep them a little longer in the oven until they appear solid. Remove them from the pan and let them cool before covering them with their lids—if the cups have lids. Do not put them in the refrigerator before they are cold.

N.B. Properly covered, the custards can be kept for several days in a refrigerator without any strong-smelling foods.

CRÈME ANGLAISE
[English Custard—Soft Custard or Custard Sauce]

Bring to a boil 1 quart of whole milk, 1 teaspoon vanilla extract, and a pinch of grated lemon peel. Add a teaspoon of arrowroot, cover, and set on minimum heat for about 25 minutes.

Meanwhile, put 10 egg yolks in a mixing bowl with 10 ounces of granulated sugar, mix well, and then beat until the yellow turns pale and, when you lift a spoonful, a ribbon forms from spoon to surface of the mixture. Add *very* gradually the *warm* milk, while stirring constantly. Pour it all back into the milk saucepan—if nothing has stuck to the bottom of it—otherwise, take a fresh saucepan.

Set the mixture on low heat and continue to stir and scrape the bottom of the pan. When the froth on the surface disappears, the sauce is ready: a wooden spoon dipped in it should come out as if painted. Strain it through fine mesh, and stir it now and then as it cools to prevent a skin forming on the surface.

N.B. Authorities who have worked in England follow the English prescription of adding brandy or another liqueur—this is not classical French practice, although allowed as a variant.

CRÈME ANGLAISE COLLÉE
[Custard Sauce with Gelatin]

This is a principal ingredient in preparing Bavarois (page 285).

For the amount of Crème Anglaise given above, soak 4 spoonfuls of gelatin (about 1 ounce) in 1 cup of cold water, and add it to the sauce the moment you remove it from the heat. Stir well until the gelatin dissolves completely. Strain through fine mesh, and stir now and then until the sauce is cool. Do not put it away in the refrigerator before it is completely cold, or you will risk lumpiness.

N.B. Leaf gelatin is recommended by the classical authorities. For this recipe you would need 10 to 12 leaves, which you should soak in cold water, then wipe dry, and finally add to the warm sauce.

CRÈME PÂTISSIÈRE
[Custard Filling]

Boil 2 cups of milk and add 1 teaspoon of vanilla extract. Cover and withdraw from the heat. Put in a saucepan 2 ounces of sifted all-purpose flour, 6 ounces of granulated sugar, and 4 whole eggs, plus a pinch of salt, and beat them together thoroughly. To this add gradually the warm or hot milk and bring to a boil, stirring without stopping and scraping the bottom of the pan. Boil for 4 minutes, then add a spoonful of unsalted fresh butter. Stir well and let cool. Chocolate or coffee is added as given for Crèmes en Petits Pots (see page 282). *Crème pâtissière* is what you fill *éclairs* and cream puffs with.

CRÈME CHANTILLY, CRÈME FOUETÉE
[Whipped Cream]

This needs care: first, the cream must not be too heavy, like the run-of-the-mill *crème fraîche* of Paris: it would turn into butter with little beating. Nor must it be too milky, for it would require very long whipping. Cream should be liquid enough *to pour*, but heavy enough to leave a coating in a cup. Whipping should be slow at the beginning and gather speed from there on. However, you must watch out for the first signs of whey and lumps appearing, which means that you have *churned* your cream into butter. It is all a matter of paying close attention. Cream is properly whipped when the beater or whisk lifted with some cream upward shows that it holds its shape.

BAVAROIS
[Bavarian Cream or Custard]

This is intermediate between custards proper and puddings. It is a mixture of custard cream with gelatin and whipped cream, flavored with vanilla, chocolate, coffee, or fruits.

Make about a quart of custard sauce with gelatin, as in Crème Anglaise Collée (see above).

Flavor with vanilla, chocolate, or coffee, as explained for Crèmes en Petits Pots (see page 282), or with fruits (these should be in rather thick puree form, and a judicious addition of a liqueur to the puree is recommended).

Before the mixture sets—i.e., when it is freshly prepared and just cool, mix it with equal amount of whipped fresh cream, cutting and folding so as to keep the air in it.

With a tasteless oil, oil a mold with a capacity of a little more than 2 quarts, and with a chimney center (to ensure even distribution of refrigeration). Chill the mold well in the refrigerator, then fill with the mixture, cover with a sheet of paper, and set to harden in the refrigerator.

POUDINGS
[Puddings]

The distinction made by French authorities between *bavarois* and puddings is subtle: essentially, the addition of other, more solid ingredients to puddings.

POUDING NESSELRODE
[Nesselrode Pudding]

This may be called "The king of puddings." Its name should be *pouding à la Mouy*, for it was invented by Mouy, the *chef de cuisine* of the famous eighteenth- and nineteenth-century Russian statesman, Count Nesselrode.

Put 1½ cups of water and 2 ounces of granulated sugar in a 3-quart saucepan. Stir to dissolve the sugar. Add 1 teaspoon of vanilla extract and stir. Shell and peel 36 fresh chestnuts, or use whole tinned ones (*marrons glacés* will not do, but excellent tinned chestnuts, ready for use and usually labeled *marrons au naturel*, are recommended). Chop the chestnuts coarsely and add to the pan. Set the pan on medium heat, bring to a boil very gradually, then boil gently, regulating the heat accordingly, for 1½ hours.

Meanwhile, put 6 ounces of raisins to soak in cool white wine, cut 15 candied cherries (*not* Maraschino) in quarters, and prepare 2 cups of Crème Anglaise Collée (page 284).

Mash the chestnut mixture into a fine puree—make this really creamy in texture—then mix the custard sauce, cherries and raisins (not the wine) with the cooling puree. Put in the refrigerator to cool and *half*-set with a sheet of paper over it to prevent the surface hardening too much. (If the refrigerator is not very cold, 1 hour should do.)

Mix with an equal amount of whipped cream (about 3 cups), folding and cutting, and add a small glass of Maraschino—almost in drops.

Line a mold with clean white paper, bottom and sides (a disc to fit the bottom, an overlapping sheet for the sides). Fill the mold with the mixture, using a spoon and shaking the mold from time to time to pack it properly yet delicately. Cover with a sheet of paper and put it in the refrigerator to congeal.

Unmolding is quite simple because the paper does not stick to the metal and can easily be peeled off the pudding. Remove the paper from the top of the mold. Put a folded, clean napkin in its place, and on top of the napkin place the serving platter, upside down. Turn it right side up, and you should be agreeably surprised.

POUDING DIPLOMATE
[Molded Custard with Candied Fruits]

Soak 4 ounces seedless raisins (black and/or white, preferably half and half) in ½ cup white wine for an hour. Drain them, then add them to a small glass of kirsch and a teaspoon of granulated sugar. Cover and let stand for 30 minutes.

Meantime, prepare 2 cups of Crème Anglaise Collée (see page 284).

Cut 4 ounces candied cherries in quarters, cut 1 spoonful of candied orange peel in slivers, and cut 6 lady fingers lengthwise to half their thickness and again twice across, and moisten them with a spoonful of kirsch.

Whip 1⅓ cups fresh cream. Reserve a few tablespoons of the whipped cream for later use (decorating the finished pudding) and mix the rest with the custard sauce, cutting and folding.

Oil a 1½-quart mold, bottom and sides, and cover its bottom with white paper cut to fit it exactly. On the bottom of the mold put a layer of raisins mixed with cherries and orange peel. Spoon the mixture of custard sauce and whipped cream into the mold to a depth of about 1 inch, then add a layer of lady fingers and raisins mixed with cherries and orange peel. Spoon on a second layer of the custard sauce–whipped cream mixture and bang the mold down on flat sur-face so the contents pack properly.

Continue to pile layer upon layer as before, banging the mold down for every layer and winding up with a layer of the custard mixture.

Place a sheet of paper over the mold, and set it in refrigerator to congeal. Unmold by wrapping a hot towel around the mold for a minute or two.

On a serving platter, decorate the pudding with whipped cream (done most easily with a pastry bag).

GLACES
[Ices, Ice Cream]

Cream is not an important—certainly not an essential—ingredient in French ice cream. The French equivalent of ice cream is really *glace à la crème* ("ice with custard") and of water ices or sherbets, *glaces au sirop* ("ices with syrup").

FOR AN ICE CREAM: Beat 10 egg yolks with 10 or 12 ounces of granulated sugar until the mixture, when the beater is held up, makes a ribbon. Dilute *very* gradually with 1 quart of boiling whole milk, then set on medium-low heat and stir until the mixture coats the spoon like paint.

The flavor is determined by what is added to the milk: for vanilla ice cream, add 1 teaspoon vanilla extract at the moment the milk boils; for fruit flavors, add at that moment a puree made of 1 pound of fruit mashed with 10 ounces of confectioners' sugar and strained.

FOR WATER ICES—I.E., ICES WITHOUT MILK OR EGGS: Make a puree of fresh fruit and strain it, then make a syrup of sugar and water by dissolving 10 ounces of granulated sugar in 1¼ cups *warm* water and boiling for 2 minutes. Let the syrup cool, and mix it with the fruit puree (to add 1 teaspoonful of a sweet liqueur does no harm).

Freezing in the ice trays of the refrigerator is more in accordance with the really old methods than freezing in the crank-freezer of our childhood. Long ago, the mixture would have been put into a sort of mold with a tight-fitting lid and laid in a deep bed of ice and coarse salt with a bit of saltpeter, and just twirled now and then. So, if the mixture in the ice tray is taken out when it is half frozen and then beaten, and again put in the freezing compartment, the result should be satisfactory, even according to very old standards.

CHARLOTTES
[Molded Creams]

CHARLOTTE RUSSE
[Molded Bavarian Cream]

Line the bottom of your charlotte mold with lady fingers cut in triangular shapes with their points meeting at the center (the sides or outer edges can remain round). Cut the long lady fingers to line the sides as straight as possible, so that they will fit tight against each other, taking care to shave the ends that touch the bottom a little aslant to allow for the slight conical shape of the mold. The other ends are trimmed with scissors to the level of the filling just before serving.

Charlotte mold

Fill the mold with Crème Anglaise Collée (see page 284), except that the gelatin there prescribed is diminished by one-fourth, to make the custard smoother. Cover with a sheet of paper, and put in a not-too-cold refrigerator for 2 hours.

Make sure the filling is set, then trim off any lady fingers that project above the surface of the filling. Hold a folded napkin against the serving platter, lay the platter upside down on the surface of the mold, and turn the whole right side up.

CHARLOTTE MALAKOFF
[Molded Almond Cream]

If you are using almonds that are shelled but unpeeled, throw 4 ounces of them into a saucepan of boiling water. Remove it from the heat but let the almonds remain in hot water for 3 minutes. Cool them in cold water; drain. Remove the skins by pressing the almonds on a flat surface with your thumb.

Line a mold with nicely tailored lady fingers as in the recipe for Charlotte Russe (see above), except that you cover the bottom with a white paper disc cut to fit it and then line *only the sides* with lady fingers.

Chop up the almonds, then grind them in a mortar with 4 ounces of granulated sugar and a teaspoon of vanilla extract, making a fine puree.

Soften 4 ounces of fresh unsalted butter with a spoon on a plate, without heating. Add the butter to what is in the mortar, and mix and mash with a pestle to make the mixture froth. Mix in a small glass of kirsch.

Beat fresh whipping cream into stiff whipped cream. Reserving some of this for topping the finished dish, blend the rest into the almond mixture, cutting and folding. Fill the mold with the mixture and place in the refrigerator. After an hour there, it may be un-molded, but, before unmolding, trim off any lady fingers that project above the surface of the filling.

Hold a folded napkin against the serving platter, lay the platter upside down on the surface of the mold, and turn the whole right side up. Remove the paper disc.

Sugar and flavor (with vanilla) the whipped cream you reserved. Top the charlotte Malakoff with it, using for this operation—if handy —a pastry bag with a fluted tube.

CHARLOTTE ESTIVALE
[*Summer Charlotte*]

Make a Génoise (see page 277) in a rectangular mold, bearing in mind for its dimensions the height of the charlotte mold you will use in the end, because instead of lady fingers you will use slices of the Génoise to line the mold.

Cut the slices from your cake once it is *cold* about the same width as a lady finger, working with a very sharp knife to get clean edges. Then glaze half of them with a white fondant flavored with kirsch and the other half with pink fondant tinted with an edible dye and flavored like the first.

Line the charlotte mold, bottom and sides, with white paper lightly brushed with tasteless oil, and having made sure that the fondants are *absolutely dry*, line the mold with the cake slices, alternating the colors, glazed face next to the paper and unglazed cake side facing inwards. Proceed likewise with the bottom. Fill the mold as directed in the preceding recipes with a Bavarian Cream (see page 289) mixed with a puree of berries and sugar to your taste, christened with a little kirsch or your favorite liqueur. Cover the top with a sheet of paper and put away in the refrigerator until *stiff*.

Before unmolding, trim any irregular edges of the cake slices. After unmolding on a folded napkin on a platter, peel off the oiled paper with great care so as not to spoil the sheen and smoothness of the glaze. A ring of berries (fresh, of course) around the base of the charlotte is a good touch.

TARTES
[*Tarts*]

The difference between one-crust pies and tarts is that the pie has the crust on top and the tart, under. The pastry mix recommended for tarts is Pâte à Foncer (see page 275) which is like the American plain pastry, with the difference that the finer French pastry cooks do not use other shortening than unsalted fresh butter of excellent quality. It is always desirable to bake the tart shells without the filling: this presents some difficulty, but it can be overcome. You can bake the shell on a pie plate upside down, and only partly baked so that you can fill it later and finish the edge to be baked again. Or, you can fill the raw tart with dried beans or rice on a disc of lightly oiled tissue paper before baking, so as to keep the center from rising off the pie plate; and you must punch holes in the bottom of the pastry, to the same end. Before baking the tart, finally, the edge all around must be brushed with beaten egg.

TARTE AUX FRAISES
[*Strawberry Tart*]

Bake the empty tart as indicated above for 20 minutes in a 400° F. oven. Let it cool after removing the beans or rice. Arrange fresh strawberries, points up, all around, and half cover them with raspberry jam moistened with kirsch. For 6 people at table you need, for the pastry, 6 ounces of all-purpose flour, 3 ounces of fresh butter, a pinch of salt, 1/2 teaspoonful of powdered sugar, and 4 to 5 spoonfuls of cold water; and 3/4 of a pound of strawberries, 4 or 5 spoonfuls of raspberry jam, and 1 spoonful of kirsch. To brush the tart you need part of 1 beaten egg. The total time required: 2 hours.

TARTES AUX FRUITS CUITS
[*Cooked Fruit Tarts*]

The standard practice is to fill the raw pastry shell with the cooked fruit, to which you add a jam or jelly of the same or of a different flavor. Also, the raw shell is filled with Crème Pâtissière (see page 284) and on top of it the sliced cooked fruit. The proportions are those given above.

LE CLAFOUTIS LIMOUSIN

This is a delicious though rough country sweet. It can be served hot, tepid, or cold; and best, right in the ovenproof pottery or china pie dish in which it is cooked. For 6 to 8 people take 1½ pounds of ripe cherries, preferably black, ¼ pound of granulated sugar, 2 ounces of all-purpose flour, 1⅓ cup of milk, 3 whole eggs, 1 teaspoon of vanilla extract and a good pinch of salt. Sift the flour into a bowl, add the sugar and 1 egg. Mix well. Add another egg and mix; add the third egg and mix. Sprinkle the vanilla and the salt over this, and then moisten with the cold milk, stirring as you pour. Make a smooth and homogeneous paste of the mixture, and then strain it through fine mesh for double security against lumps. Remove the stones from the cherries but save the juice; distribute the cherries over the pie dish with the juice. Finally, pour the paste all over the cherries, distribute the sugar over all, and set it in a 375° F. oven to bake for 30 to 40 minutes.

COMPOTES ET FRUITS CUITS
[*Compotes and Cooked Fruits*]

POMMES AU FOUR
[*Baked Apples*]

Choose apples that are sound, without spots, and not too ripe. Wash, dry, and core them; and prick the skin around the middle, and set on a generously buttered ovenproof dish.

Fill the bottom of each hole with ½ inch of soft, moist, doughy bread (as a stopper) and the rest of the hole with brown sugar mixed with half its quantity of fresh butter and a generous sprinkling of powdered ginger.

Bake in 400° F. oven for 40 minutes, basting with the pan juice after the first 20.

Serve hot or cold, with a few drops of apple liqueur (Calvados) or applejack.

COMPOTE D'ABRICOTS
[Compote of Apricots]

Make a syrup of sugar and water (8 ounces of sugar to 1 quart cold water) and boil it for 30 minutes. Remove from the heat.

Meanwhile, cut the apricots in two. Add them to the syrup and bring it to a boil, then reduce the heat to keep it simmering for 8 minutes. Lift the fruit with a skimmer to a plate and peel it delicately, while keeping the syrup on increased heat to reduce it to half its volume.

If you like, you may crack the shells of the pits, remove the kernels inside, and place these in the centers of the apricots halves.

Pour the syrup over the apricots on a platter and let cool completely.

COMPOTE DE CERISES
[Compote of Cherries]

Make a syrup by mixing ½ cup of good red wine, ½ cup of warm water, and 6 ounces of granulated sugar.

Remove the stones of 1½ pounds of red cherries (not black), taking care not to smash them and saving all the juice. (An ordinary straight hairpin does the trick if you do not have a pitter.) Crush the stones in a mortar, tie them up in a piece of cheesecloth, throw them and the cherries into the syrup, and bring the liquid to the boil. Lower the heat and simmer for 8 minutes.

Lift the cherries with a skimmer to a bowl and cover them, then reduce the syrup with the stones to half its volume by gentle but steady boiling, then strain it into the bowl with the cherries. Add a small glass of kirsch and let cool.

N.B. If the syrup is too sweet, add water to your taste, but then bind the liquid with arrowroot (see page 65).

COMPOTE DE REINES-CLAUDES
[Compote of Greengages]

Make a syrup with 6 ounces of granulated sugar and 1 cup of warm water. Bring to a boil, and add 1½ pounds of greengages, which you have washed and dried (without peeling or pitting). Cook for 8 minutes.

Withdraw from the heat, add a few drops of essence of bitter almonds or pistachio, and cover. After 10 minutes, remove the fruit with a skimmer to a bowl. Taste the syrup for sweetness: if not sweet enough, boil down to your taste.

Pour the syrup over the fruit and let cool.

N.B. If you are very finicky about pits and skins, the former can be removed after 3 minutes of cooking and the latter after the end of cooking; but with them you will remove a good deal of the flavor.

COMPOTE DE PÊCHES
[Compote of Peaches]

Make a syrup with 6 ounces of granulated sugar and 1 cup of warm water. Bring to a boil.

Meanwhile, peel 6 to 8 peaches (if you rub the skins with the *back* of a small knife you loosen them and they come off quite easily) and cut them in halves. Put the peaches in the boiling syrup—skins and pits and juice—and after 6 or 7 minutes remove the pan from the heat and lift the peaches to a bowl.

Add a few drops of Cognac to the syrup and strain it over the peaches.

POIRES EN COMPOTE AU VIN ROUGE
[Compote of Pears in Red Wine]

Choose undamaged, quite ripe pears that stand up straight.

Make a syrup of half water–half good red wine (Bordeaux preferably), sugared to your taste (better not very sweet because you
will boil it down later and thus increase the sweetness). Make enough
syrup to cover the pears to two-thirds their height when they are
standing upright in the syrup in a saucepan.

Peel the pears, leaving no mark of the knife and *not* cutting off the
stem. Rub each peeled pear with half a fresh lemon to keep it from
browning, and snip off the little black navel at its bottom.

Bring the syrup to a boil. Place the pears carefully in the pan with
the boiling syrup. (If you are afraid of burning your fingers, stand
the pears side by side in a *warm* empty pan, pour the boiling syrup
over them, and set this pan on high heat to boil quickly.) Temper
the heat to make boiling continuous for 30 minutes, then turn off
the heat.

After 10 minutes, lift the pears by their fruit stems—with pincers,
if your fingers are too delicate—to a plate or shallow bowl. Boil down
the syrup to the desired sweetness, and then pour over the pears. Let
cool.

This is the most delicate way of cooking pears, for the subtle flavor
of the fruit is in no way altered by the syrup, but enhanced.

PRUNES ET BRUGNONS EN COMPOTE
[Compote of Plums and Nectarines]

Follow the recipe for Compote de Reines-Claudes (see above),
except cook 2 minutes longer and omit the essence of pistachio or
bitter almonds.

PART II

Menus

THAT MENUS are the product of their times is undeniable. To a person of mature years, home menus today seem scant when compared with the five-course dinner of the turn of the century. Contrariwise, a present-day youngster laughs with scorn at the "groaning board" of that time. However, we did not gorge then: the digestive capacity has not shrunk; helpings were smaller then and variety greater—that is all.

Another coefficient in the composition of menus is geography. In the United States home fare was probably always simpler, class by class, than in Europe, the very richest being an exception because they copied the Europeans in their manner of living. In France the domestic menu was always more elaborate and varied than elsewhere in Europe. The passage of time has tended to narrow the difference. A notable influence has been the changing ideas about feminine beauty, especially in the minds of the feminine population: women set the fashions—or, at any rate, men do not—and the men vie for their favors according to what fashion proclaims to be the stars. So the menu has shrunk, even in France.

Then there is the science of medicine, especially as reported in the newspapers. A brave British doctor recently announced that people coddled themselves *to make life safe for senility*. From a gastronomic point of view he is a prophet, a hero. At the two poles of life there is seldom much gastronomic appreciation; and the sacrifice of good things for insipid existence is anathema to us.

Our menus should suit individual preferences, deferring in civilized practice to the wishes of those who join us at table. Broadly speaking, our menus should conform also to the society we frequent and its habits. Ample midday meals among people inured to snacks at that hour are a reversal of established order. So, even though gastronomy would favor dining at midday and supping at night, the menus suggested below will toe the "business" line. (Gastronomy assumes that it is more important than "business" and therefore that when we are most vigorous, at the apex of the day, is when we should feast.)

Great cooks, the princes of the profession who have written the great cookery books, have been the *chefs de cuisine* of famous restaurants or of great potentates, or of both. Their menus have been suitable for the given circumstances. But a restaurant menu even of the present day needs picking and choosing to adapt it to home use. Here again considerable progress is to be noted: moderation is gaining ground; and even at state dinners at the Elysée, menus are anything but copious.

Brillat-Savarin, whose pronouncements on gastronomy have been frequently and respectfully quoted by authors on this subject, ruled that the more substantial foods should precede the lighter ones. Nevertheless, a glance at almost any menu elaborated by these authors shows that they have paid only lip service to their master. He was obviously right in thinking that when the stomach is relatively empty it can digest more easily than when it is full, and therefore that foods requiring greater digestive efforts should be tackled first. But the great Escoffier prescribed, on the same menu, shellfish cream, then salmon, then roast veal, then chicken, then lamb, then pheasant and partridge; nor did he respect the rule with regard to foie gras which he served *after* a grand succession of rich dishes.

A charming and very wise American cookery book gives a lunch menu consisting of soup and salad. For those who have a hearty breakfast, tidbits at cocktail time, and a hearty dinner, this would be

adequate. And if they arrived in Paris on a trip and upset their digestive habits with two hearty meals (plus unaccustomed wines), who
would blame them for harking back to the soup-cum-salad lunch
menu? But we are not dealing here with such extremes. Here we will
try to give reasonable lunch and dinner menus for home use, particularly the entertaining of friends in varying numbers.

Certain fundamental principles should be respected:

1. More than one *hearty* dish should not be served at the same
meal—e.g., a *bouillabaisse* or a *matelotte* or a *brandade de morue*
should not be followed by a *navarin de mouton* or an *estouffade à la
provençale* or a hot meat pie.

2. Two *sautés* should not be served at the same meal—e.g., a
sautéed fish should not be followed by a sautéed meat.

3. If the first dish has a creamy sauce, the second dish should not.
One creamy dish at one meal is enough, including the dessert.

4. If a farinaceous dish, such as any substantial Italian macaroni
preparation, is served, the rest of the menu should not contain any
pastry or other farinaceous food.

5. A highly spiced dish should not precede a more delicately
flavored one. This applies to dishes strongly flavored with garlic.

6. Green salads should not be served with "sauced" meats, even
on a side dish or plate; and vegetables that ooze liquid, of whatever
nature, should never accompany meats with sauces.

7. A profusion of vegetables on a serving dish with a nicely carved
joint in the center is very pretty; but, actually, with a roast it is
better to serve one vegetable plus a border of a farinaceous food—
e.g., little potatoes browned in butter or potato puree out of a pastry
bag or little mounds of rice, and green beans served apart. Thus the
beans can be appreciated to advantage. The old French custom of
serving a vegetable as a separate course *after* a roast is certainly
recommendable when the vegetable deserves the honor, such as tiny
garden peas, tender green beans, tiny whole carrots, etc. (This does
not apply to vegetables cooked with meats in a stew where the object
is to blend their flavors.) And the old-fashioned American custom of
little side dishes ("birdbaths") with vegetables has ample gastronomic
justification.

8. Fried foods are not suitable for evening meals of any importance

(for any meal, of course, it is better to avoid these foods because they are not the most digestible). And stews should be served rather at midday than at any evening meal; likewise for "casserole" dishes, which are very "informal," no matter how succulent.

Some, perhaps many, of my readers will complain that the party menus suggested hereafter are too copious. It is quite simple to omit any dish judged unnecessary. For family menus this is expected, of course.

Alexandre Dumas in his *Grand Dictionnaire de Cuisine* states that the kitchen has its own language. Hence, no apologies are offered for what the French would call *une belle salade* of English and French in the menus.

LUNCH MENUS FOR COLD WEATHER

Soufflé of Finnan Haddie
Boeuf à la Mode
Carrots, Turnips, and Small Onions
Cheese
Compote of Greengages

Scrambled Eggs à l'Uribe
Grilled Chicken
Braised Endives
Cheese
Tarte aux Pommes

Grilled Fresh Sardines
Roast Shoulder of Lamb
Stuffed Tomatoes
White Rice
Cheese
Tarte aux Poires

❧

Huîtres au Naturel
Steak and Kidney Pudding
Cheese
Pineapple Ice au Curaçao

❧

Poached Eggs, Sauce Mornay
Baked Halibut Steaks
Boiled Potatoes
Petits Pots de Crème au Chocolat

❧

Soufflé aux Épinards
Rognons de Veau Flambés
Purée de Pommes de Terre
Baba au Rhum

❧

Shirred Eggs à la Lorraine
Curry of Lamb
White Rice
Mango Chutney
Bombay Duck
Glace à l'Orange

❧❧❧

Cherrystone Clams on the Half Shell
La Poule au Pot
Cheese
Vanilla Soufflé

❧❧❧

Ravioli à la Genoise
Escalopes de Veau Flambées
Purée of Sorrel
Cheese
Baked Apple

❧❧❧

Artichoke Hearts in Vinaigrette
Pork Chops
Purée de Marrons
Cheese
Tarte aux Pommes

❧❧❧

Melon
Coulibiac de Saumon
Cheese
Glace Moka

❧❧❧

Gnocchi Parisienne
Harengs Grillés, Beurre Mâitre d'Hôtel
Ananas au Naturel

DINNER MENUS FOR COLD WEATHER

❧

Consommé à la Royale
Fillets of Sole Portugaise
Culotte de Boeuf Braised in Red Burgundy Wine
Pudding Diplomate

❧

Potage à la Reine
Carrelet à la Dugléré
Boiled Smoked Ham, Sauce Madère
Épinards en Branches
Glace au Chocolat
Petits Fours

❧

Oxtail Soup
Poached Gray Mullet, Beurre Blanc
Roast Veal (boned rack),
Sauce Espagnole
Glace à la Vanille
Petits Fours

❧

Blinis au Caviar Pressé, Melted Butter, Sour Cream
Borsch
Roast Woodcock
Cherries Flamed with Kirsch

❧

Potage Crécy
Lobster Thermidor
Roast Quail
Polenta
Compote of Apricots

❧

Potage Parmentier
Alose à l'Oseille
Tournedos Rossini
Glace aux Fraises
Petits Fours

❧

Potage Crème de Riz
Merlan à la Dieppoise
Roast Haunch of Venison, Sauce Poivrade
Braised Celery
Blueberry Ice

❧

Potage Dubarry
Cabillaud à la Portugaise
Roast Pheasant, 2 Bread Sauces
Glace aux Abricots

❧

Potage Condé
Fillets of John Dory à la Mazatlán
Pintade Rôtie
Tomates Farcies
Crêpes Suzette

❧

Consommé Madrilène
Bar Rôti
Petites Pommes a l'Anglaise
Roast Prime Ribs of Beef
Yorkshire Pudding
Watercress Salad
Soufflé aux Fraises

❧

Bisque de Homard
Wild Duck, Rouennaise
Wild Rice
Soufflé au Citron

❧

Cockyleekie
Poached Salmon, Drawn Butter
Sliced Cucumbers
Roast Young Partridge
Compote of Pears in Red Wine

LUNCH MENUS FOR WARM WEATHER

❧

Salade Niçoise
Poulet Sauté Parmentier
Cheese
Fresh Fruit

❧

Soufflé au Fromage Surprise
Cold Boeuf à la Mode
Green Salad
Cheese
Fresh Fruit

❧

Cold Asparagus, Sauce Gribiche
Poulet Sauté Marengo
Cheese
Tarte aux Fraises

❧

Chaud-froid de Volaille
Salade de Cresson et Laitue
Cheese
Framboises Fraîches

❧

Quiche Lorraine
Escalopes de Veau Flambées
Laitues Braisées
Cheese
Fresh Fruit

❧

Pipérade
Roast Chicken
Potatoes Château
Green Salad
Cheese
Tarte aux Pêches

❦

Quenelles de Brochet, Sauce Américaine
Poulet Poché à l'Estragon
White Rice
Cut-up Fruit in Kirsch

❦

Cooked Vegetables Salad, Vinaigrette
Bouillabaisse
Cheese
Tarte à l'Orange

❦

Warm Green Asparagus, Hollandaise
Pâté de Veau Parisienne
Cheese
Fresh Fruit

❦

Moules Marinière
Escalopes de Veau Viennoise
Nouilles
Courgettes Farcies
Tarte aux Abricots

❦

Oeufs Froids à la Reine
Grilled Double Prime Lamb Chops
Braised Lettuce
Cheese
Clafoutis Limousin

DINNER MENUS FOR WARM WEATHER

❧

Consommé Froid au Madère
Mousse de Merlan, Sauce Américaine
Selle de Mouton
Petits Pois à la Française
Charlotte Russe

❧

Potage Saint-Germain
Galantine de Volaille
Cresson
Charlotte Estivale

❧

Saumon Froid, Sauce Verte
Noisettes d'Agneau, Sauce Espagnole
Haricots Verts
Petits Pots de Crême à la Vanille

❧

Truite de Rivière en Gelée
Tournedos à la Louis
Braised Celery
Charlotte Malakoff

❧

Poached Striped Bass, Sauce Moutarde
Pommes Vapeur
Roast Rack of Lamb
Petits Pois à la Française
Pudding Nesselrode

⋖§⋗

Aspic de Filets de Sole au Vin Blanc
Ris de Veau à la Grenelle
Glace aux Fraises Fraîches

⋖§⋗

Coquilles Saint-Jacques à la Dieppoise
Épigrammes d'Agneau
Carottes Nouvelles
Bavarois aux Fraises

⋖§⋗

Cold Poached Lobster, Sauce Mayonnaise
Veal Chops en Papillottes,
Sauce Tomate
Glace à la Framboise

⋖§⋗

Crabe à la Beatrix
Poulet Sauté Archiduc
Purée de Céleri-Rave et Pommes de Terre
Glace à l'Orange

⋖§⋗

Cold Poached Fresh Sardines, Sauce Gribiche
Canard aux Navets
Bavarois au Chocolat

❧

Homard à la Newburg
Filet de Boeuf Rôti
Haricots Verts
Glace au Sirop des Abricots Frais

❧

Homard à l'Américaine
Pintade en Chartreuse
Compote of Plums and Nectarines

PART III

Foreign
and
Exotic
Dishes

LIKE ALL GREAT CITIES, Paris harbors a multiplicity of races and na-
tionalities. Sooner or later even the poorest immigrants seek and find
their own kind of home cooking, and, as the enticement of gain appears before the eyes of the more alert among them, little food shops,
then modest cafés, and later bold-faced restaurants sprout all over.
It is possible that, barring some anthropophagous Kanakas, every
nationality in Paris has its own gastronomic consulate. One of the
most reputable *guides* lists seventy-three such establishments repre-
senting no less than twenty-three countries—by no means an all-in-
clusive register; at first sight one is aware of some lacunae. And, then,
of course, many fashionable Paris restaurants of unimpeachable Gallic
pedigree serve non-French dishes, sometimes admirably executed,
doubtless because of their fashionable international patronage. Although on the *guide* just mentioned only one "British" restaurant
appears, English and Scottish dishes are to be found on famous restaurant menus almost daily. Here only a modest non-French repertory
will be given, comprising in some cases dishes from far away lands
that—alas—can not be obtained in Paris but that the author, having
sampled them on their native heath and learned to prepare them,
would like the reader to try.

ITALIAN

MACCHERONI
[Macaroni]

Under *maccheroni* the Italians list not only what in English we know as macaroni but spaghetti, *lasagne*, *fettuccine*, etc.—all the varieties of preparations based on wheat flour and water or flour and eggs or all three combined, of course seasoned with salt. Macaroni wheat is different from bread wheat: the latter makes inferior macaroni and the former inferior bread.

It is advisable to have a large saucepan with boiling salted water (1 spoonful of salt for 3 or 4 quarts of water) into which you throw the macaroni. Do not cover, as unless the water is quite low in the pan it will boil over before you know it. Stir the bottom, now and then, to keep the macaroni from sticking and test the degree of cooking to your liking at the end of 20 minutes. (The Italians like it *al dente*—i.e., rather crisp to the tooth.) Withdraw it from the heat and cover it to let the macaroni swell for a few minutes: thus they do not stick together. Drain it just before serving and butter it to your taste, unless you serve it with a sauce with an olive oil base, in which case a little oil just before serving helps the unctuousness of the pasta.

Fettuccine and *tagliatelle* are noodles and the most delicate of this family, being made of flour and eggs without water. Spinach, cooked, squeezed dry, and strained is used to color them green when so desired. (For a recipe for noodle paste, see page 47). The famous Alfredo alla Scrofa in Rome served his excellent *fettuccine* with finely grated cheese—whether Parmesan or Romano *pecorino* he never told. No sauce was needed, as the cheese literally melted into the fine pasta.

Vermicelli are preferably combined with tiny clams called *vongole* and sauced with tomatoes and a suspicion of garlic in olive oil. This is a specialty of Jewish restaurants in Rome. No grated cheese should be added.

Spaghetti, the national dish of Naples, is served with Neapolitan sauce preferably and also with Bolognese sauce, the latter, originating in northern central Italy, not being quite orthodox for the *conoscenti*. Variations of both sauces may be found in authoritative Italian cookery books and the length and breadth of the country: an imaginative cook can invent his or her own twist, provided he or she does not neglect the indispensable tomato.

Lasagne are wide (1½ inch and more) strips of pasta made as for noodles—i.e., with eggs and flour without water. The addition of spinach as given above makes them attractive without changing their flavor. A very flavorful dish is *lasagne alla bolognese*: butter an oven dish and spread a layer of boiled (as above) *lasagne*, then a layer of Bolognese sauce, then another layer of boiled *lasagne*, then a layer of Sauce Béchamel (see page 8), then another layer of *lasagne*, another of Bolognese sauce, a final layer of *lasagne*, and a good covering of Sauce Mornay (see page 9), topped with flakes of butter, to brown in the oven.

In all these preparations the affinity of sweet basil and tomato must be kept in mind.

Cappelletti are little discs of pasta filled with ground meats and herbs and shaped like little hats (hence the name), cooked in boiling water for 20 minutes just before serving in a meat broth.

Of all pasta dishes the most demanding preparation is that of *ravioli*, the crowning glory of Genoese cuisine. It deserves at least the following recipe.

RAVIOLI ALLA GENOVESE
[Ravioli Filled with Calf's Brains and Borage]

Contrary to expectations, the *pasta* is made with more water than egg: to 1 pound of flour add 1 egg and 1 good wineglass of water, plus ½ teaspoon of salt, to make a rather floppy dough that should be worked thoroughly and then covered to let rest for an hour or so.

Meanwhile sauté in a wineglassful of oil and 2 spoonfuls of rendered suet (veal kidney fat) ½ pound of beef round with 1 small chopped onion, half a clove of minced garlic and 1 teaspoon of ground rosemary. When it is well browned on both sides, moisten it with enough red wine to cover (about 1½ cups) and let this be almost entirely absorbed. Add 1 cup of chopped tomatoes (peeled, seeded, squeezed of their water) and ½ cup tomato puree (tinned).

Let all this cook, stirring from time to time, while you boil in salted water 1 large head of escarole lettuce (thoroughly well washed in advance), and 1 well-packed cup of borage leaves (*this is the tricky ingredient*); put these through a strainer after cooling under the tap and squeezing the water out. To this puree add one-half its volume of calf's brains (½ calf's brain) cooked in 1 cup of vinegar court-bouillon (see page 51); ½ cup cooked, ground-up white chicken meat; and some of the beef from the first preparation—plus 2 ounces of sausage meat; 1 whole egg (to bind it); pinches of chopped basil, parsley, and thyme leaves; salt and pepper; and cooked lamb fries—all ground up and pureed. The predominant ingredient—mark you—is the green one, in a 2 to 1 proportion: this is the filler or stuffing, which you place in little heaps on the thin, rolled-out sheet of pasta that you have already marked like a checkerboard in 2-inch squares with a roweled pastry cutter. To each little heap add a good pinch of grated Parmesan cheese (some masters insist upon mixing the puree with milk curd).

Cover this sheet of pasta (with the little heaps) with another sheet of pasta, equally thin; pinch down the joints of the checkerboard and then cut them with the roweled cutter. Make sure each square is well sealed, and when everybody is at table throw them in a large pan with boiling salted water for 5 or 6 minutes. Serve the ravioli on very hot plates and cover them with the sauce made with the first preparation and plenty of grated Parmesan cheese.

N.B. Of course the meat with the tomatoes and wine, etc., is put through the grinder. Also, *never* add spinach to the filler: absolutely against Genoese rules.

MINESTRONE
[*Vegetable Soup*]

Minestra is the Italian for a soup with vegetables and *Minestrone* is the augmentative, therefore a grand soup containing many ingredients. Every town and city in Italy has its own *minestrone*: the northern cooks, excepting the Genoese, omit the pasta; the Genoese, possibly through their maritime intercourse with Naples, are pasta eaters. Practically all add beans, dried or fresh, and tomatoes. So, you can invent your own *minestrone* by starting with beans which have soaked for 2 hours if they are dry and cooked in water or broth with onion and garlic and a piece of bacon, and continuing with any vegetable at hand, beginning with those that require longer cooking and winding up with the tenderer varieties. The vegetables must not disintegrate. Cut macaroni or rice can be added, or pieces of toasted bread, preferably of the rougher varieties. Peeled, seeded, and squeezed tomatoes should come toward the end. And, of course, generous helpings of grated cheese, Parmesan or old *pecorino*.

RISOTTO

Lombardy and the Piedmont are the land of the *risotti*. There the rice used is short grained, and its mission is to enrich the sauces or flavors with which it is cooked. Simon-pure *risotto alla milanese* is this short-grained rice thrown into a saucepan, where a chopped onion is cooking in butter and beef marrow, stirred briefly, then moistened with boiling salted water or broth, *which is replaced* as soon as it is consumed, so as to obtain a gummy texture but not a mush. Saffron is added at mid-cooking—two or three filaments ground in a small mortar and moistened with warm water for a pot of rice—a little more butter, and finally grated Parmesan.

POLENTA

East of Milan and over the Veneto yellow cornmeal, called *polenta*, is the staple food. Dribbled over boiling salted water while with the other hand it is constantly stirred, the polenta is then simmered for 25 or 30 minutes, buttered generously, and finally well mixed with a generous amount of slivers of Fontina cheese and seasoned with white pepper. Whiter cornmeal is used to prepare *gnocchi*: boiled in the same way, sometimes in milk, it is mixed with whole eggs very thoroughly and seasoned with salt and white pepper; it is spread out on a moistened flat surface to an even thickness of ¾ to 1 inch, cut with a round pastry cutter about 1¼ inches in diameter, set in a buttered ovenproof dish well dusted with grated Parmesan, covered with very hot butter and more Parmesan, and lightly browned in a 350° F. oven.

OSSOBUCO
[Braised Veal Knuckle]

Perhaps the best-known Italian meat dish is *ossobuco*, again a northern Italian preparation. This is knuckle of veal sawed in sections 1½ inches to 2 inches long (the marrow remaining inside), and then braised on a bed of onions and carrots (chopped), half a clove of garlic, and herbs, with wine and consommé. Tomatoes (peeled and seeded and squeezed) are added, also tomato paste, and the sauce is thickened after straining with butter and flour or with arrowroot (not very Italian), and a little grated lemon peel is sprinkled over all.

VITELLO TONNATO
[Veal with Tuna Sauce]

Italy can boast of a cold meat dish that can vie with any of the best in the world: *vitello tonnato* or *vitello uso tonno*, which is veal cooked with anchovies and tuna in oil (tinned).

Take a 2-pound slice of veal from the top of the round and lay it on finely sliced onions in a rather flat and oval pan with a good lid. Cover the veal with the tuna (5 to 6 ounces) and 4 anchovy fillets (washed of their brine or tinned with oil) cut in little pieces and distributed about. Carefully pour in enough white wine to cover the meat, then put on the lid and set the pan on medium heat. When a boil is reached, turn down the heat to keep the liquor simmering for 1½ to 1¾ hours.

Make sure the meat is cooked but not falling apart; then remove it to a dish that more or less fits it and spread over it the strained contents of the pan with a little fruity olive oil and lemon juice well amalgamated. Cover and leave to cool for 24 hours—*not* in the refrigerator.

N.B. This is a delicious hors d'oeuvre.

SALTIMBOCCA
[Veal and Ham Sauté]

Veal again is used in the Roman dish (originally from Brescia, some fifty-five miles east of Milan) *saltimbocca*. These (yes, the word is plural) are small and very thin slices of veal from the top of the round that are pinned together with a wooden sliver (a wooden toothpick) to an equally fine and small slice of raw ham with a fresh sage leaf sandwiched in between, sautéed in butter, turned over once. The pan is deglazed with hot water or wine and water for a sauce.

There are two outstanding Italian gastronomic practices that are highly commendable: (1) beginning the midday meal with a green salad; and (2) finishing a meal with ripe pears and fresh Parmesan cheese in the piece. For the English-speaking person a well-seasoned lettuce or vegetable salad goes admirably well after cocktails or gins-and-bitters, while it poses a problem for the wine at the end or toward the end of lunch: obviously, the vinegar in the dressing ruins the mouth for the wine. As for the Parmesan with ripe pears dessert, the Italians have a rather endearing ditty:

> *Al contandin' non far sapere*
> *Com' è buon il caccio con le pere.*

> Don't let the farmer know
> How good cheese is with pears.

RUSSIAN

BLINIS
[Leavened Pancakes]

Modern cooking appliances do not lend themselves to the preparation of blinis, because they should be cooked in a little iron pan
without handles sitting on an old-fashioned stove with heat distributed evenly all over. However, Russian refugees all over the
world manage with their typical incredible adaptability to produce
them in holes in the wall. So, why not try?

Bliny pan

In ½ cup of warm milk, dissolve 1 ounce of yeast completely.
Add this to 11 ounces of buckwheat flour in a bowl and beat to mix
well. Let rise, well covered and in a warm spot, for 2 hours. Beat
again and add 6 ounces of wheat flour, 2 lightly beaten egg yolks,
and ⅔ cup of thick cream. Sprinkle with ½ teaspoonful of salt, then
mix well and beat lightly to get a creamy, not-too-thick mixture. Add
2 egg whites beaten stiff, cutting and folding, and 2 spoonfuls of
whipped cream. Cover and let stand for 25 minutes.

Brush at least two very small (they *should* be about 5 inches in
diameter!) skillets with clarified butter (see page 10) and get them
hot. Take a spoonful of your mixture from the top of the bowl and
drop it on each pan, without stirring the bowl, and laying the spoon
on a plate beside it until the next pair so as not to stir the mixture.
Each bliny should spread by itself, and after it solidifies should be
brushed lightly with the clarified butter and then turned over with

a spatula. As soon as they are golden in color they should be re-moved to a hot plate (preferably silver) and covered. Continue the operation until all the blinis are cooked.

With the quantities given here you should have about 20. They should be served piping hot with heavy sour cream and caviar (pressed caviar is recommended): the caviar may be spread over a bliny, another bliny put on top, and the cream poured overall.

N.B. Many authors spell "bliny" in English *bleeny*, which is perfectly acceptable, as the *i* is longer than in *in*, though perhaps not quite as long as the *ee*. Here the spelling current on restaurant menus has been followed. Note also that blinis are a special dish for the last week of the Carnival—i.e., Lent.

PÍROSHKI

[Meat-Filled Patties]

Píroshki (again, the spelling should be *pirozhki* in English, but this complication has been sidestepped in the vernacular) are little soft patties with meat filling. They make delicious hot hors d'oeuvres (a current yet absurd term because to be at their best they should be cooked just before they are eaten) before lunch, or even a light supper with a plate of soup. The dough may be used for Koolyebyaka (spelt *koulibiac* or *kouliebiac* or *coulibiac*) (see below). No better recipe for American readers than that of Princess Alexandra Obolensky, as below.

Soften 6 ounces of butter (or 3 ounces of butter and 3 ounces of oleomargarine) and 6 ounces of cream cheese at room temperature and add 2 cups of sifted all-purpose flour, working with your fingers in a bowl until you make a ball that does not stick to its sides. Wrap this in waxed paper and put it away in the refrigerator's fruit and vegetable compartment—i.e., least cold portion. When ready to use, let it stand at room temperature to acquire the necessary soft-ness to be shaped. Dust your pastry slab or board with flour and roll out the dough to a 1/8-inch thickness. Mark with a pastry cutter 2½ inches in diameter as many patties as your dough can make, and lay a spoonful of filling (see below) in the center of each—in an oval shape—so that when you cut out each patty you can fold it over the filling and, with your fingers moistened in cold water, pinch the edges together to enclose the filling. Brush the surface with beaten egg, punch little holes with a sharp-tined fork (to let the steam escape while baking and thus prevent cracking of the patty), and bake in a 375° F. oven for 35 or 40 minutes.

For the filling take 1 pound of ground beef (better done at home than at the butcher's: you know what you are getting), 1 large onion (chopped fine), 2 hard-boiled eggs (also chopped fine), 1 teaspoon of dill weed, and ½ cup beef consommé. Mix all this thoroughly, adding the consommé gradually: the filling must be quite hard, so do not use all the consommé if you see it soften. Also, if the consommé is not salted or is lightly salted, add a pinch of salt.

BORSCH

[Beef and Beet Soup with Sour Cream]

Borsch is a soup, but it is given here because blinis and píroshki are eaten about the same time as borsch—sometimes before, some-times after, but more or less at the beginning of a meal. Borsch is a sour soup—made sour by the generous addition of soured beet juice; so if you cannot or will not obtain this ingredient, as is most likely, you will add a good portion of *sour cream*, which actually improves the soup for Western palates.

Take, then, 1½ pounds of brisket of beef, 1 pound of bacon, and 2 large onions and chop them in large dice; put them in a soup pot to brown lightly with 2 spoonfuls of butter; add 1 large cabbage (minus its stem and well washed), 3 or 4 leeks (likewise), and 4 or 5 large beets (carefully peeled), and all sliced quite fine. Cover the whole with water and consommé in the proportion of two-thirds of the first and one-third of the second. Verify the salt seasoning and add 1 teaspoon of peppercorns. Set on high heat and skim as gray scum rises with the boil, and boil steadily but not violently for 2 hours, or until the chunks of beef are cooked. Add the desired amount of sour cream: 4 spoonfuls or so.

KOOLYEBYAKA
[Coulibiac]

Here will be considered only the salmon and rice *coulibiac* (this is the easiest spelling after all). So, take ½ cup of rice and cook it as on page 45. Then sauté lightly in butter 2 or 3 (depending on size) salmon steaks 1½ inches thick and remove the bones. Sauté likewise 2 or 3 spoonfuls of chopped shallots and sprinkle them generously with dill weed and white pepper.

Now take *piroshki* (see page 322) paste in the quantity given in that recipe and make two equal-sized balls; then shape each one into a square block. Roll these out with your rolling pin into twin sheets twice as long as they are wide. On the center of one put a layer of the cooked rice, keeping it 1½ inch from the edges, and on this the boned and sautéed salmon steaks sprinkled with the sautéed shallot and dill. Sprinkle a pinch of salt over each steak. Cover all this with the other sheet and pinch the two sheets together, moistening your fingers with cold water. Make a few vent holes all over to let the steam escape and brush the surface with beaten egg. Put into a buttered and floured roasting pan and bake in a 300° F. oven for 40 minutes.

N.B. Hard-boiled eggs, halved or chopped up, may be added to good effect. Also, wherever Russian delicatessens have *vesiga*, it should be boiled gently and minced, then added to the sautéed shallots: 6 ounces will suffice.

GAVIÁDINA PA STRÓGANOVSKY
[Beef Stroganoff]

Slice 1 pound of beef tenderloin ⅛ inch thick and then cut the slices into pieces 1 inch wide and 3 inches long. Season them with salt and pepper and let them stand for 1 hour, then make a brown binding by melting 1 spoonful of butter, adding to it 1 spoonful of all-purpose flour, stirring, letting this puff up, stirring again, and repeating the operation until the mixture is brownish. Add 1 tin of beef consommé, stirring on medium-low heat, and then 1 spoonful of tomato paste and 2 spoonfuls of sour cream. Cover and set aside while you sauté the slices of beef in hot butter with finely chopped shallots for 5 minutes on each side. Add the sauce and remove the pan to low heat to allow it to simmer for 10 minutes. Serve on very hot plates.

BRITISH

OXTAIL SOUP
[English]

The real English recipe is this:

Take 2 skinned oxtails and cut them across at the joints of the vertebrae; put them in a large cocotte, rather high than wide, with 1 thick slice of raw ham, 2 spoonfuls of butter, 2 or 3 carrots (peeled and cored), 1 well-washed leek (minus its root base), 2 or 3 turnips (peeled), 1 well-washed bunch of celery *green leaves*, 3 onions (roughly sliced), 2 bay leaves, 2 sprigs of fresh thyme (or ½ teaspoon dried), several stalks of parsley, and 1 teaspoon of salt. Add 1½ cups of cold water and set on high heat. When the liquid boils, skim the gray froth that comes up. Add 2½ quarts of boiling water and 1 spoonful of peppercorns, then turn the heat down so that the liquid simmers to cook thus for 3 to 4 hours, at the end of which lift the pieces of tail onto a warm plate.

With 2 spoonfuls of butter and 2 spoonfuls of all-purpose flour, make a dark yellow binding, which you then dilute with the soup, *little by little*. Bring to a boil and skim again, then strain through fine mesh into another cocotte. Add 2 spoonfuls of ketchup and half a wineglassful of tawny port. Verify the seasoning. Turn the sections of oxtail back into the soup and bring to a boil, then remove from the heat and serve.

COCKYLEEKIE, COCK-A-LEEKIE
[*Scotch*]

Put a mature fowl (preferably a cock) in a soup pot with a well-fitting lid, along with the white portions of 12 to 15 medium-sized leeks and cold water just to cover the fowl. Set on high heat and skim carefully as the liquid comes to a boil. Add 1 cup of concentrated beef consommé and 1 spoonful of peppercorns and bring to a boil again, then reduce the heat to simmer the liquor, covered, for 3½ hours. Lift the fowl and carve it as you would a roast chicken. Put it back, bones and all, into the pot, and, 30 minutes before serving, add 12 prunes.

The moment before serving, cut the meat of the fowl into smaller pieces and serve them *without the bones* but with what is left of the leeks and the prunes, and the soup poured over them.

STEAK AND KIDNEY PUDDING
[*English*]

For this you need a pudding bowl or basin and about 24 inches of good rough muslin, which you should dip in warm water, squeeze out, and lay on the bowl with its edges hanging over the rim. Dust the muslin with all-purpose flour.

Make a dough with 3 cups of flour and ⅔ of a cup of finely chopped raw suet (the ball of fat enclosing veal kidneys) without any membrane, adding enough cold water, with ½ teaspoon of salt and a pinch of baking powder, and kneading it, to make it homogeneous. Roll into a ball.

Now throw one large onion (finely sliced) into *melted* butter on medium heat and cook until it is yellow (not deep brown). Add 1½ pounds of beef top of the round in thin slices about 4 inches long and well dredged in flour. Turn them over once one side is browned, stirring to keep the flour from catching, and once both sides are brown add enough beef consommé to cover them by about 1 inch. Turn the heat down to keep this simmering and stir from time to time. After 1 hour of cooking, add ½ teaspoon of salt, some freshly ground pepper, a bay leaf, and 1 sprig of fresh thyme (¼ teaspoon dried). Cover and cook for 1 hour longer, simmering.

Cut two veal kidneys, freed of all membrane and fat, into ¾-inch-thick pieces across and sauté them lightly in hot butter until they are grayish brown on both sides. Season them with salt and pepper, then mix them with the cooked beef slices and the gravy. Spread out the dough in a round shape and set it on the floured muslin in the bowl so its outer edge will overlap the brim of the bowl. Turn the meats and gravy into the middle of the dough and then gather dough and muslin over them into a bag that you then tie securely with several turns of white cotton string, leaving one long strand of string. Use this to lift the loaded bag and put it into a pan containing furiously boiling water. Cover the pan, leaving a chink to prevent boiling over and keeping the string hanging over the side to lift the bag when the pudding is done. Boil steadily for 3½ hours, then lift with the string and a skimmer to the bowl, which should be kept warm, after untying the bag on a plate and putting the bowl upside down on the pudding.

Serve with powdered English mustard moistened with water into a paste.

STEAK AND KIDNEY PIE
[English]

Cook the meats as for the pudding above and put them in an ovenproof earthenware dish. Cover this with plain pastry (see Pâte à Foncer, page 275), brush with beaten egg, and bake for 35 minutes in a 375° F. oven. Serve with mustard as above.

BOILED LEG OF MUTTON, CAPER SAUCE
[English]

If the mutton is *boiled* exactly 15 minutes to the pound, and when that time elapses removed instantly from the water to a hot dish, the juice of the meat will compare favorably with a roast leg of mutton and the meat will be more uniformly rosy.

In order to obtain this result, the leg must be trimmed at the hip joint and of all extra fat, but left with its skin on. Then it should be weighed carefully and the pounds multiplied by 15: you will have the exact time of *boiling*. Put it in a kettle and cover it with cold water, then lift it without losing any of the water: this is to make sure you have sufficient water. Add 1 spoonful of rock salt, 1 spoonful of crushed (in a mortar) rosemary leaves, 2 onions (stuck with 1 whole clove each), 1 pound of turnips (peeled and quartered), ½ pound of carrots (peeled and cored), 2 bay leaves, 2 sprigs of fresh thyme (or ½ teaspoon dried), several stalks of parsley, and (sneak in) half a clove of garlic.

Set your kettle on high heat and bring the water to a boil. Now calculate at what time you are to serve the meat, and, allowing a leeway of 10 minutes for the water to boil again, put the leg into the boiling water, leaving a long string out to lift it with when done, and clap on the lid. Count your precise time from the moment the water boils again and lift the meat out the moment the time is up. Lay it on a hot serving platter or a carving board on a platter: the juice will overflow the board. Lift the vegetables out and crowd them around the meat.

Serve with boiled potatoes and a Sauce Béchamel (see page 8) in which you shall have mixed 2 or 3 spoonfuls of capers.

YORKSHIRE PUDDING
[English]

This is the classical accompaniment for roast ribs of beef.

Take 1 cup of all-purpose flour and 1 cup of milk and mix them thoroughly, then add 1 teaspoon of salt and 2 beaten eggs. Beat the whole with a mechanical egg beater for 2 minutes by the clock.

Have a round pie plate heated in a 350° F. oven with some beef fat; pour your mixture into it and bake at that heat for 35 to 40 minutes. It should puff up and become golden brown.

Serve with the roast juices poured over it.

SPANISH

POTE GALLEGO
[Galician Pork and Vegetable Soup]

The rustic edition of this soup comprises white beans, turnip greens, cabbage, potatoes, a bit of rancid bacon, and a pig's tail! Countess Pardo-Bazan in her delightful book *Ancient Spanish Cuisine* says that, when the peasants can afford to have a pig's tail "dancing in the pot," they break into song with joy. But, those were other days. Now the *pote* or *caldo gallego* is made with the aforesaid vegetables, a piece of raw ham (a slice off a picnic), and potatoes. An improvement is to use small, fresh lima beans cooked in cold water to cover with a spoonful of butter to 1 cup of beans, an onion (peeled), half a clove of garlic, and 4 ounces of bacon (cut in 2 or 3 pieces); boil for 1 hour and then add 1 quart of water, 2 handfuls of well-washed turnip greens, and 1 medium-sized cabbage (roughly chopped up), 1 bay leaf, and a few peppercorns. Cook at a steady boil for 40 minutes, add 4 thick chunks of raw shoulder (picnic) ham, cook for 20 minutes longer, and serve.

N.B. Potatoes, boiled, can be added at the last minute while still hot.

PAELLA À LA VALENCIANA
[Casserole of Chicken, Vegetables, Fish, and Rice]

The casserole here must be a wrought-iron shallow pan with two handles; the fish must be sections of skinned eel and clams; the vegetables, onion (chopped up), well-pared artichoke hearts (preferably precooked), tomatoes (peeled and seeded), and sweet peppers (peeled and seeded and cut into thin slices).

First, sauté in pork lard or olive oil the vegetables, without making them mushy. Then add pieces of chicken, beginning with the dark meat (without the bone), and then the seafood. When everything is golden—half cooked—add 1 cup of rice and stir it all over without damaging the contents of the *paella*, then, after 3 or 4 minutes, moisten it with 2 cups of boiling chicken broth. Stir lightly and cover for a few minutes.

As soon as the liquid is absorbed, withdraw the *paella* from the heat to a warm place, covered quite tightly.

N.B. The rice should be of the short-grain variety, and not mushy when cooked. Small red Spanish sausages called *chorizos* can be added when the rice is moistened with the broth. Also, a variant calls for a little saffron dissolved in hot water.

BACALAO A LA VIZCAINA
[In Basque, Makalua-Bizkai-Arauz—Salt Cod à la Basque]

This is perhaps the most famous of all Spanish fish dishes, yet, as the Basques insist that they are a nation apart, it may be considered improper to list it under this heading.

Anyway, for 4 persons:

Take $1\frac{1}{2}$ pounds of salt cod and soak it for 24 hours in cold water; after 3 or 4 hours it should be soft enough to cut in pieces 2 by 3 inches, which should be put back to soak. After the 24 hours, drain the cod and and put it in a pan with cold water to cover and 1 bay leaf; set the pan on high heat and when a white froth begins to rise—i.e. just before the water breaks into a boil—take the fish out but keep the water. Scrape off any scales stuck to the skin and pick off all bones without breaking up the pieces, which you set aside between two plates.

Fry in a cupful of olive oil some garlic cloves and a spoonful of bacon dice, and when both are light brown lift them out with a skimmer and replace them with 4 or 5 onions (cut in fine rings, about $2\frac{1}{2}$ pounds of onion) to fry until golden yellow; remove the pan from the heat, and while the oil cools slightly cut up 10 sweet Spanish peppers (tinned) in very fine strips and 4 or 5 tomatoes (peeled and seeded), which you throw into the oil. Return the pan to high heat and add 4 or 5 thick slices of white bread (without the crust), $1/2$ teaspoon sugar, and 2 spoonfuls of toasted almonds (pounded fine in a mortar with a pestle). After cooking for 15 minutes, strain through a colander: you should have a thick sauce. Verify the sea' soning as to salt, and, if the water you boiled the cod in is not too salt, add some of it to thin down the sauce: all depends on your taste.

Heat the fish in the sauce before serving (preferably in low earthenware dishes).

N.B. Whatever bits of bacon remain are not served.

PIPÉRADE
[In Basque, Piparrada Zarauztarra—Scrambled Eggs with Sweet Peppers, Tomatoes, and Ham]

Zarauz is a famous sea bathing resort in the Basque country of Spain, and there can be found very special sweet peppers, both green and red. For this dish—which is scrambled eggs with sweet peppers, tomatoes, and raw ham—put the peppers on a pie plate in the oven until the skin wrinkles up, then peel them, seed them, and cut them up in long thin strips. Peel and seed the same amount of tomatoes, and cut them up.

Sauté the peppers in olive oil for 15 minutes, turning them over when done on one side, then lift them out to a plate with a skimmer and replace them with the tomatoes. When these are half cooked— i.e. before they turn mushy—add beaten whole eggs and strips of raw ham and diminish the heat. Stir constantly to obtain a creamy consistence, then add the peppers and the tomatoes, verify the salt and pepper seasoning, and serve on hot plates.

GREEK

DOLMADES
[Stuffed Vine Leaves]

30 vine leaves (fresh or dried)
2 pounds ground pork
2 oz. rice, washed in boiling water and drained
3 oz. finely chopped onion
Parsley, fennel, salt and pepper

Wash vine leaves well. Wilt them by placing them for a few minutes in boiling water. In a mixing bowl, place your meat, rice, onions and seasoning. When well blended, roll a small portion of the mixture out and wrap well in a vine leaf. Continue until all the meat is thus parceled out.

Place the dolmades in a fairly deep kettle in one layer. Pour in 1 cup of water. Set on high heat and let come to a boil. Boil until the water is practically absorbed, then add enough water to come up almost to the top of the dolmades. *Simmer* for 1 hour.

Sauce:
1 ounce butter
2 egg yolks
Juice of 1 lemon
3 tablespoons of flour
1 cup of warm milk

Melt butter in a small saucepan and add the flour. Stir and cook for a few minutes until the mixture begins to change color, then add warm milk and salt gradually while stirring, and at the first boil withdraw from the heat. It should be a creamy mixture. Whip the egg yolks to a froth and add the lemon juice to them; to this add the creamy mixture gradually and stirring.

Lift the dolmades from their saucepan with a skimmer to a clean napkin to drain, then to a warm platter, and serve with the sauce.

(Mrs. Thomas Wildman's recipe.)

(continued)

N.B. Greek vine leaves, accompanied by a light sauce, are available in tins. They need no wilting in boiling water.

INDIAN

On his first visit to India early in 1919, the author made two bad mistakes on his first morning in Calcutta: wishing to visit the city's great bazaar, he directed the taxi driver to take him to the Lal Bazaar, which to his humiliating horror he found to be the police headquarters; and, then, after repairing somewhat his ruffled dignity, he bid the driver to take him where he could buy some seed of the curry "plant": he was taken to a large marketplace, where he finally found the spices, etc., but to his dismay discovered that there is no curry plant. Many months later, at Mahaberatenni Estate in Ceylon, his planter host had his Tamil cook teach him how to make curry. Here is the Western adaptation.

In teaspoonfuls: ½ of powdered ginger, ¼ of powdered cardamom seeds, ¼ of powdered mustard, ¼ cayenne pepper, ¼ powdered white pepper, 1 of powdered fenugreek, 1 of powdered coriander seed, 2 of powdered cumin seed, 2 of powdered turmeric. These powders, readily available in the United States at the better food stores, should be mixed together thoroughly and kept in well-stoppered jars.

The best planter's curry was made of roast mutton cut up in 2-inch chunks and sautéed in a saucepan with *ghee* (liquid and quite rancid butter) into which as many heaping spoonfuls of the above mixture had been put and stirred for 2 or 3 minutes, then moistened with enough water to cover the meat. The heat was turned down to keep the sauce simmering for 30 minutes.

Excellent Patna rice was served with it; and the garnishes put on the table were very hot *dhal* (a dried pea mush spiced with the curry mixture surcharged with red pepper), *poppadums* (thin curd bean-flour and rice-flour wafers), mango chutney, and Bombay duck (dried *bommaloe* fish fillets). Grated coconut was served with curry at the Galle Face Hotel, Colombo, a garnish never added in the subcontinent.

There are, of course, many varieties of curry in India and Ceylon and wherever the British Raj extended its customs in the East. In the exiguous kitchens of British planters the powders indicated above were replaced by pastes made in the native mortars from most of the ingredients, which are roots and fruits.

JAPANESE

The cuisine of Japan is possibly the most delicate in the world. The same could be said for the Japanese table setting and general philosophy regarding food. It is a pity that all this has been unfavorably affected by Western influences since World War II; and even many years before there had been some vitiation of the old mores by the introduction of beef, such as in the really non-Japanese s'kyaki (generally written sukyaki).

TEMPURA

Tempura is a dish that can be prepared wherever fresh, preferably live prawns or large shrimps are obtainable. At the Asakusá Amusement Park (a sort of Coney Island) in Tokyo there was a tiny bar where this delicacy was prepared to perfection. A bowl the size of a circle made by your two arms was kept full of boiling sesame oil. A smaller bowl sat beside it on the small counter with some whitish batter. The fat cook behind it dipped prawns into the batter, dropped them into the hot oil and almost instantly scooped them out with a wire skimmer. No better prawn or shrimp dish in the world! Of course, part of the merit was the proximity of the consumer to the cook.

The batter is made by beating an egg (whole), and while beating adding a cup of rice flour, a little salt, and then enough cold water to dilute it all *without excessive mixing.* The oil should be so hot that a pellet of flour and water thrown into it will rise immediately to the surface. Japanese restaurants serve a sauce of soy beans, sodium glutamate, and broth—quite unnecessary and not recom-mended.

N.B. As the boiling oil spreads its smell, which the cooking of the shrimps make stronger, this dish had better be tried outdoors.

CHINESE

Forty years ago the author was invited to dine by friends who had lived for many years in Peking at a famous restaurant back of the Grand Hotel de Pekin. That meal with quite different from any other he ate in Peking, Shanghai, Tientsin, or Hong Kong in private houses or restaurants, not to mention his experience with Chinese restaurants in Paris, London, and New York. The outstanding dishes were, of course, lacquered duck and sharks' fins soup: they were good, but not to be compared with American black duck or even Rouen duck "à la presse" and any of the fine *potages* of the French repertory. At that dinner he was informed that chop suey was not a Chinese dish but one invented for Western con-sumption, and that chow mein was more or less coolie food. Of course, the contempt of northern Chinese for their southern countrymen was obvious, so these dishes, which are Cantonese (if not foreign to China), were spoken of in appropriate emotional terms.

As here an attempt has been made to bring to the reader the authentic recipes of non-French dishes from various lands, this apologia for not entering into the subject is submitted.

NORWEGIAN

Norway is famous for its *smorgaas*,—i.e., its hors d'oeuvres. No attempt will be made here to give recipes for the numerous prepara-tions of that kind. Here only one similar dish will be given: smoked eel (cold) with spinach (hot). Nothing simpler: cook the spinach the ordinary way (see page 98) and serve it with sections of smoked eel. It is as good as rarely known.

TAHITIAN

AI-ÏOTA
[Raw Tuna Pickled in Lemon Juice]

Cut 1½-inch cubes of raw, fresh tuna (bonito will do at a pinch), put them in a bowl and cover them with lemon juice with 2 spoonfuls of salt (in Tahiti they use sea water from the lagoon). Cut one or more onions in medium-thin slices and lay them on top of the water to extend over the whole surface. Set aside in a warm place for 4 or 5 hours: the tuna will turn from red to white.

Cut up the meat of a coconut (make sure it is white and not rancid) and put it, without the brown skin, through your meat grinder; collect all the cream that oozes out and put the ground meat in a clean napkin and squeeze the rest of the cream out of it. After the first squeeze, moisten the ground meats in the napkin with a little water and try squeezing again. Discard the onions; drain off the lemon juice; serve the fish cubes with the coconut cream.

N.B. In Tahiti this is eaten with baked breadfruit, which can be procured now and then in the United States; but the dish is excellent without it as an hors d'oeuvre.

POLYNESIAN BARBECUED PIG

Although it would be most exceptional to find this preparation in Paris or any other city, the item deserves mention in case an enterprising reader should wish to undertake it somewhere in the country. A pit is dug about 4 feet deep, 4 feet long, and 3 feet wide and well lined with large pebbles (or small boulders) on which a very hot fire is made.

Meanwhile, the pig has been killed, disemboweled, and washed (scraping is not necessary). When the fire dies down and the stones are burning hot, the pig is laid on them, roughly wrapped in green banana leaves. Quickly a few more of these leaves are stretched over it and then earth is shoveled in to close the pit. After 3 hours the pit is carefully dug up, the earth brushed away from the banana leaves, and the pig lifted out with hooks: it is perfectly roasted or, rather, baked. The old Spanish-American *barbacoa*, anglicized into "barbe-cue," bears only a superficial resemblance to this baking method, and is really a roasting system: the pit is dug and the fire is made in it, but the pit is left open and across it are placed green branches on which the meat is spitted or laid.

SPANISH-AMERICAN

PUCHERO
[*Argentine*]

To the French Pot-au-Feu (see page 57) add a fowl and a piece of ham or bacon previously blanched to remove excessive salt. Like all such preparations it is based on the Spanish *olla podrida*, meaning "rotten pot;" but it is very far from being rotten and, in fact, is a succulent dish for a hungry man.

ASADO AL ASADOR
[*Argentine*]

Meat spitted on an iron bar stuck in the earth on which a fine bed of embers is burning. The bar or rod is stuck aslant and turned now and then. Several of these bars are kept going at the same time at smart parties, and the men serve the ladies by slashing off morsels from half carcasses of lamb deliciously roasted.

CHUPE DE PESCADO
[*Chilean*]

This is a fish stew of considerable merit. You "melt" a finely sliced onion in clarified butter, and just before it begins to turn yellow you add 1 teaspoon of sweet Spanish red pepper (or paprika) and immediately as much all-purpose flour as you put butter to begin with. Stir until the mixture turns light yellow, then add hot milk, sufficient to make a creamy sauce, while stirring. Add 4 or 5 sweet Spanish peppers pureed through a strainer and 2 spoonfuls of Parmesan cheese (grated). Set aside after thorough stirring.

Meanwhile, bake for 20 minutes in a 350° F. oven a 1½-pound piece of halibut or scrod; cut it up in several pieces and add it to the sauce, together with 5 or 6 spoonfuls of cooked crab meat (tinned), and 2 spoonfuls of heavy cream. Verify the seasoning and serve with boiled potato balls.

RAPINGACHOS
[Ecuadorian]

Potato patties the size of the hollow of your hand with a fried egg on top, covered with peanut sauce.

Make potato balls with mashed potatoes mixed with grated Gruyère-type cheese and flatten them to patty shapes. "Melt" finely sliced white onions or scallions in pork lard until they begin to turn yellow, slowly. Chop up the same quantity of peanuts as of onion and crush them in a mortar with a pestle; add them to the onions and moisten with milk to make a sauce, then season with salt and white pepper.

Fry an egg in pork lard and at the same time a potato patty; lay the fried egg on the patty and cover both with the sauce. Chilies are sometimes added to the sauce: Tabasco sauce could do duty for them.

HUNGARIAN

GOULASH

Goulash or *gulyas* is a beef stew (there is also a goulash soup which is a liquefied form of the same thing plus sausages and other meats of your choice).

Take 2 pounds of beef from the plate, without bones, and cut it into finger-length pieces. Sauté them in 3 or 4 spoonfuls of clarified butter with some coarsely sliced onions (preferably tender spring onions), on medium low heat until the onions begin to turn yellow.

Meanwhile, peel and seed 1 pound of ripe tomatoes. Sprinkle over the meat 1 spoonful of good paprika (it must be the real thing, very aromatic and not very peppery), ½ teaspoon of salt, and a dash of white pepper. Stir well. Add the tomatoes, 1 bay leaf, a sprig of fresh thyme (or ¼ teaspoon dried), and some stalks of parsley. Cover and cook in a 250° F. oven for 1 hour.

Meanwhile, peel 1 pound of potatoes and cut them in quarters. Keep them in cold water until the stew has cooked 1 hour in the oven, then add them, with boiling water to cover them. Put the cocotte back in the oven and raise the heat to 350° F. After 10 minutes, inspect to see that the liquid is boiling and verify the salt seasoning. Continue boiling steadily for 15 minutes. To serve, dish out the potatoes and the meat and pour over them the sauce through a strainer—if you are very refined. Otherwise, just serve as it comes out of the cocotte.

N.B. If the sauce is too liquid, thicken it with arrow-root (see page 65) just before serving. This dish has a good variant: do not add potatoes, but cook noodles separately (see page 47), drain them, and add them to the stew 5 minutes before serving.

Stock and Equipment for a Small Kitchen

IT IS ADVISABLE to have the following ingredients on your kitchen shelves or in your kitchen closet or larder:

1. Natural sea salt, both fine and coarse (in America the latter is obtained in its best form under the label of "kosher" salt—a small bin or a jar is best for coarse salt); onion salt, and celery salt. Shakers should not be held above steaming pans: this cakes the salt. Never keep metal spoons in the salt bin.

2. Pepper: both white and black, both ground and whole (peppercorns). A pepper mill.

3. Bay leaves, thyme (preferably not powdered), rosemary, basil, chervil, tarragon, dill (powdered or in dried leaves). Leaves to be kept in well-wrapped packages or jars.

4. Whole cloves, grated nutmeg, ground mace.

5. Saffron, preferably powdered.

6. Curry spices (powdered): Cuminseed (2), Turmeric (2), Coriander seed (1), Fenugreek (1), Ginger (1), Mustard (½), Cayenne pepper (½). (The figures indicate the proportions for a hot curry powder mixture in, say, spoonfuls.) When buying, make sure of freshness by the strong aroma of each; and, when storing, keep lids well screwed down.

7. Olive oil, preferably French, in bottles (kept in a cool place). Flavorless vegetable oil (to prevent butter from burning, and for frying): peanut, cotton-

seed, corn, sesame, or other, if flavorless. Vinegar, both white (malt, wine, or cider) and red (wine). Tarragon (wine) vinegar is excellent for salads.

8. White sugar: granulated, confectioners' (powdered), and lump or tablet; brown sugar (to be kept in well-stoppered jars to prevent caking).

9. All-purpose wheat flour. Long-grain rice.

10. Canned beef consommé (6 tins always on hand); canned clear chicken bouillon or broth and/or chicken bouillon cubes; tomato paste in small jars or tins (it spoils quite quickly, once opened, unless kept in the refrigerator). Flat anchovy fillets in small tins.

11. Parmesan cheese, either grated or in the piece, to be grated as needed (keep in a well-stoppered jar in the refrigerator).

12. Irish potatoes, 2 or 3 pounds, preferably small, and the same quantity of medium-sized yellow onions. 1 garlic bulb (if unobjectionable!).

13. 1 bottle at least of the following: dry white wine such as Chablis (once uncorked, must be kept in refrigerator), Madeira, sherry (pale), port, and French cognac (Three Stars quality). All wines must be good. So-called "cooking" wines are not advisable.

Equally necessary are the following utensils:

1. A set of 5 enameled iron saucepans from $8\frac{1}{2}$ down to $4\frac{1}{2}$ inches in diameter. These should never be put on heat empty and are kept best hanging on hooks within easy reach; and each should have its own close-fitting lid. Enameled iron has the advantages of not discoloring sauces and of not being affected by minerals contained in some waters.

2. A set of 5 heavy enameled cast-iron shirring or oven dishes, oval in shape, from 14 down to 9 inches in length. These can be used in the oven as well as on the top of the stove, and are most valuable because food does not burn easily in them, as in lighter pans.

3. Two *round*, heavy enameled cast-iron "cocottes" with their own lids, 9 to 7 inches in diameter; two *oval* "cocottes" of the same capacity, with their own lids; one or two small oval "cocottes" about 5 inches long, also with own lids; one shallow dutch oven of the same material, with its own lid and preferably divided into three compartments.

4. Two iron frying pans—one to be kept solely for omelettes, wiped clean but not washed. Their diameter should not be greater than 9 inches.

5. Two enameled iron fish kettles, about 16 down to 14 inches long, with inner racks or trays if possible.

6. One heavy enameled cast-iron roasting pan, or one sheet-iron roasting pan (which can be kept less clean and not show it).

7. Individual egg-shirring dishes, preferably of enameled cast iron to with-

stand cooking directly on top of the stove. The number of them is to be determined by the user's needs.

8. Roasting racks or trivets to set in the roasting pans. The best are round in outline and have very short feet.

9. Two white enameled iron strainers (not wire mesh), 1 medium and 1 small; 1 "Chinese" (*chinois*) conical strainer with small holes and another one with wire mesh; one fine sieve for flour.

10. One hand-operated mechanical vegetable grinder or masher (*mouli*), with plates coarse to fine.

11. One meat grinder, preferably electrically powered, with mixer attachments for whipping eggs and cream, etc., and grating and slicing attachments. If that is not possible, a hand-operated meat-grinder, an egg beater, and a hand-operated grater are necessary.

12. One or two soup ladles (stainless steel); 1 wire skimmer; 1 steel and 2 wooden spoons with quite long handles; 2 or 3 two-tined kitchen forks with long wooden handles; 2 or 3 vegetable peelers; 1 apple corer; 1 potato masher; one rolling pin; 1 or 2 can openers; a dozen skewers for "brochette" preparations; 2 or 3 spatulas with long handles; 2 large, 2 medium, and 2 small knives.

N.B. Stainless-steel knives can be resharpened and lose their silvery sheer only along the sharpened edge. They are easier to keep clean than plain steel knives.

13. Reliable scales; 2 or 3 measuring cups (glass).

14. Half a dozen kitchen plates; 2 or 3 wire-mesh dish covers; several washable pot holders; a dozen good-sized dish towels; 2 or 3 sink brushes; soap dish with lid; good supply of garbage bags; order pad and sharp pencils.

15. A mortar and pestle.

About Wines, Words, Mealtimes, Appetizers, and Lobsters

WINES TO ACCOMPANY FOOD: TASTES CHANGE

LISTENING TO MOST ARBITERS of gastronomy today, one is under the impression that a sort of Decalogue was handed down from Above prescribing the inviolate rules governing what wines should be served with what dishes, at least since many centuries back. Such is *not* the case.

For instance, quite recently—since the latter part of the nineteenth century—the taste for Champagne has changed considerably. In France at that time, Champagne of decidedly sweet flavor was the wine that topped the meal. Elsewhere in Western Europe and in the United States sweet Champagne had by then begun to lose favor. "Dry" on the label was mandatory, then "Extra Dry," and later Goût Américain ("American taste"). From a dessert wine it moved up to the middle of the meal, where we find it accompanying substantial meat dishes in 1880–1890. Then, with the increasing *dryness* of the wine, came a decrease in its popularity as a dinner wine, while demand for it in bibulous later hours at the cabarets increased. "Great Britain Reserve" was the next step, moderating the extreme dryness and returning Champagne to the one-wine menu. More recently "Brut"—meaning "untampered with"—has gained top favor and is especially consumed before lunch, even an hour or so before.

Illustrating the serving of champagne with red meat I have a menu of the

Complimentary Dinner to Hon. A. A. Sargent, Minister to Berlin, given by John H. Mitchell at Welcker's, Washington, D.C., on March 1, 1882. Filet de Boeuf was washed down by Mumm and Pommery "Sec."

At that same ten-course dinner, Château d'Yquem was served with the oysters! And two years earlier, at the Annual Supper of the Kinnickinnick Gun Club, the Blue Points were accompanied by "Claret St.-Julien." (The only other wine mentioned on that menu is Amontillado sherry, served with the fish, a "boiled halibut, oyster sauce.")

Lest my readers reject these evidences of the gastronomic fashion of that time as untutored practices in obscure establishments, I will cite the menu of the dinner "In Honor of Hon. S. W. Dorsey given by Citizens of New York at Delmonico's, February 11th, 1881." The committee was headed by John Jacob Astor, J. Pierpont Morgan, John A. Stewart, and Levi P. Morton, among the notables of international experience. The oysters were washed down with Haut Sauternes; the fish, with Johannisberger; the filet of beef and saddle of mutton with Pommery Champagne.

At Welcker's again, in Washington and three years before the Mitchell banquet, oysters were accompanied by Chablis, which probably a large proportion of gastronomes today would approve. But, between the saddle of mutton and Château Lafite and a Burgundy with a capon, Champagne (no mark mentioned) was served with a *suprême* (breast of) pheasant, stewed terrapin, and stuffed artichokes *à l'italienne*. And yet another year before, at the same establishment, Liebfraumilch went with brook trout and cucumber-and-tomato salad, then Pommery Champagne with braised beef, then chaud-froid (cold, of course) of game and stewed terrapin with 1800 Madeira, then Château Lafite with woodcock and lettuce salad.

A Parthian shot: even the great Escoffier lists on a menu of a dinner given at the Élysée by President Loubet for King Edward VII, May 2, 1903, port wine at the beginning.

TIPS ON SERVING WINE

1. Every bottle is an individual. So, never pour into a half-empty glass wine from a different bottle, regardless of the label.

2. White wines should be served cold: sweet white wines, *very* cold; Champagne, *very* cold; dry pale sherry, *very* cold. Red wines should never be heated in any way: they should be kept several hours before uncorking in a comfortably warm room and uncorked 1 or 2 hours before they are drunk—unless they are very old wines, which spoil quickly with oxidation.

3. Red wines over six years old, unless very light, should be decanted. If in doubt how much of the bottom to sacrifice, pour out into a glass what you hope to salvage: if muddy, throw it away.

4. Wines are very seldom (practically *never*) "corky" if they are limpid in the glass. A bad taste out of a good bottle is always possible, due to ordinary human error in bottling and corking; and a wine fine for some palates may taste bad on other palates. Also, what you have had in your mouth before drinking a wine may ruin or improve it—e.g., asparagus, artichokes, or salad dressing with vinegar will ruin it, while a good cheese will improve it.

5. It is wise to drink a rather light, young wine daily and to reserve the older and richer bottles for occasional indulgence. In that way the palate is not jaded.

6. The war between the grape and the grain has many angles. One or two gin drinks of very mild flavor are likely to produce some euphoria in the prospective diner, and therefore to predispose the consumer to appreciate a meal. This can be said about whisky and, yes, brandy (of fine quality, of course). But excessive preprandial drinking, even of water, obviously has the opposite effect. As the consumption of alcohol dehydrates the body, a heavy drinker does not want to eat: he wants to drink more.

7. It is reasonable that stronger wines should come after lighter and more delicate wines when more than one wine is served. If you serve a white wine meal, the full-bodied, more flavorful wines are better after the more subtle kind: a Quincy, or a Muscadet, or a very dry Graves would go better with oysters or fish, to be followed by a Montrachet with a *chaud-froid de volaille;* and, to cap such a meal, a sweet Sauternes or Barsac with the dessert. If you serve a completely red wine meal, you may find that a St.-Estèphe will accompany salmon very nicely, to be followed by a red Graves with the red meat—or a red Burgundy with game. But there are many highly civilized people—especially ladies—who stick to reds right through a meal, including fish. *De gustibus* . . .

GOURMET AND GOURMAND

Words are being corrupted today speedily, at random, arrogantly, even vengefully. "Sophistication"—which means adulteration and false quality—is used by our "technocrats" to mean refinement, superscientific design, which is diametrically the contrary. "Multiple" means arithmetically a figure that contains another figure a number of times exactly—12 is a multiple of 6, and 6 is of 2—precisely the reverse of the present-day meaning on Wall Street—i.e., the number of times the earnings of a company's stock is multiplied to make the quoted price. "Prestigious" means practicing juggling or legerdemain, cheating, deceptive, illusory: practically the opposite of what our newspapers intend to convey when they tack this adjective to a prominent person or institution. To "compound," according to the *Oxford English Dictionary* and the *Century Dictionary* (U.S.), means to mix, put together, join, combine, settle amicably on certain terms—not at all what a famous "columnist" had in mind when he used it to denote to complicate or pile up, which fine example has been followed by many of his profession. Probably this was the way that the Latin of Cicero was corrupted into *vulgar Latin*.

In gastronomy perhaps the worst case of this is the confusion between "gourmet" and "gourmand." People who fancy themselves as masters in such matters make a point of explaining that gourmet is a laudatory term meaning a person who is a connoisseur of fine food and *not* a gourmand, who gorges. No greater error. A gourmet may be said to be a connoisseur of wines and spirits, and a gourmand a connoisseur of food. The French word *gourmet* is derived from the English word "groom" and was originally "groumet"—the domestic who looked after the cellar; but in its present form, properly used, it is applied to *gourmets piqueurs*, "those who taste wines and spirits" (Bouillet, *Dictionnaire des Sciences et des Arts*).

Anthelme Brillat de Savarin (commonly known as Brillat-Savarin) is as good and widely recognized an authority on the subject as anyone. He does not mention the word "gourmet." But he expatiates on the subject of "gourmand" and "gourmandise." In his *Physiology of Taste*, which he wrote in his mature years after the storm of the French Revolution and his three-year sojourn in the then-youthful United States, he devotes two chapters— *in toto* the longest —to this subject. And that is as it should be.

Brillat-Savarin makes a fine point in speaking of women as *gourmandes* and enjoys describing their physiognomy—their somatological characteristics, as we might say today. But he does not make them out to be big eaters, gluttons. (No one seems to have thought of inventing the word *gourmette*—which actually shocks the ear—to indicate a discriminating female gastronome. Nor could it be defensible, properly speaking, since a female could hardly be a groom— i.e., a *gourmet piqueur*—who is strictly a masculine employee.)

Moreover, he roundly condemns those who equate gourmand with glutton. He says: "Gourmandising is inimical to excess . . . cannot be designated by the Latin word *gula* nor the English word *gluttony* . . ." "*N'est pas gourmand qui veut*," he says—i.e., not just any one can be a gourmand—one must be predestined by Nature. You will find him, he says, among the financiers, the physicians, the men of letters, the divines; he is blessed with wit and prone to longevity; he contributes to the general welfare of society by stimulating trade in the provision of foodstuffs; and he obeys the mandates of God by appreciating the good things of the world. A better charter of merit could hardly be asked or more eloquently expressed.

How, then, can the *Oxford English Dictionary* assign a pejorative sense to "gourmand"? Dr. Johnson himself subscribes to this error by defining a "gormand"—note the spelling—as a greedy eater. This definition *and* spelling are repeated in the great *American Century Dictionary*.

Against these English and American lexicographers, Brillat-Savarin says: "I have gone over dictionaries on the word *gourmandise* and I have not been satisfied at all with what I found there. It is only a perpetual confusion of *gourmandise* proper and *gluttony* and *voraciousness*." He condemns anyone "who stuffs or gets drunk" and proclaims "La Gourmandise" as "the enemy of excess." My reader will judge who is the better arbiter, the lexicographers or the great authority on gastronomy.

MEALTIMES AND SNOBBERY

In the United States, people who invite you to Sunday *dinner* at 1 P.M. are marked down by snobs as "hicks," ignorant rustics, common, uncivilized. Upper-class people, they say, call the meal at that hour "lunch," or perhaps "luncheon"; dinner is the evening meal. As in so many things, the snobs are quite mistaken on this point.

Dinner is and has always been the principal meal of the day and therefore the fullest one. The term has no necessary connection with the hour this meal is served. The confusion has come from the vulgarization—if you wish— of the manner of living of the well-to-do. When such people feasted in the middle of the day, they called the meal dinner and, until about the last quarter of the eighteenth century, so was it called. The evening meal was called "supper" and was generally lighter. Lunch was a light meal—as light as meals could be in those days—taken some two or three hours after breakfast, which was a substantial repast until quite recently.

Luncheon was called "muncheon" in the eighteenth century—also "munchin" and even "moonshine" (believe it or not). It consisted originally of cold dishes, with perhaps a hot one thrown in for good measure. In the United States, particularly in the West, the word "lunch" has retained this old meaning and is applied regardless of the hour of day or night to what is almost universally called now a "snack." In a word, only the hard-working businessman and the slimming lady speak correctly, in the old sense, in calling their midday meal "lunch."

One might say with reasonable certainty that breakfast is the only meal that has kept regular hours—i.e., the time of arising in the morning or shortly thereafter. The other meals have shifted as much as four hours in one gen-eration. But breakfast has changed its nature, even among conservative Eng-lishmen, not to speak of the French workingman's breakfast, which consists generally of a smallish cup of coffee laced with rum.

In the grand days of the British Raj in India, even as recently as fifty years ago, a planter's day began with a 6 A.M. cup of tea, rarely accompanied by a small biscuit. Then came *chota hazri*, or "small breakfast," with more tea, toast, and fruit, about 8 or 9. Then followed about 11 A.M. a good English breakfast, called *hazri*. *Tiffin* was served about 1: a two-course affair ending up invariably with a curry. Tea, of course, came at 4 to 5 P.M., and dinner at 7— a substantial meal often washed down with French wines. What now seems a Gargantuan feeding schedule was merely a manifestation of conservatism far away from the metropolis: an echo of a bygone age.

Conservatism is also evident in that most conservative of Western Euro-pean countries, Spain, with regard to the hours of meals and their designations. The midday meal, called *comida*—i.e., "dinner"—is taken at 2 or 3 P.M.; and the evening meal, called *cena*—i.e., "supper," at 10 or 11 at night. The Spaniards have not, as some snobs think, affected late hours: they have merely stuck conservatively to the old timetable—that is all.

APPETIZERS AND PRE-MEAL DRINKS

A strong cheese—judged by aroma or flavor—on a cracker or bit of fried toast is not likely to prepare one's palate for a delicate meal. Such strong flavors should be reserved for the end, or toward the end, of the meal. They can, of course, constitute an entire meal—not an introduction to a delicate one. The same may be said of any highly spiced mixtures: it is all very well before a curry or a hearty roast, but not advisable before a carefully planned dinner.

The same principle applies to drinks. A highly flavored cocktail or neat (or slightly diluted) spirits is better by itself—or with highly flavored ap-petizers. As a foundation for a delicate meal . . . better not. What applies to quality here applies also to quantity: if you gorge on appetizers, you are not likely to be eager for your dinner. If you consume enough alcohol—or even water—you will not care what—or whether—you eat.

Cocktails with very little flavor, and likewise neat or very diluted spirits, in *small* cocktail glasses (or medium small tumblers for whisky and soda or water) are advisable, because repetition will not be so dangerous. Two or three such drinks will be plenty for the majority of people accustomed to alcohol. More will make most of them indifferent to the meal that follows. (Remember the wit's remark: One drink is fine, two is too much, and three is not enough!)

So with solid appetizers: three at the most, and small. And let the flavor be subdued. A cracker or a piece of fried bread the size of a half-dollar, spread over with anchovy paste and sour cream, or with an anchovy fillet sprinkled lightly with finely chopped hard-boiled egg and parsley, or with a tiny (and well-cleaned) boiled shrimp; or olives, green and ripe; or foie gras on Delmonico toast; or caviar—if one can afford it: these and the like are pleasant and even exquisite things to nibble with a preprandial drink that will not spoil the full enjoyment of a fine meal.

ON KILLING LOBSTERS

Ada Boni, the late distinguished Italian author of *The Talisman of Happiness* (*Il Talismano della Felicità*), quotes the French poet Achille Ozanne on this subject:

> *Prenez un beau homard, puis sur la carapace*
> *Posez une main ferme, et, quelques sauts qu'il fasse,*
> *Sans plus vous attendrir à des regrets amers*
> *Découpez tout vivant ce Cardinal des mers.*

Which an English poetaster mauled into:

> "Take a fine lobster, and upon its shell
> Place a firm hand, and, though it jump and writhe,
> Don't let your heart on vain compassion dwell:
> Cut up the Cardinal of the blue seas alive."

Bibliography*

Athenaeus: *Les Quinze Livres des Deipnosophists.* 1580.
Apicius: *Les Dix Livres de Cuisine d'Apicius* (Trad. B. Guigan, 1933).
L'École de Salerne (Trad. Levacher de la Feutrie) 1782.
L'École de Salerne (Trad. en vers français Ch. Maux de Saint-Marc) 1880.
The Queen's Closet Opened. 1664.
Louis Lemery: *Traité des Aliments.* 1705.
L'École Parfaite des Officiers de Bouche. 1716.
Les Délices de La Campagne. 1761.
Le Ménage des Champs et de La Ville. 1732.
La Science du Maître d'Hôtel, Cuisinier. 1768.
La Cuisine Bourgeoise, suivie de l'Office. 1771.
Grimod de la Reynière. *Manuel des Amphitryons.* 1808.
Magiron. *Le Nouveau Cuisinier Universel.* 1812.
Utrecht-Friedel. *Le Confiseur Royal.* 1821.
Carême. *Le Cuisinier Parisien.* 1828.
————. *Le Maître d'Hôtel Français.* 1823.
————. *The Royal Pastry Cook.* 1834.
Viart (Viard). *Le Cuisinier Royal.* 1844.
Hippolyte Etienne. *Le Livre de la Phagotechnie.* 1852.
A. Soyer. *The Pantropheon.* 1853.

* N.B. These are some of the books on my kitchen shelf.

Carême. *Le Pâtissier Pittoresque*. 1854.

Urbain Dubois and Émile Bernard. *La Cuisine Classique*. 1856.

————. *La Cuisine de Tous les Pays*. n.d.

A. de La Fizelière. *Vins à la Mode et Cabarets du XVII S.* 1866.

Robert Tomes. *The Champagne Country*. 1867.

A. Gogué. *La Cuisine Française*. 1869.

Jules Gouffé. *Le Livre de Cuisine*. 1870.

Alexandre Dumas. *Grand Dictionnaire de Cuisine*. 1873

Jules Gouffé. *Le Livre de La Pâtisserie*. 1873.

Isabella Beeton. *The Book of Household Management*. 1880.

Paput-Lebeau. *Le Gastrophile*. 1883.

Will H. Coleman. *La Cuisine Creole*. 1885.

Charles Ranhoffer. *The Epicurean*. 1894.

Chatillon-Plessis. *La Vie à Table à la Fin du XIX S.* 1894.

Louis Maillard Genève. *La Cuisine des Familles*. 1912.

A. Filippini. *The International Cook Book*. 1911.

L. E. Audot: *La Cuisine de la Campagne et de la Ville*. 1905.

Pierre Lacam. *Le Mémorial de la Pâtisserie*. 1919.

Bertrand Guégan. *La Fleur de la Cuisine Française*. 1920.

Auguste Escoffier. *Le Guide Culinaire*. 1921.

————. *Le Livre des Menus*. 1912.

————. *Ma Cuisine*. 1934.

Urbain Dubois. *Nouvelle Cuisine Bourgeoise*. n.d.

Tante Marie. *La Veritable Cuisine des Familles*. n.d.

Countess Pardo Bazan. *La Cocina Española Antigua*. n.d.

70 Medecins Français. *Le Tresor de la Cuisine du Bassin Mediterranéen*. n.d.

L. Domenech. *La Cocina Vasca*. n.d.

A. Petit. *Traité de la Cuisine Russe*. n.d.

E. Molokhovets. *Podarok Molodim Khozyaikam*. (Photostat.) n.d.

A. Brillat-Savarin. *La Physiologie du Goût*. n.d.

Cassell's Dictionary of Cookery. n.d.

Arnold Palmer. *Movable Feasts*. 1952.

Alfred Suzanne. *150 Manières d'Accommoder les Restes*. n.d.

James Woodforde. *The Diary of a Country Parson*. (New printing: 1952.)

Henri Pellaprat. *La Pâtisserie Pratique*. n.d.

————. *Good Food from France*. 1951.

Ada Boni. *Il Talismano della Felicità*. 1931.

Henri Paul Pellaprat. *L'Art Culinaire Moderne*. 1936.

Phineas Beck (Samuel Chamberlain). *Clementine in the Kitchen*. 1946.

Samuel Chamberlain. *Bouquet de France*. 1952.

Samuel and Narcissa Chamberlain. *Calendar of French Cooking.* 1957 and 1958.

Narcissa Chamberlain. *The Omelette Book.* 1956.

Dr. Alfred Gottschalk. *Histoire de l'Alimentation et de la Gastronomie.* 1948.

Ambrose Heath. *Madame Prunier's Fish Cookery Book.* 1939.

Celine Vence and Robert J. Courtine. *Les Grands Maîtres de la Cuisine Française.* 1972.

Andre L. Simon. *A Dictionary of Gastronomy.* 1949.

Mme. E. de Ste.-Ange. *Le Livre de Cuisine.* 1927.

A 35-Year Resident. *The Indian Cookery Book.* (Calcutta.) 1931.

Index

(Page numbers in *italic* refer to menus)

[355]